T0256985

Semantic Software Design
A New Theory and Practical Guide
for Modern Architects

Eben Hewitt

Beijing · Boston · Farnham · Sebastopol · Tokyo

Semantic Software Design

by Eben Hewitt

Copyright © 2020 Eben Hewitt. All rights reserved.

Published by O'Reilly Media, Inc., 1005 Gravenstein Highway North, Sebastopol, CA 95472.

O'Reilly books may be purchased for educational, business, or sales promotional use. Online editions are also available for most titles (*http://oreilly.com*). For more information, contact our corporate/institutional sales department: 800-998-9938 or *corporate@oreilly.com*.

Acquisitions Editors: Ryan Shaw and Chris Guzikowski	**Proofreader:** Charles Roumeliotis
Development Editor: Alicia Young	**Indexer:** Ellen Troutman-Zaig
Production Editor: Kristen Brown	**Interior Designer:** David Futato
Copyeditor: Octal Publishing, LLC	**Cover Designer:** Karen Montgomery
	Illustrator: Rebecca Demarest

October 2019:   First Edition

Revision History for the First Edition

2019-09-25:   First Release

See *http://oreilly.com/catalog/errata.csp?isbn=9781492045953* for release details.

The O'Reilly logo is a registered trademark of O'Reilly Media, Inc. *Semantic Software Design*, the cover image, and related trade dress are trademarks of O'Reilly Media, Inc.

The views expressed in this work are those of the author, and do not represent the publisher's views. While the publisher and the author have used good faith efforts to ensure that the information and instructions contained in this work are accurate, the publisher and the author disclaim all responsibility for errors or omissions, including without limitation responsibility for damages resulting from the use of or reliance on this work. Use of the information and instructions contained in this work is at your own risk. If any code samples or other technology this work contains or describes is subject to open source licenses or the intellectual property rights of others, it is your responsibility to ensure that your use thereof complies with such licenses and/or rights.

978-1-492-04595-3

[LSI]

Table of Contents

Part III.   Operations, Process, and Management

Preface

Thank you kindly for picking up *Semantic Software Design*. Welcome.

This book introduces a new method of software design. It proposes a new way of thinking about how we construct our software. It is primarily focused on large projects, with particular benefit for greenfield software projects or large-scale legacy modernization projects.

A software project is said to fail if it does not meet its budget or timeline or deliver the features promised in a usable way. It is incontrovertible, and well documented, that software projects fail at alarming rates. Over the past 20 years, this situation has grown worse, not better. We must do something different to make our software designs more successful. But what?

My assumption here is that you're making business application software and services to be sold as products for customers or you're working at an in-house IT department. This book is not about missile guidance systems or telephony or firmware. It's not interested in debates about object-oriented versus functional programming, though it could apply for either realm. It's certainly not interested in some popular framework or another. And for the sake of clarity, my use of "semantic" here traces back to my philosophical training, and as such, it concerns the matter of *signs*. "Semantic" here refers more to *semiology*. It is not related or confined to some notion of Tim Berners-Lee's concept of the Semantic Web, honorable as that work is.

The primary audience is CTOs, CIOs, vice presidents of engineering, architects of all stripes (whether enterprise, application, solution, or otherwise), software development managers, and senior developers who want to become architects. Anyone in technology, including testers, analysts, and executives, can benefit from this book.

But there is precious little code in the book. It is written to be understood, and hopefully embraced, by managers, leaders, intellectually curious executives, and anyone working on software projects. That is not quite to say that it's *easy*.

The ideas in this book might appear shocking at times. They are likely to irritate some and perhaps even infuriate others. The ideas will appear as novel, perhaps even foreign and strange in some cases; the ideas will surface as borrowed and recast in other cases, such as in the introduction to Design Thinking. Taken in sum, it's my bespoke method, cobbled together over many years from a wide array of disparate sources. Most of these ideas stem from my studies in philosophy in graduate school. This book represents a tested version of the ideas, processes, practices, templates, and practical methods that together I call "semantic design."

This approach to software design is proven and it works. Over the past 20 years, I have been privileged to work as CTO, CIO, chief architect, and so on at large, global, public companies and have designed and led the creation of a number of large, mission-critical software projects, winning multiple awards for innovation, and, more important, creating successful software. The ideas presented here in a sense form a catalog of how I approach and perform software design. I've employed this approach for well more than a decade, leading the design of software projects for $1 million, $10 million, $35 million, and $50 million. Although this might seem a radical departure from traditional ways of thinking about software design, it's not conjecture or theory: again, it's proven and it works. It is not, however, obvious.

We are forced to use the language we inherit. We know our own name only because someone else told us that's what it was. For reasons that will become clear, in this book I sometimes use the terms "architect" or "architecture" *under erasure*, meaning it will appear with a strike, like this: ~~architect~~. That means that I am forced to use the word for clarity or historical purposes to be communicative, but that it is not presented as the intended meaning in the current context.

The first part of the book presents a philosophical framing of the method. We highlight what problem we're solving and why. This part is conceptual and provides the theoretical ground.

The second part of the book is ruthlessly pragmatic. It offers an array of document templates and repeatable practices that you can use out of the box to employ the elements of this method in your own daily work.

The third part provides an overview of some ways you manage and govern your software portfolio to help contain the general entropy. The book ends with a manifesto that summarizes concisely the set of principles and practices that comprise this method.

Taken altogether, the book represents a combined theoretical frame and a gesture toward its practice. It is not closed, however, and is intended to be taken up as a starting point, elaborated, and improved upon.

This book was written very much as a labor of love. I truly hope you enjoy it and find it useful as you apply the method in your own work. Moreover, I invite you to contribute to and advance these ideas. I'd be honored to hear from you at *eben@aletheastudio.com* or *AletheaStudio.com*.

Conventions Used in This Book

The following typographical conventions are used in this book:

Italic
> Indicates new terms, URLs, email addresses, filenames, and file extensions.

`Constant width`
> Used for program listings, as well as within paragraphs to refer to program elements such as variable or function names, databases, data types, environment variables, statements, and keywords.

`Constant width bold`
> Shows commands or other text that should be typed literally by the user.

`Constant width italic`
> Shows text that should be replaced with user-supplied values or by values determined by context.

 This element signifies a tip or suggestion.

 This element signifies a general note.

 This element indicates a warning or caution.

Using Code Examples

Supplemental material (code examples, exercises, etc.) is available for download at *https://aletheastudio.com*.

This book is here to help you get your job done. In general, if example code is offered with this book, you may use it in your programs and documentation. You do not need to contact us for permission unless you're reproducing a significant portion of the code. For example, writing a program that uses several chunks of code from this book does not require permission. Selling or distributing a CD-ROM of examples from O'Reilly books does require permission. Answering a question by citing this book and quoting example code does not require permission. Incorporating a significant amount of example code from this book into your product's documentation does require permission.

We appreciate, but do not require, attribution. An attribution usually includes the title, author, publisher, and ISBN. For example: "*Semantic Software Design* by Eben Hewitt (O'Reilly). Copyright 2020 Eben Hewitt, 978-1-492-04595-3."

If you feel your use of code examples falls outside fair use or the permission given above, feel free to contact us at *permissions@oreilly.com*.

O'Reilly Online Learning

 For almost 40 years, *O'Reilly Media* has provided technology and business training, knowledge, and insight to help companies succeed.

Our unique network of experts and innovators share their knowledge and expertise through books, articles, conferences, and our online learning platform. O'Reilly's online learning platform gives you on-demand access to live training courses, in-depth learning paths, interactive coding environments, and a vast collection of text and video from O'Reilly and 200+ other publishers. For more information, please visit *http://oreilly.com*.

How to Contact Us

Please address comments and questions concerning this book to the publisher:

O'Reilly Media, Inc.
1005 Gravenstein Highway North
Sebastopol, CA 95472
800-998-9938 (in the United States or Canada)
707-829-0515 (international or local)
707-829-0104 (fax)

We have a web page for this book, where we list errata, examples, and any additional information. You can access this page at *https://oreil.ly/semantic-software-design*.

To comment or ask technical questions about this book, send email to *bookquestions@oreilly.com*.

For more information about our books, courses, conferences, and news, see our website at *http://www.oreilly.com*.

Find us on Facebook: *http://facebook.com/oreilly*

Follow us on Twitter: *http://twitter.com/oreillymedia*

Watch us on YouTube: *http://www.youtube.com/oreillymedia*

Acknowledgments

Thank you to the gloriously perspicacious Mike Loukides, whose guidance and encouragement has helped to shape these ideas and bring this work to fruition. I am very grateful to know you and work with you. Thank you for all that you do to advance the discourse in our field.

Thank you to the incredibly diligent, detail-oriented, assiduous Alicia Young, my development editor at O'Reilly. Your partnership throughout the creation of this book has been terrific; you've done so much to improve and focus it. It's a pleasure to work with you.

Thank you to Mary Treseler, Neal Ford, Chris Guzikowski, and the entire Software Architecture Conference team at O'Reilly. These venues you have created make the space and atmosphere where these ideas can be further explored and challenged. Thank you to Tim O'Reilly, for the awesome wonder that is O'Reilly Media.

Thank you to our outstanding enterprise architecture team at Sabre. Andrea Baylor, Andy Zecha, Holt Hopkins, Jerry Rossi, Tom Murray and Tom Winrow, I am grateful to work with each of you and for the joy of all of the beautiful, rigorous systems we make together. Thank you to Jonathan Haynes for your reviews of early drafts and your brave comments that helped improve this work. Thanks goes to Clinton Anderson and Justin Ricketts for all of your support.

Thank you to my parents, for inspiring in me the joy and practice of writing.

Thank you to my teachers, in particular Christine Ney and Bryan Short. I cherish you for caring enough about the world of ideas to push your students so hard.

Thank you to Alison Brown for the many important ideas you contributed here and for your amazing nurturing and support of this work. This is for you, as if to say elsewise would make it unso.

Episteme: The Philosophy of Design

In everything, there is a share of everything.
   —Anaxagoras

In this part, we explore the figure of design itself. We examine in new light how our work designing software came to be shaped, and challenge some received views in our industry. We reimagine architecture as the work of creating concepts, and see how to express those concepts working with teams to create effective software designs.

CHAPTER 1

Origins of Software Architecture

We are most of us governed by epistemologies that we know to be wrong.
—Gregory Bateson

The purpose of this book is to help you design systems well and to help you realize your designs in practice. This book is quite practical and intended to help you do your work better. We must begin theoretically and historically. This chapter is meant to introduce you to a new way of thinking about your role as a software architect that will inform both the rest of this text and the way in which you approach your projects moving forward.

Software's Conceptual Origins

We shape our buildings, and thereafter they shape us.
—Winston Churchill

```
FADE IN:

INT. A CONFERENCE HALL IN GARMISCH GERMANY, OCTOBER
1968 — DAY

The scene: The NATO Software Engineering
Conference.

Fifty international computer professors and crafts-
people assembled to determine the state of the
industry in software. The use of the phrase soft-
ware engineering in the conference name was delib-
erately chosen to be "provocative" because at the
time the makers of software were considered so far
from performing a scientific effort that calling
```

```
themselves "engineers" would be bound to upset the
established apple cart.
                    MCILROY
        We undoubtedly get the short end of
        the stick in confrontations with
        hardware people because they are the
        industrialists and we are the
        crofters.
        (pause)
        The creation of software is backwards
        as an industry.

                    KOLENCE
        Agreed. Programming management will
        continue to deserve its current poor
        reputation for cost and schedule
        effectiveness until such time as a
        more complete understanding of the
        program design process is achieved.
```

Though these words were spoken, and recorded in the conference minutes in 1968 (*http://homepages.cs.ncl.ac.uk/brian.randell/NATO/nato1968.PDF*), they would scarce be thought out of place if stated today.

At this conference, the idea took hold was that we must make software in an *industrial* process.

That seemed natural enough, because one of their chief concerns was that software was having trouble defining itself as a field as it pulled away from hardware. At the time, the most *incendiary*, most *scary* topic at the conference was "the highly controversial question of whether software should be priced separately from hardware." This topic comprised a full day of the four-day conference.

This is a way of saying that software didn't even know it existed as its own field, separate from hardware, a mere 50 years ago. Very smart, accomplished professionals in the field were not sure whether software was even a "thing," something that had any independent value. Let that sink in for a moment.

Software was born from the mother of hardware. For decades, the two were (literally) fused together and could hardly be conceived of as separate matters. One reason is that software at the time was "treated as though it were of no financial value" because it was merely a necessity for the hardware, the true object of desire.

Yet today you can buy a desktop computer for $100 that's more powerful than any computer in the world was in 1968. (At the time of the NATO Conference, a 16-bit computer—that's two bytes—would cost you around $60,000 in today's dollars.)

And hardware is produced on a *factory line*, in a clear, repeatable process, determined to make dozens, thousands, millions of the same physical object.

Hardware is a commodity.

A commodity is something that is interchangeable with something of the same type. You can type a business email or make a word-processing document just as well on a laptop from any of 50 manufacturers.

And the business people want to form everything around the efficiencies of a commodity except one thing: their "secret sauce." Coca-Cola (*http://bit.ly/2mlnZOY*) has nearly 1,000 plants around the world performing repeated manufacturing, putting Coke into bottles and cans and bags to be loaded and shipped, thousands of times each day, every day, in the same way. It's a heavily scrutinized, sharply measured business: an internal commodity. Coke is bottled in factories in identical bottles in identical ways, millions of times every day. Yet only a handful of people know the secret *formula* for making the drink itself. Coke is copied millions of times a day, every day, and bottled in an identical process. But making the recipe a commodity would put Coke out of business.

In our infancy, we in software have failed to recognize the distinction between the commodities representing repeated, manufacturing-style processes, and the more mysterious, innovative, *one-time work* of making the recipe.

Coke is the recipe. Its production line is the factory. Software is the recipe. Its production line happens at runtime in browsers, not in the cubicles of your programmers.

Our conceptual origins are in hardware and factory lines, and borrowed from building architecture. These conceptual origins have confused us and dominated and circumscribed our thinking in ways that are not optimal, and not necessary. And this is a chief contributor to why our project track record is so dismal.

The term "architect" as used in software was not popularized until the early 1990s. Perhaps the first suggestion that there would be anything for software practitioners to learn from architects came in that NATO Software Engineering conference in Germany in 1968, from Peter Naur:

> *Software designers are in a similar position to architects and civil engineers*, particularly those concerned with the design of large heterogeneous constructions, such as towns and industrial plants. *It therefore seems natural that we should turn to these subjects for ideas about how to attack the design problem.* As one single example of such a source of ideas, I would like to mention: Christopher Alexander: Notes on the Synthesis of Form (Harvard Univ. Press, 1964) (emphasis mine).

This, and other statements from the elder statesmen of our field at this conference in 1968, are the progenitors of how we thought we should think about software design. The problem with Naur's statement is obvious: it's simply false. It's also unsupported. To state that we're in a "similar position to architects" has no more bearing logically, or truthfully, to stating that we're in a similar position to, say, philosophy professors, or writers, or aviators, or bureaucrats, or rugby players, or bunnies, or ponies. An argument by analogy is always false. Here, no argument is even given. Yet here this idea took hold, the participants returning to their native lands around the world, writing and teaching and mentoring for decades, shaping our entire field. This now haunts and silently shapes—perhaps even circumscribes and mentally constrains, however artificially—how we conduct our work, how we think about it, what we "know" we do.

Origins

To be clear, the participants at the NATO conference in 1968 were very smart, accomplished people, searching for a way to talk about a field that barely yet existed and was in the process of forming and announcing itself. This is a monumental task. I hold them in the highest esteem. They created programming languages such as ALGOL60, won Turing Awards, and created notations. They made our future possible, and for this I am grateful, and in awe. The work here is only to understand our origins, in hopes of improving our future. We are all standing on the shoulders of giants.

Some years later, in 1994, the Gang of Four (*http://bit.ly/2mp16ua*) created their *Design Patterns* book. They explicitly cite as inspiration the work of Christopher Alexander, a professor of architecture at University of California at Berkeley and author of *A Pattern Language*, which is concerned with proven aspects of architecting towns, public spaces, buildings, and homes. The *Design Patterns* book was pivotal work, one which advanced the area of software design and bolstered support for the nascent idea that *software designers are architects*, or are "like" them, and that we should draw our own concerns and methods and ideas from that prior field.

This same NATO conference was attended by now-famous Dutch systems scientist Edsger Dijkstra (*http://bit.ly/2lW5UXM*), one of the foremost thinkers in modern computing technology. Dijkstra participated in these conversations, and then some years later, during his chairmanship at the Department of Computer Science at the University of Texas, Austin, he voiced his vehement opposition to the mechanization of software, refuting the use of the term "software engineering," likening the term "computer science" to calling surgery "knife science." He concluded, rather, that "the core challenge for computing science is hence a conceptual one; namely, *what (abstract) mechanisms we can conceive* without getting lost in the complexities of our own making" (emphasis mine).

This same conference saw the first suggestion that software needed a "computer engineer," though this was an embarrassing notion to many involved, given that engineers did "real" work, had a discipline and known function, and software practitioners were by comparison ragtag. "Software belongs to the world of ideas, like music and mathematics, and should be treated accordingly." Interesting. Let's hang on to that for a moment.

```
      * * *

      Cut to:

      INT. PRESIDENT'S OFFICE, WARSAW, POLAND — DAY

      The scene: The president of the Republic of Poland
      updates the tax laws.
```

In Poland, software developers are classified as creative artists, and as such receive a government tax break of up to 50% of their expenses (see Deloitte report (*http:// bit.ly/2ko2zAa*)). These are the professions categorized as creative artists in Poland:

- Architectural design of buildings
- Interior and landscape
- Urban planning
- Computer software
- Fiction and poetry
- Painting and sculpture
- Music, conducting, singing, playing musical instruments, and choreography
- Violin making
- Folk art and journalism
- Acting, directing, costume design, stage design
- Dancing and circus acrobatics

Each of these are explicitly listed in the written law. In the eyes of the Polish government, software development is in the same professional category as poetry, conducting, choreography, and folk art.

And Poland is one of the leading producers of software in the world.

```
      Cut to: HERE—PRESENT DAY.
```

Perhaps something has occurred in the history of the concept of structure that could be called an event, a rupture that precipitates ruptures.

This rupture would not have been represented in a single explosive moment, a comfortingly locatable and suitably dramatic moment. It would have emerged among the ocean tides of thought and expression, across universes, ebbing and flowing, with fury and with lazy ease, over time, until the slow trickling of traces and cross-pollination reveal, only later, something had transformed. Eventually, these traces harden into trenches, fixing thought, and thereby fixing expression and realization.

What this categorization illuminates is the tide of language, the patois of a practice that shapes our ideas, conversation, understanding, methods, means, ethics, patterns, and designs. We name things, and thereafter, they shape us. They circumscribe our thought patterns, and that shapes our work.

The concept of structure within a field, such as we might call "architecture" within the field of technology, is thereby first an object of language.

Our language is constituted of an interplay of signs and of metaphors. A metaphor is a poetic device whereby we call something something that it isn't in order to reveal a deeper or hidden truth about that object by underscoring or highlighting or offsetting certain attributes. "All the world's a stage, and all the men and women merely players" is a well-known line from Shakespeare's *As You Like It*.

We use metaphors so freely and frequently that sometimes we even forget they are metaphors. When that happens, the metaphor "dies" (a metaphor itself!) and *becomes* the name itself, drained of its original juxtaposition that gave the phrase depth of meaning. We call these "dead metaphors." Common dead metaphors include the "leg" of a chair, or when we "fall" in love, or when we say time is "running out," as would sand from an hourglass. When we say these things in daily conversation, we do not fancy ourselves poets making metaphors. We don't see the metaphor, or intend one. It's now just The Thing.

In technology, "architecture" is a nonnecessary metaphor. That word, and all it's encumbered by, directs our attention to certain facets of our work.

Architecture is a dead metaphor: we mistake the metaphor for The Case, the fact.

There has been considerable hot debate, for decades, over the use of the term architect as applied to the field of technology. There are hardware architectures, application architectures, information architectures, and so forth. So can we claim that architecture is a dead metaphor if we don't quite understand what it is we're even referring to? We use the term without quite understanding what we mean by it, what the architect's process is, and what documents they produce toward what value. "Architect" means, from its trace in Greek language, "master builder."

What difference does it make?

Copies and Creativity

No person who is not a great sculptor or painter can be an architect. If he is not a sculptor or painter, he can only be a builder.
　　—John Ruskin, "True and Beautiful"

Dividing roles into distinct responsibilities within a process is one useful and very popular way to approach production in business. Such division makes the value of each moment in the process, each contribution to the whole, more direct and clear. This fashioning of the work, the "division of labor," has the additional value of making each step observable and measurable.

This, in turn, affords us opportunities to state these in terms of SMART goals (*https://en.wikipedia.org/wiki/SMART_criteria*), and thereby reward and punish and promote and fire those who cannot meet the objective measurements. Credit here goes at least in some part to Henry Ford, who designed his car manufacturing facilities more than 100 years ago. His specific aim was to make his production of cars cheap enough that he could sell them to his own poorly compensated workers who made them, ensuring that what he could not keep in pure profit after the consumption of raw materials— his paid labor force—would return to him in the form of revenue.

This way of approaching production, however, is most (or only) useful when what is being produced is well defined and you will make many (dozens, thousands, or millions) of copies of identical items.

In *Lean Six Sigma*, processes are refined until the rate of failure is reduced to six standard deviations from the mean, such that your production process allows 3.4 quality failures per million opportunities. We seek to define our field, to find the proper names, in order to codify, and make repeatable processes, and improve our happiness as workers (the coveted "role clarity"), and improve the quality of our products.

But one must ask, how are our names serving us?

Processes exist to *create copies*. Do we ever create copies of the software itself? Of course, we create copies of software for *distribution* purposes: we used to burn copies of web browsers onto compact discs and send them in the mail, and today we distribute copies of software over the internet. That is a process facilitating distribution, however, and has little relation to the act of creating that single software application in the first place. In fact, *we never do that*.

Processes exist, too, in order to repeat the act of doing the same *kind* of thing, if not making the same exact thing. A software development methodology catalogs the work to be done, and software development departments have divisions and (typically vague) notions of the processes we undergo in the act of creating any software product or system. So, to produce software of some kind, we define roles that participate in some aspect of the process, which might or might not be formally represented, communicated, and executed accordingly.

This problem of determining our proper process, our best approach to our work, within the context of large organizations that expect measurable results according to a quarterly schedule, is exacerbated because competition and *innovation* are foregrounded in our field of technology. We must innovate, make something new and compelling, in order to compete and win in the market. As such, we squarely and specifically aim *not* to produce something again that has already been produced before. Yet our embedded language urges us toward processes and attendant roles that might not be optimally serving us.

Such inventing suggests considerable uncertainty, which is at odds with the Fordian love of repeatable and measurable process. And the creation of software itself is something the planet has done for only a few decades. So, to improve our chances of success, we look at how things are done in other, well-established fields. We have embraced terms like "engineer" and "architect," borrowed from the world of construction, which lends a decidedly more specification-oriented view of our own process. We created jobs to encapsulate their responsibilities but through a software lens, and in the past few decades hired legions of people so titled, with great hopes.

More recently, we in technology turned our sights on an even more venerable mode of inquiry, revered for its precision and repeatability: science itself. We now have data "scientists." Although the term "computer scientist" has been around perhaps the longest, no one has a job called "computer scientist" except research professors, whose domain all too often remains squarely in the theoretical sphere.

The design of software is no science.

Our processes should not pretend to be a factory model that we do not have and do not desire.

Such category mistakes silently cripple our work.

Why Software Projects Fail

As I mentioned earlier in this chapter, software projects fail at an astonishing rate:

- In 2008, IBM reported (*https://ibm.co/2kQHGxP*) that 60% of IT projects fail. In 2009, ZDNet reported (*https://zd.net/2m28U4B*) that 68% of software projects fail.

- By 2018, Information Age reported (*http://bit.ly/2mncfeX*) that number had worsened to 71% of software projects being considered failures.

- Deloitte characterized our failure rate as "appalling." It warns (*http://bit.ly/2lVXrDQ*) that 75% of Enterprise Resource Planning projects fail, and Smart Insights reveals (*http://bit.ly/2mgqn9E*) that 84% of digital transformation projects fail. In 2017 Tech Republic reported (*https://tek.io/2XbQgZ0*) that big data projects fail 85% of the time.
- According to McKinsey (*https://mck.co/2kQnVq0*), 17% of the time, IT projects go so badly that they *threaten the company's very existence.*

Numbers like this rank our success rate somewhere worse than meteorologists and fortune tellers.

Our projects across the board do not do well. Considering how much of the world is run on software, this is an alarming state for our customers, us as practitioners, and those who depend on us.

Over the past 20 years, that situation has grown worse, not better.

A McKinsey study (*https://mck.co/2knAHvZ*) of 5,600 companies found the following:

> On average, large IT projects run 45 percent over budget and 7 percent over time, while delivering 56 percent less value than predicted. Software projects run the highest risk of cost and schedule overruns.

Of course, some projects come in on time and on budget. But these are likely the "IT" projects cited in the McKinsey study, which include things like datacenter moves, lift-and-shift projects, disaster-recovery site deployments, and so forth. These are complex projects (sort of: mostly they're just big). I have certainly been involved in several such projects. They're different than trying to conceive of a new software system that would be the object of design.

The obvious difference is that the "IT" projects are about working with actual physical materials and things: servers to move and cables to plug in. It's decidable and clear when you're done and what precise percentage of cables you have left to plug in. That is, many CIO IT projects of the back-office variety are not much more creative than moving your house or loading and unloading packages at a warehouse: just make the right lists and tick through them at the right time.

It's the CTO's *software projects* that run the greatest risk and that fail most spectacularly. That's because they require the most creative, conceptual work. They demand making a representation of the world. When you do this, you become involved in signs, in language, in the meaning of things, and how things relate. You're stating a philosophical point of view based in your epistemology.

You're inventing the context wherein you can posit signs that make sense together and form a representation of the real world.

That's *so much* harder.

It's made harder still when we don't even recognize that that's what we are doing. We don't recognize what kind of projects our software projects are. We are in the semantic space, not the space of physical buildings.

The McKinsey study demarcates IT projects as if they are all the same because they are about "computer stuff" (I speculate). The results would look very different if McKinsey had thought better and saw that these IT projects should be lumped in with facilities management. The creation of a software product is *an entirely different matter*, not part of "IT" any more than your design meetings in a conference room are part of the facilities company you lease your office space from.

But creative work need not always fail. Plenty of movies, shows, theatrical productions, music performances, and records all get produced on time and on budget. The difference is that we recognize that those are creative endeavors and *manage them as such*. We think we're doing "knife science" or "computer science" or "architecture": we're not. We're doing *semantics*: creating a complex conceptual structure of signs, whose meaning, value, and very existence is purely logical and linguistic.

This assumes that everyone from the executive sponsors to the project team had fair and reasonable understanding of what was wanted, time to offer their input on the scope, the budget, the deadline. We all well know that they do not. Even if they did, they're still guessing at best, because what they are doing by definition has never been done before. And it's potentially endless, because the world changes, and the world is an infinite conjunct of propositions. Where do you want to draw the line? Where, really, is the "failure" here?

Because software is by its nature semantic, it's as if people who aren't software developers don't quite believe it *exists*. These are hedge fund managers, executives, MBA-types who are used to moving things on a spreadsheet and occasionally giving motivating speeches. They don't *make anything* for a living.

Software projects often fail because of a lack of good management.

The team knows from the beginning the project cannot possibly be delivered on time. They want to please people, they worry that management will just get someone else to lie to them and say the project can be delivered on the date that was handed to them.

As a technology leader in your organization, it's part of your job to help stop this way of thinking and have the healthy, hard conversations with management to set expectations up front. They can have *some* software in six months. It's not clear what exactly that will be. Software projects succeed when smart, strategic, supportive executives understand that this is the deal and take that leap of faith with you to advance the business. When greedy, ignorant executives who worry about losing a deal or getting fired themselves dictate an impossible deadline and tremendous scope, you must refuse it. This is in part how the failed software of the Boeing 737 Max (*https://nyti.ms/2koeYUJ*) was created.

The McKinsey study goes on to state the reasons it found for these problems:

- Unclear objectives
- Lack of business focus
- Shifting requirements
- Technical complexity
- Unaligned team
- Lack of skills
- Unrealistic schedules
- Reactive planning

These are the reasons that software projects fail.

If we could address even half of these, we could dramatically improve our rate of success. Indeed, when we focus on the semantic relations, on the concept of what we are designing, and shift our focus to set-theorizing the idea of the world that our software represents, our systems do better.

Of these reasons, the first *five* could be addressed by focusing on the *concept*: the idea of the software, what it's for, and the clear and true representation of the world of which the software is an image. The remaining three are just good old fashioned bad management.

The Impact of Failures

So perhaps now we can say there is a rupture between our stated aims, the situation in which we find ourselves as technologists, and how we conceptualize and approach our work. We are misaligned. The rupture is not singular. It shows itself in tiny cracks emerging along the surface of the porcelain.

But what does it mean for a software project to fail? Although metrics vary, in general these refer to excessive overruns of the budget and the proposed timeline, and whether the resulting software works as intended. Of course, there are not purely "failed" and purely "successful" projects, but not meeting these three criteria means that expectations and commitments were not met.

And even when the project is done (whether considered a failure or not), if some software has shipped because of it, the resulting software doesn't always hit the mark. Tech Republic cites a study (*https://tek.io/2mjR1hW*) showing that in 2017 alone, software failures "affected 3.6 billion people, and caused $1.7 trillion in financial losses and a cumulative total of 268 years of downtime."

Worse, some of these have more dire consequences. A Gallup study (*http://bit.ly/2moAk56*) highlights the FBI's Virtual Case File software application, which "cost U.S. taxpayers $100 million and left the FBI with an antiquated system that jeopardizes its counterterrorism efforts." A 2011 Harvard Business Review (*http://bit.ly/2kooQ0R*) article states that the failures in our IT projects cost the US economy alone as much as $150 billion annually.

The same HBR article recounts the story of an IT project at Levi Strauss in 2008. The plan was to use SAP (a well-established vendor and leader in its technology) and Deloitte (a well-known, highly regarded leader in its field) to run the implementation. This typical project, with good names attached, to do nothing innovative whatsoever, was estimated at $5 million. It quickly turned into a colossal $200 million nightmare, resulting in the company having to take a $193 million loss against earnings and the forced resignation of the CIO.

Of course, that's small stakes compared with what President Obama called the "unmitigated disaster" of the HealthCare.gov project (*https://en.wikipedia.org/wiki/HealthCare.gov*) in 2013, in which the original cost was budgeted at $93 million, soon exploding to a cost 18 times that, of $1.7 billion, for a website that was so poorly designed it was able to handle a load of only 1,100 concurrent users, not the 250,000 concurrent users it was receiving.

Discovering a root cause in all this history will be overdetermined: there are failures of leadership, management, process design, project management, change management, requirements gathering, requirements expression, specification, understanding, estimating, design, testing, listening, courage, and in raw coding chops.

Where are the heroes of architecture and Agile across all this worsening failure?

Our industry's collective work on methods, tooling, and practices has not improved our situation: in fact, it is only becoming markedly worse. We have largely made mere exchanges, instead of improvements.

It's also worth nothing that we in software love to tout the importance of failure. Failure itself, of course is horrible. It is not something to be desired.

What people mean, or at least should mean, when they say this, is that what is important is to *learn* and to do something new to address the aspects that helped lead to a failure, and that sometimes (often) failure accompanies doing something truly new. It's easy to repeat a known formula, but we must be supported in attempts to try something different, and take a long view.

The importance of failure, in this context, is not to celebrate it. It is to underscore that we are not doing good enough work. We can do better. There is no easy fix. As Fred Brooks stated in his follow-up essay to 1975's excellent book, *The Mythical Man Month: Essays on Software Engineering*, there is no silver bullet.

But there is a way.

It starts with a question. What would our work look like if instead of borrowing broken metaphors and language that cripple our work, we stripped away these traces, and rethought the essence of our work?

What we would be left with are *concepts*, which are at the center of a semantic approach to software design. The next chapter unpacks the idea of concepts as they apply to our proposed approach to your role in designing effective software.

CHAPTER 2

The Production of Concepts

The external character of labor for the worker appears in the fact that it is not his own, but someone else's, that it does not belong to him, that in it he belongs, not to himself, but to another.

—Karl Marx

Semantics and the Software Factory

The manufacturing process requires a system. The process of making a system for anything itself requires a system. This is a meta-model: a way of making models.

In 1844, German economist Karl Marx wrote about the problems of the division of labor in his *Economic and Philosophical Manuscripts*. By dividing work into many jobs, each with only one distinct responsibility, the work within each field becomes repetitive, rote, and is drained of opportunity for creativity. Such is the fate of industrial workers—our forebears in computer hardware factories from which software has separated only in its physical space of production, but not entirely in our minds as developers and designers. And certainly not in the minds of corporate leaders.

In the built world, architecture as a field is concerned with the transformation of raw materials within a given site to create a concrete space, fit to a stated purpose. This space might be a resort, a concert hall, a cathedral, a theater, an office building, a bridge, a tunnel, or a park. The building architect starts with the ground, the *site* on which the building will be built. The site is clearly defined and preestablished in no uncertain terms by real estate ownership and zoning laws. Humans have had homes and offices and hotels and formal gowns and luggage and many of the objects of architecture and design for thousands of years. The ideas of going to work in an office with others, or attending a musical performance, or traversing a body of water safe and dry, these are well-understood human functions that have been going on for thousands of years, across all cultures across the entire settled world.

We in software and systems have chosen for our conceptual parents "architecture" and "design." These are the words we use to describe our work. We print them on business cards, and they rest in the fields of endless human resources databases to describe our job functions. Our field is prescribed by their inherited language and conceptual models. This is understandable, but perhaps inadequate.

It's understandable because the building architect is concerned primarily with making something that must be sturdy, usable (fit to purpose), and delightful. The conceptual miss comes, I assert, because these fields are not predominated by a concern for something *novel* (an innovation, the expounding of an *idea* that is new). Put bluntly, building architects make rather an object that did not exist before, within a tightly prescribed realm of human interaction.

However, when something is new *as an idea*, and not merely a latest realization of a very old idea, we call it an invention. Or art. In this way, the term *architecture*, the nonnecessary *metaphor* that has been carried over time onto our mental model of how we think of our work, how we talk about it, and what we think our responsibilities are with respect it, has converged into a dead metaphor, perhaps constraining or hampering our work more than it any longer enables and supports it.

What if, in that moment decades ago, as encapsulated at the NATO Conference in 1968, in that moment as fumbling around for how to assign metaphors to ourselves to understand our work, in an effort to bootstrap our field, we had instead adopted the term "composer," or conductor, or play director, or writer? *They were on the table.* It's not *unthinkable*. But our entanglement, our fusion, at the time with the manufacturing processes in hardware, have led us down a path that has created many wonderful programs and advances in software.

But perhaps these advances are in spite of, not because of, these industrial metaphors? Or rather, that they were critical at the time, but no longer as useful?

The world has changed in these many decades since the NATO Conference in 1968. The world is more synthetic. Jobs must move up the value chain. A faculty member of the Arizona State University School of Architecture recently told me that the unemployment rate for architects in the Phoenix area is higher than 50%. In fact, the best way to face the highest possible unemployment rate for yourself is to go to architecture school (*http://bit.ly/2ly7PSa*). It's not a job that creates enough value in the world of physical buildings because computers and civil engineering codes aid lower-level modelers. Such a fate is coming for architects in software who cannot determine how to move up in the chain of value creation for customers.

We have been altogether too inward facing, burdened by thinking the job was to create an enterprise ontology, or fill out the chart of a Zachman framework and think we have done something useful. We have not. We have merely complied with one available method of trying to understand our own place in the world, justifying an existence, the frame of a field grappling with its own identity. This was a necessary stage to move through, yet we cannot remain in stasis there.

To be clear, I am not merely arguing for us to all have a title change and get on with the same practices. But because the name begat practices that don't fit our work, it stands to reason we might learn from having new ones.

The Myth of Requirements

In system design, we speak of the "requirements." This word creates a false center, a supposed constant, which creates problems for our field. These problems come in the form of a binary opposition set up between the product management team and the development team. It supposes, in the extreme form, that the product management team knows what to build and that the development team are passive receptacles into whom we insert this list of what they are required to build. Within an Agile method, some freedom is perhaps allowed to the development team in how to design within that list of requirements.

The requirements, however, do not exist. But the requirements, like everything else of value, are just made up by someone. They are not first known and then told. They are *invented*.

Part of the work of the new architect-creative is to help create those requirements, both functional and nonfunctional. To see what needs to be done, what might work, what structure accounts for what we think we want the system to do, or what we think someone else we've never met might want or need the system to do three years from now when it's harder to change and how to accommodate that.

How do we know that Indiana Jones is the archaeology professor who finds the Lost Ark of the Covenant? Because George Lucas invented a character named Indiana Smith, and Steven Spielberg didn't like the name so he changed it to "Indiana Jones." And all of a sudden there is a world of the 1930s and a man standing in it and he needs to go do something and someone needs to get in his way and how might that work? That's how requirements are made, in the movies and in software. People make stuff up.

When you make stuff up as a software designer, that world, like the world of the movie into which you posit a character with a conflict, is your context. It's the place where you posit signs that have meaning in relation to one another. It's your semantic field.

Semantics and Software Architecture

This book has a single primary purpose among many purposes: to help you better design software. To do so, it advances a new model, a new approach, a new set of ideas and tools called *semantic software design*.

Why "semantics"?

Semantics, as a field, is concerned with the production of meaning, and how logic and language are used. It is "the linguistic and philosophical study of meaning, in language, programming languages, formal logic, and semiotics. It is concerned with the relationship between signifiers—like words, phrases, signs, and symbols—and what they stand for in reality."[1] It is about sets. It is about relations, and the possibilities that language itself creates, performs, and cuts off.

This *precisely* describes the role that ~~architects~~ designers should be playing, the kind of work they should be doing. The logic demanded by the compiler and the business requirements remain logical problems, set theoretical problems. Everything the developer does is expressed in language.

Semantics = logic + language.

That sounds *exactly* like the work we do when we are allowed to do our best work as software developers. But we've been trained around these incorrectly conceived metaphors. So we don't have a set of practices to even see where we are making the little mistakes that accrue toward failed projects. We have practices that rather discourage the kind of thinking we must embrace to make successful designs.

The problem with software—a chief reason our projects fail—is a failure of our language. We are *not architects*. Not even close. We do not build buildings with an obvious and known prior purpose, which is an approximate copy of the same kind of building people have been making and using for thousands of years, using tangible commodity materials on a factory line. Quite the opposite.

Our *only* material is that of language and ideas, names and meanings, signifiers and signifieds. Our only material is *semantics*.

When we design software we are designing the semantics of a demarcated field of signifiers and signifieds.

That is our primary activity. It takes its material expression in a collection of classes or functions as syntax in some language. But these languages are interchangeable enough. And the syntax is not the message.

---

1 *https://en.wikipedia.org/wiki/Semantics*

The *semantic field* comprises the set of sets of interplaying linguistic terms that form the idea our software represents from a comprehensive systems view. It's the nouns and verbs in your domain, how they relate, and how in your software system design that complete set of ideas acts as an overlay representing the "real" world.

We are haunted by our inherited language. It's the air we breathe: it's ubiquitous and invisible. It has both shaped and deformed our thinking, and our software suffers.

Semantics is the missing step. This is the piece that we skip because we did not know it was required. Because our inherited conception of our field took us to the factory lines, away from language and epistemology (the study of what is knowable, and how we can know what we know), and philosophical categories.

To perform semantic software design, you perform these steps:

1. Define its semantic field.
2. Produce your concept within it.
3. Deconstruct the concept to improve it.
4. Design the system according to the deconstructed concept and its semantic field.
5. Write the software and realize the attendant systems and processes.

Where we fall short is in rigorously creating a concept of our software as above. When we do this, our software succeeds. When we do not, we endure a thousand minor missteps, many of which we don't even see, that over time add up to larger failures of our projects and systems.

The rest of this book unpacks these ideas and illustrates how to apply them to make more successful software systems and projects.

The Semantic Field

A *proposition* is a declaration about what is the case. It represents the set of possible worlds or states of affairs in which it obtains truth-value, in which it is true.

The universe is an infinite conjunct of propositions.

As an infinite conjunct of propositions, the universe is a (very long) list of all of the statements that result in a truth-value. Because time keeps passing, that list is infinitely long.

The conjunctive is just the logical connector "and." We could say "this is true and this is true and this is true..." If we said only true things, and said all the true things, we would have a complete image of the entire universe across time and space. If we could iterate every proposition across space and time, we would have an exhaustive representation of the universe.

Representing some aspect of the actual world in its true propositions is the work of the software designer.

If the scope of our software was to represent the entire universe, we would translate the infinite list of propositions into executable statements. This would be straightforward because computers understand the true/false binary.

But someone has to pay for this project. And they don't have infinite time and they don't need all that scope. Just some of it. We use logic and language to form a concept. Our concept is the collection of our propositions. We carve out a space from that infinite conjunct of propositions representing the world. We create a boundary separating the scope of our software, its domain, from the rest of the universe. There are things we represent and things we will not. This is how we define that semantic field.

Because we do not have time and scope and budget or need to represent the entire universe, we carve off the scope of our domain. All software for certain and by necessity will have this boundary. This is the edge of your semantic field, that place where your software stops representing the world. At this boundary, you will suffer border skirmishes between your representation and what you've cast out or left out beyond the horizon. We are forced to round our thought off in a not-entirely-consistent way.

If we did not draw such a line around the domain, our work would be to represent All The Things, our scope would be infinite, our representation would be of the entire universe in eternity, and our software would be the actual lived world and we would be God. Because this is not the case, we have to stop making representations, and that's our semantic boundary, and that makes inconsistencies in our logic and language, our semantics. But if we consider that boundary consciously, because we're aware of it, because we understand that our work is actually semantics and not engineering or architecture, we will make the logic and language better. And because they are only building blocks in software, our software will be better.

The main thesis of this book is that software fails because of improper understanding of the world, because of an improper understanding of our role—we have thought we were engineers and architects instead of philosophers and semanticists—and this results in unclear objectives, undue complexity, incorrect and changing requirements, lack of alignment, lack of focus, wasted effort, churn, and disarray—many of the top reasons the McKinsey report states that software projects fail.

Software is a linguistic and logical endeavor. If we think we are the semanticists or philosophers of our systems, we will make better language and use better logic. And because those are the only tools of software design, our software will be better.

The semantic field allows for the possibility of concepts.

Designers Are Producers of Concepts

To be engaged with architecture is to be engaged with almost everything else as well: culture, society, politics, business, history, family, religion.
—Paul Goldberger

Vitruvius is the first Roman architect of record, working in the first century BC.

He wrote *de Architectura*, now known as *Ten Books on Architecture*, which is still taught to this day at university. It would be nearly 1,500 years before another book on architecture was written. Vitruvius declares that the architect should be versed in drawing, geometry, optics, history, philosophy, astronomy, music, theater, medicine, law, and other fields.

Building architects are told this sort of thing all the time: that they must engage with all of culture, all schools of thought and academic disciplines, and understand many disparate fields in order to do their work. The lineage of this assertion comes from *de Architectura*.

Yet we in software somehow find ourselves exempt. As the world in general becomes more and more specialized, we frequently find ourselves satisfied to recount the variants of Big O notation and argue the virtues of MergeSort over QuickSort, or (heaven forbid) this JavaScript framework over that one.

This should not be the case.

Thinking only from our own perspective as computing practitioners leaves our design tepid, derivative, inefficient, incomplete, untrustworthy, unstable, and costly to expand and maintain.

We must begin with the concept.

The concept must support integrity and harmony. It must provide for, as Vitruvius asserts, the three critical components: stability, utility, and beauty.

Technology Strategy Patterns

Please see this book's companion volume, *Technology Strategy Patterns*, for a more in-depth discussion of an architect's attributes and how architecture and strategy best work together in a tech organization.

Designing Concepts

Good designs do not merely execute the stated requirements.

The creative architect will first create a coherence and an integrity to the concept.

First, we design the concepts. The concepts inform, provoke, and support the local designs that they encompass. For the effective enterprise architect, these might be designs of software systems, integrations, infrastructure, organizations, the use of data, and business processes.

Proceeding from the concept, all the elements can work together in a coherent system of signs.

We are not merely drawing deployment diagrams. We ask ourselves, what is your theme, your point of view? What design principles can a user intuit from your work without being told them?

Thinking in systems means that you observe the entire system. Step back far enough to see all of it, the whole thing. You need to see all the parts to form an understanding of the relations between all the parts, both within the bounds of the system and the universe of systems that it touches and in which it participates. Then, in a double-action, use that knowledge to understand each part on its own. Considering each part as its own integral system, without a view of those relations, what new light does it emit? What new understanding can you find in the observance?

Now strip it down further: consider the object of the system as a thing-in-itself, relieved of our assumptions about what it is and why it is.

Now build the system up again, suspending your prior knowledge, reaching each object itself, and see how the relations reveal themselves anew. Reexamine how the relationships could be improved, augmented, destroyed, and rearranged based on this violent investigation.

Only now can you proceed with confidence that you have considered for your client the forces at work, the justifications for their presence in the system, their organization, and the context in which this system will operate and others within which it possibly could.

The behavior your system exhibits reveals the web of all of these interrelated and interdependent subsystems. There are many decisions to be made, whether by you, your team, or the participating team (the application developers or those working in the process).

The ~~architect~~ is the chief philosopher of their system.

The work and the joy of the architect is to create a concept, then clarify it, then communicate it for realization.

What Is a Concept?

So architecture is art and it is not art; it is art and it is something more, or less. This is the paradox and its glory, and always has been.
—Paul Goldberger

A *concept* is a complex idea consisting of compounded abstractions over a variety of related ideas. A concept is an interpreted representation of some aspect of the world.

Concepts are *not facts*. They are attempts to explain something. Your software might not appear to be an attempt to explain something about the world. But it is in fact the result of a concept. That concept might be very poor: it might be logically unsound, ethically problematic, or aesthetically challenged. One of the arguments of this book is to foreground the concept given that you have no material to carve, no plot of land to build on with concrete and steel. You are defining concepts. That's the job of the software designer.

A concept is always a concept *of something*: it is a representation. As such, you are necessarily *interpreting* what is important about the world, what requires independence, what merits refining, what earns a place at the table of competing representations, who gets a voice and a name and a fully rounded character and who doesn't. You are making value judgments, ethical judgments, aesthetic judgments, telling and participating in a story about the world, whether you're doing so consciously or not.

A concept is *nonobvious*. It's a complex of ideas and abstractions mixed with judgments. It is the product of thinking. A simple and direct referent is not a concept. Saying "My software system is an ecommerce website" is not a concept. That is obvious, understood, undistinguished from any of the other millions of ecommerce websites. Saying "My software system is an ecommerce website that lets people barter (trade goods and services) with each other instead of paying with money" is one step closer. It's more distinct, refined, and complected.

A concept can be *argued against*. A reasonable person could argue that your concept is incorrect, that your representation is incomplete, shoddy, or misguided. This is an easy test to see whether your concept is forming. If no one would argue the opposite of your statement, you haven't done anything but cheer a marketing slogan.

If I were to ask you to draw a picture of a "pet," what would you draw? Perhaps a big, fat snuggly kitty. Or a skittish and playful kitten. Or a bird, an iguana, a dog, a ferret. There are many different ideas that complect into a concept. Foregrounding metacognition, or thinking about how you think, helps you recognize these kinds of differences, including your own biases. It's an important step to doing these more consciously. That, in turn, is an important step in creating compelling concepts that are the hallmark of truly innovative software.

Accomplish, Avoid, Fix

To be useful in a typical software project, your concept will generally be about one of three things: accomplishing something, avoiding something, or fixing something:

Accomplish

> This might mean that your user can make a contribution, or can take advantage of a new opportunity in an emerging market. Projects involving accomplishing are about doing something new, different, exciting. They're about making more cakes.

Avoid

> Your project might be about helping you avoid something negative, like fraud or noncompliance, or averting risk. They're about more fairly dividing up the cake you already have.

Fix

> Software projects often arise in order to address some sins of the past, and "simplify" or "streamline" some particularly messy process. They're not really about cake.

Your new software project probably is not about all three, or even two of these. If it seems that way, your concept might be too sprawling, unruly, and too poorly constrained. You should refine it.

Outlining Your Concept on the Concept Canvas

To start to work with your concept in a more practical way, you can outline it.

Consider something that you do know about the project. Think in terms of something your customer might want to accomplish, avoid, or fix. In a sentence, answer this question:

> *Who wants what by when and for what reason?*

These are basically the aspects of the "reporter" questions, and are very similar to the structure of a user story. Your organization might have a "one pager" or "Business Requirements Document" that is intended to answer these kinds of questions. Your design concept is most immediately informed by the business idea: some application or major update that product management or other executives want to make. It is informed too by the overall business strategy, your technology strategy, and the creative work you perform in designing the concept.

These are interrelated, and shown in a cluster of associated ideas, as illustrated in Figure 2-1. They should inform one another in a continuous cycle, and not unidirectional or only top down. The design concept for your local application can be robust and rich and innovative enough to reinform and at times even reinvent the technology strategy and business strategy.

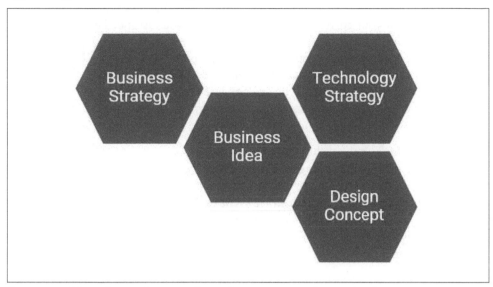

Figure 2-1. The relations between these elements are not hierarchical

To support your concept, and this richer cycle, consider what the need behind the need is. Consider how they would like to accomplish this. Typically the "business" will come up with what needs to be done, and expect architecture to describe how it should be done. This is fine. There is greater value in the designer who can shape the technology concept such that it informs and changes and perhaps even reimagines the business idea.

What are the salient bullet points across People, Process, and Technology? Consider the strengths your organization can build on, and challenges to overcome.

Constraints are often found to be frustratingly constricting in other models of software design. They are welcome in our world, however, because they give us an anchor, something real to help orient us.

Divergent and convergent thinking

As you work through your concept, you should go through two stages, *divergent thinking*, followed by *convergent thinking*.

With divergent thinking, you generate a list of candidate solutions that should be very different from one another, and very different from what exists today. Then, in a second, distinct stage, use convergent thinking to conflate these ideas, throw out the ones that won't work, and come up with your concept based on this refinement:

Divergent thinking

Generate a wide variety of possible solutions. They should have variety and be distinct across the array of candidate solutions. What solutions do not neatly conform with your current application or business landscape? How can you follow your curiosity? How can you imagine a solution that is prompted outside the field of the local software problem, such as by a bit of music, art, an opera, a toy, a game, something entirely outside the domain? Are you taking a risk? You should be clear on what the risk is. If you are not sure what it is, you might not be doing something sufficiently interesting. Capture your solution candidates in a list that becomes part of your lookbook or scrapbook.

Convergent thinking

After your divergent thinking exercise has generated a list of candidate solutions, it's time to narrow this field to a coherent single concept. Here, you are creating a set of filters or lenses by which to view your related ideas so that you can clarify and refine these scattered lists into what will become your working concept. To do so, ask yourself and your team the following types of questions for each candidate solution:

1. What absolute constraints are known?

2. How might these candidates fit within a budget, if known?

3. How might these candidates fit within a timeline?

4. What known elements of the business or technology strategy do these candidates support?

5. What new opportunities does this create?

6. What positive and negative elements of our current landscape of People, Process, and Technology does this enhance or aggravate?

7. What people or roles would need to approve or work together with these candidates?

There are many questions and conversations your team will have that might be more relevant to this process for your situation. These are just to get you started.

The convergent thinking exercise will result in a few key components. There might be three to seven of them. These are the main ideas that together form the concept. Later in executive briefings, marketing slides, customer-facing product decks, interviews, and other forms of communication, you'll use the statement and then these main bullet points as the "elevator pitch" to quickly and concisely express the concept—what this system is about, why it exists, and whom it benefits.

Your ideation work at this stage can be captured in this template, which I call the "Concept Canvas." Figure 2-2 depicts this.

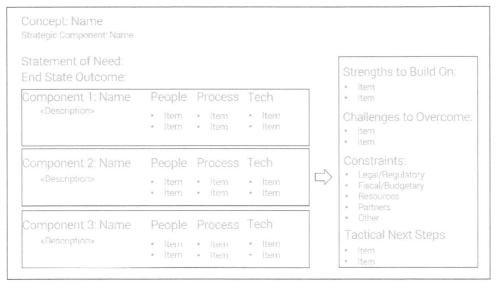

Figure 2-2. Capturing your concept in the Concept Canvas

Of course, companies don't have concepts: people do. Get your team together for a morning and work through the Concept Canvas. This can then serve how you put together the project plan and create the detailed design.

In our practice, we don't do "architecture," for reasons we discussed. Rather, in Semantic Software Design we are producers of concepts, designers of concepts. We express them in a way that allows others to be inspired and participate and understand the boundaries.

In summary, a rough guiding outline for how to work with your concept at this early stage is as follows:

1. **Concept statement**: A single sentence or phrase. This is like the melody of a tune you can hum. It's not the whole song; it's a memorable image that helps you communicate the basic subject.

2. **Statement of need**: Captures who wants what by when for what reason. This ensures that you are striking the right balance between being creative and curious and not going off on a tangent that has no business value. Who are the customers, end users, business partners, and internal executives who stand to benefit— or could stand in the way?

3. **Alignment with strategy**: You will have a greater chance of relevance, impact, and support if it is very clear that your concept relates and advances at least one element of the business and technology strategies. You should identify this explicitly.

4. **Idea components**: These are the highly cohesive idea components that work together to form the concept. Consider them each through the lenses of People, Process, and Technology.

5. **Path forward**: After you have your basic concept, you want to consider how you will bring it into the world as a real system. There is of course considerable work to be done yet. At this point, you have only a complex set of ideas that together form your concept. The remainder of this book is devoted to showing how to turn that concept into a designed system that can be implemented as fantastic software. But you need a bridge to help cross this gap between concept and designed system. The *path forward* captures circumstances in the real world and tactical next steps that you want to take in order to advance your concept into a system design and working software.

You capture these in your single Concept Canvas. You can then add this to your parti, as we discuss shortly.

Ideas Are Captured in a Lookbook

In the fashion and design world, there's something called a *lookbook*. This is a collection of photographs that a designer will use to showcase their work for a particular line or season or campaign. It gives viewers possible suggestions on how to pull together a few components from the new season's line, such as these jeans, that sweater, and these boots to form a look or a personal style.

John Malkovich Lookbook

Venerable actor John Malkovich has turned his talents to designing his own fashion line, and you can find an example of his lookbook here (*https://www.johnmalkovich.com/lookbooks*).

In fashion, this is a collection of images illustrating the concept. At first, you can use it that way, too. Eventually, your *lookbook* will become a compilation of design sources, inspirations, and otherwise random-seeming documents. It's your idea diary, and it helps you to recall all the aspects of the concept you're working with as you form it. It helps you as a concise compendium to show others so that you can collaborate on the design.

Your lookbook might have many of the following items:

- Informal sketches
- UML-type diagrams, but nothing formal or definitive-looking
- Images
- Mind maps
- Snippets of thoughts
- Key customers
- Relevant quotes
- Stories
- Links
- Videos
- Colors
- Materials

Your lookbook is like an active journal in collage form. There will be many sources of inspiration along the way that might have informed your concept. Simply capture them in this single place so that you have them to refer back to. This single place might just be a growing Word document, a special page on the wiki, a OneNote file, a web page, or whatever you like.

You might be working with a set of themes, the way a composer would have a set of themes for different characters or events. One might be "craftsmanship." How would you express that to your team or think of it yourself? You might consider some of the following:

- The Mercedes-Benz AMG "one man, one engine" philosophy, as shown in this video (*http://bit.ly/2kH4qjU*). Every AMG engine bears the signature of the one man who made it.

- A master seamstress making a tiny replica of the Miss Dior Dress from the 1950s in this video (*http://bit.ly/2kTQbIv*).

- A master cobbler making a pair of Prada shoes in this video (*http://bit.ly/2kQkboz*).

If one of your themes was about radically rethinking historical approaches, you might include the Google X Moonshot Thinking video (*http://bit.ly/2kIGWuK*), and so forth.

Initially, the audience for your lookbook will be the other folks on your team, but it's probably not useful outside that at first. It should feel a bit personal, as if to share it, you'd be revealing something, a bit of your attitude, tastes, inspirations, understanding, limits of that understanding, some part of yourself. You might feel a slight pang of nerves to do so. That's good. This means that you're doing something that matters to you, something you're truly engaged with.

As it becomes more refined, you can use it as a catalog from which to pull particular views that help you communicate the design to the variety of diverse collaborators who might include UI/UX folks, developers, executives, managers, and customers.

Fit to Purpose

> *As an artist, yes, I have constraints. Gravity is one of them.*
> —Frank Gehry

The Walt Disney Concert Hall opened its doors in Los Angeles in 2003 to become the new home of the Los Angeles Philharmonic. After being designed by architect Frank Gehry, it was constructed over the course of four years.

At the time of its opening, the following story was told by *Los Angeles Times* music critic Mark Swed:

> When the orchestra finally got its next [practice] in Disney, it was to rehearse Ravel's lusciously orchestrated ballet, *Daphnis and Chloé*. … This time, the hall miraculously came to life. Earlier, the orchestra's sound, wonderful as it was, had felt confined to the stage. Now a new sonic dimension had been added, and every square inch of air in Disney vibrated merrily. Toyota says that he had never experienced such an acoustical difference between a first and second rehearsal in any of the halls he designed in his native Japan. Salonen could hardly believe his ears. To his amazement, he discovered that there were wrong notes in the printed parts of the Ravel that sit on the players' stands. The orchestra has owned these scores for decades, but in the Chandler no conductor had ever heard the inner details well enough to notice the errors.

Figure 2-3 shows this fantastically expressive building.

This is architecture at its best: inventive, coherent, clear in concept, expressive, in conversation with its context, multivariate, improvisational, alive. The building appears as moving music itself. To support the quality of sound that it does, and the comfort and clarity it affords patrons, is astonishing. Gehry's building is brilliant, beautiful. Moreover, as the story about the misprinted music sheets reveals, the building is incredibly well fit to purpose. So must our concepts be.

Figure 2-3. The Walt Disney Concert Hall in Los Angeles by architect Frank Gehry (photo: Wikipedia)

In an interview, Gehry states that in architecture, you must ask, "Then what?" You can love the clients, love the city, hit the budget, be polite, be good to work with. These things are merely the table stakes. So you must ask yourself, "Then what?" to get the real value out of your work.

We must push ourselves to deliver something truly special, something of such wonderful function that we help our users hear notes they never heard before. We can astonish and delight.

The Concept Is Expressed in a Parti

> *It is better to enter a turn slow and come out fast than to enter a turn fast and come out dead.*
> —Dr. Ferry Porsche

Building architects have space, a neighborhood, and a building to build. They can start with physical objects, like a sculptor: a block of marble.

We in technology cannot do this. We have no space, no material but our logic, our language, and how we employ semantic signs to produce a concept.

The concept is the first moment of our work, and the one most often skipped and ignored because we did not even know it should be part of our work. Because we started with the "architect" metaphor. This causes us to make many other local category mistakes that accrue toward the failure of our projects.

Our work is to *produce a concept*. That concept produces a *system design*. That system design is comprehensive to create the best context for writing valid and sound requirements, both functional and nonfunctional, and for allowing them to be viewed together. The concept also informs a *designed project model*. Because our view is comprehensive, we design the project plan every bit as much as the software system. Because they go together in symbiosis. Taken together, our projects then have a far higher chance of succeeding than software projects have over the past 25 years or so. Such a program model produces working *software* that is innovative, delights customers, and features outstanding support for nonfunctional requirements. It also offers the most rewarding opportunity for the people on these teams to have fun and make a meaningful contribution that they are excited and delighted to do. With our approach, we stand a better chance to light a fire *within* people instead of under people.

The advent of the microprocessor meant that we had to conceive of how to create sturdiness, and fitness to purpose, and beauty, in a nonphysical realm. This is the realm of the philosopher more than of the architect.

As we have discussed, one reason so little software is properly functional or pleasant to use is that when we were busy borrowing metaphors, perhaps we picked the wrong one. And after we did, even then we skipped a part, and an important one: the *parti*.

The parti is short for "parti pris," meaning a "decision taken" in French. It is an image expressing the general organization of a design. The parti takes the Concept Canvas, the lookbook, and the ongoing changes and reveals of the project over time as inputs and refines them over the course of the project into a decision log of the key components. The parti is the first representation of high-level executable system components that can be built as software modules.

Partis are never reused because they are particular to this design challenge, these constraints, this context.

A straightforward, simple example comes from NASA (though they don't call it a parti), which you can see in Figure 2-4.

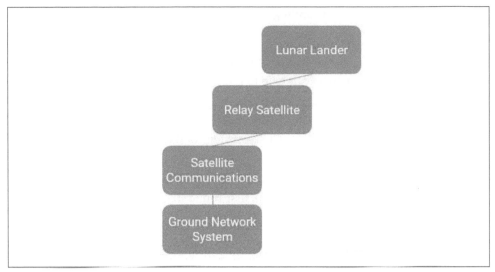

Figure 2-4. A concept sketch for a lunar landing system

This is enough to have hard discussions with as you focus your concept. It is at a high level. It focuses on the comprehensive system context, not one subsystem.

An Example

Imagine that we're to begin work on a new machine learning–based software project for the travel industry. We might create a parti for this software based on Athena. She is the Greek goddess of wisdom, strategy, craft, the harvest, and war, and advisor to travelers.

We ask, what possibilities does this suggest? Where does it direct our focus and attention? How can this create a theme for our design that supports coherence? Many things come to mind:

- The machine learning must not be tacked on to one aspect, but must be natively relevant in the entire scope.

- The Strategy pattern can be used to inject ever more implementations of stated algorithms. The system must create a new context for the business to pivot and support alternate growth.

- A focus must remain on craftsmanship and careful adherence to resilience.

- The system will bring the harvest, the new capabilities in retailing and offers.

- The system should offer exceptional user support through its interfaces, offering creative and just-in-time advice to travelers.

Now you have the basis, a grounding, for thinking about ways in which such ideas might be realized in the architecture. Pulling together these high-level contours under a single unifying personage as "Athena" makes sense. Capturing your concept in a unifying character, figure, name, or readily expressible idea will help you communicate your ideas with others who can help to refine the concept.

Define one supporting pole around which your idea can find another idea to enter a dialogue. Where do these ideas argue? On what basis? What do they try to persuade each other of? Where can they agree? Use that tension to create a space for the circulation of ideas.

Pick one pole, and design that entire pole. Now you have something to hang other ideas on, something that has survived the first round of interrogation. This will help prepare other aspects of the system.

Adding Aspects to the Parti

At this point, you've explored how one aspect of the system might work, how it can be useful, and powerful. Now change dimensions and design across the whole field, but only one inch deep so that you can see where the boundaries might be. You don't need to define them all firmly yet, but you've put a line on the horizon. You have one aspect thought through, and many others as points identified on the field.

You do not need to express the parti directly or map all of these elements to something concrete. It acts as an organizing principle and should be useful to you as you continue to mentally process and further explore and imagine the system. Eventually, your parti will find its way into a variety of concrete documents with design decisions, and the trick is to keep it in mind as you create these:

- Use case diagrams
- A deck outlining the design
- Class and component diagrams for key areas
- A complete architecture definition document

We address these in further depth in Chapter 5. The parti should not burden, but ignite.

The Parti Is Based on a Series of Reveals

> *I have always felt that if you know what you're going to do in advance, then you won't do it. Your creativity starts with whether you're curious or not.*
> —Frank Gehry

The parti must reveal, moment by moment, the key aspects of the story. It is nothing but a silly flight of fancy without a concrete realization. The parti is a disposable bridge toward human use. It can lend an organizing principle to your design that allows people to intuit it better and support you in providing more ways to serve the customer, the human user, as they want to be, and as they might not yet have imagined they want to be.

A *reveal* is the careful dosage to the implementing teams of what they can understand. It is your job, not theirs, to provide the concrete links to the parti within aspects of the design. Eventually the parti will fall away altogether, having blossomed from abstraction into design diagrams into a working system.

Make the system for the extreme users: both the experienced power user who is able to do everything, like make their own macros, and the novice user who only cares about 10% of the functions should be able to easily and readily do the obvious jobs. Consider the extremes up front and play them against each other to provide something that works for both of them. Consider other spectra for extreme users: old and young, native speakers and nonnative speakers, women and men, short and tall, those who need the deep details and those who need the quick summary.

Know what and where your reveals are. Consider the people on your project and how you will implant the parti into everyday life.

Look for opportunities to express the concept in every aspect, across the templates you make, the hiring practices, the culture of the project team, the development life cycle, the milestones, the management, the ordering and prioritizing.

Do not expect too much of the parti. It has its moment of real value in capturing the concept, and then will fade away. New requirements, laws, and constraints will emerge. Change it or abandon it if and when necessary and reconceive based on new things you've learned. You must do this in order to retain the holistic integrity of the concept, not the original concept or your parti.

Let the system begin to speak to you. Enter into a dialog with your concept that hourly gains greater embodiment, through ever more avenues: the system diagrams, the use cases, the goals, and the ways to achieve them.

Let it change your course as it takes on more life of its own. You make the child, name it, teach it. Then, as the child grows, they show you that they're not a tiny version of you, but have their own values, desires, and methods; the child becomes your teacher.

As Eisenhower said, "Planning is indispensable. Plans are useless."

Understanding Ideas

Every block of stone has a statue inside it and it is the task of the sculptor to discover it. I saw the angel in the marble and carved until I set him free.
—Michelangelo

We do not understand the idea that represents our system. That is because it is incomprehensible. But also because it has not been our aim.

Michelangelo might have viewed his work as revealing the angel already within the marble. But the marble existed, and the only work was to chisel. The creative architect starts with emptiness, with nothing. And before him, a world of infinite conjuncts, a field, in which to assert some object anew. We have no marble.

When we approach system design in attempting to understand, we subvert our best efforts because we cannot understand what we have yet to invent.

We therefore seek instead to understand the idea of ideas, not the idea of our system or the solution we think we're making, but ideas themselves. Are we quite sure we know what an idea is?

Sense Certainty

See this? This is this. This ain't something else. This is this.
—Robert DeNiro, *The Deer Hunter*

We receive sensory data, a multiplicity of inputs, constantly. A filmed motion picture typically runs at 24 frames per second. The pictures are all still photographs. But as with a flip book, our minds fill in the transitions that are not truly there to give us the illusion of motion and continuity.

This is not thinking, but sensing. We do not have an idea. We have not mixed this stream of sense data with our own apprehension and conclusions. We have only complected sense. Nineteenth-century German philosopher Hegel calls this "sense-certainty," and it's sometimes called "picture-thinking."

We can, in this mode, believe that they understand utterances like "here," "now," and "this," concretely, as if they were direct referents—as if we think there is a fixed, understood definition of "here" or "now" or "this."

To be blunt, when we say these words, we believe we are saying something meaningful and that we know what we are talking about, when in fact we do not. Parsing these very commonly used words is almost impossible.

The distinction is critically important because our software projects are filled with the words of the requirements, the words of the design, and the words of the code. We must be crystal clear (as much as possible) that we are saying what we mean. When we start to try to express what we have observed about the world in language, mixed with our ideas about their coherence, we begin to form concepts. These are the basis of strong designs.

Metacognition

One of the most important skills you can have as a designer is to cultivate your meta-cognitive ability. You notice yourself thinking about *how* you think, as you do it. You see not only your concepts, but you form more complex concepts and notice the manner in which you constructed them.

When you think about how you think, you call into question a variety of things:

- The sensory data you take in, respond to, recall, and retain, and how you respond to it, what you pick out, prioritize, conjoin, and disjoin.
- How you synthesize this data to represent it back to yourself as interpreted ideas.
- Your own understanding of yourself as a stable identity that can perform this apprehension consistently, with clarity.

Foregrounding your metacognition puts you in a dialog with yourself. Being in a dialog with yourself as if you were two people, perhaps arguing, will help you to quickly shape nothing into something. And that "something" will be better, more interesting, higher performing because you are considering it more carefully, more richly, with fewer assumptions and biases.

You can practice this by batting your concepts back and forth between seemingly disparate characteristics. Consider the following:

- Sturdiness and flexibility
- Distribution and performance
- Security and ease of use
- Simplicity and complexity
- Tall and short
- Wide and narrow
- Bright and dark
- Solid and void
- Stasis and circulation
- Presence and absence
- Software and hardware

- Business and philosophy

- Architecture and art

How are you privileging one term in the binary pair? What sense data, history, ideas, subliminal suggestions, constraints, laws, cultural norms, biases, stereotypes, and viewpoint led you to this privileging? How can you find the concept that unifies both terms in each pair, such that the trade-offs you make become no apparent trade-off at all?

Then, after you have incorporated the competing concerns and satisfied the constituent members of the British parliament arguing in your head to the point where you feel there are no longer opposites, you have a concept with integrity, harmony, and sturdiness, and one that is closer to bringing the design to its truth of the matter.

Criticize your own mental processes. Stand back and observe how you intake data, from where, and why. You are always absorbing data; this data continually shapes your mental space, the field which harvests thought. What can you observe about what you're taking in, to perform a habitual act of synthesis?

How can you then subvert or overturn that synthesis with a new perspective of apparently disparate or seemingly unrelated things? How is a raven like a writing desk?

Go shopping or to the park or to see a movie or listen to music or a lecture on something entirely unrelated to your design challenge. Not as a field trip with a stated aim, but as a quotidian act of noticing how your daily commute informs your design, how a crumpled paper might beget Gehry's Disney Concert Hall. All of these will inform your thinking, what you see as possibilities of relations, and give you raw material and metaphors to work with as you hone your concepts about the design and light a path toward what concepts your design in turn affords the world.

It is an act of pattern recognition, synthesis, and subversion.

Software is often broken, and often broken from the start, in its conceptual understanding of the world. As we have discussed, a software design represents our conception of a portion of the real world. Yet we cannot design and make the software that represents the world of infinite conjuncts; we would never be finished and go to market. So we must draw a line, a border, create a margin around some subset of this world as we conceive it to limit our scope to have something to build. And that we will call the domain. This is the set, the scope of the software, and it is at this horizon, the gap between our concept and our created field imposed on top of the phenomenological world, that computers must act rationally, decidably, given their inputs. Their inputs are only those within the field we demarcate, and their outputs only those that we allow. Despite our best efforts, at some point, the point of this horizon, we must stop and ship the software. And there is ambiguity at these borders, the meeting points of the phenomenological world and our artificially superimposed field.

For example, we might be called upon to make a system to predict the price of homes. So, naturally, we define, among others, the class "House." We spend a million dollars on sophisticated machine learning projects to make better predictions. We do not understand why our prediction so often fail us. We included the attributes of age, square feet, acreage. But, fatally, did not include the attribute "proximity-to-the-beach": because we curtailed our semantic field there.

We cannot conceive of all the things. We cannot include all that we can conceive of. At some point, we must stop and make a compromise. Make these moments of compromise *conscious*, and this will mitigate the blow of the lie we're telling our system about its origins and context. This is the key aspect to better concepts, which are the supporting substructure of better software.

Context

Always design a thing by considering its next largest context: a chair in a room, a room in a house, a house in an environment, and environment in a city plan.
    —Finnish architect Eliel Saarinen

There are only two kinds of problems in the world: trivial and nontrivial.

A trivial problem is straightforward. Its cause is direct, simple, and obvious. Its span of influence is small. Examples include pricking your thumb, or running out of paper towels. Its solution is similarly clear, direct, and simple. These are simple systems and the behavior of the constituent elements of simple systems is predictable.

We are not interested in those here.

A nontrivial problem is almost always more complex than at first it seems. Trendy practitioners will tell you to "Keep It Simple, Stupid." This is a useless and empty phrase. The problem is not simplicity versus complexity, and developers "making things complex." Sometimes things are in fact complex.

Imagine you are designing an ecommerce system. You have a database of Products, wherein you assign an ID and name and description. We know when we add products to our cart, we are asked for a quantity. So we add a column to the Products table for "quantity." That's the simplest thing to do. But this is absurd.

We learn from our quick trip into sets that here there are two concepts at work: the product, and the product-as-object-during-shopping-by-a-particular-customer. And that is a related, but different matter.

This thing has certain properties that are its essence, and then there are other new properties that are obtained only in the process of shopping; those cannot be separated from that idea. There is no abstract quantity. So you must create something new. You might invent the *InventoryItem* or *CartProduct* to express this new relation: you have the user. The pencil doesn't have quantity=3; that decorating idea must exist to capture ideas that are not metadata about the product but are first-order properties of the shopped item.

This is the purpose of item *variants*. We think there is a "shirt." But a shirt is an abstraction. You can't sell it until you know its size and maybe its color and maybe its intended gender. Are we to make three rows for small, medium, and large shirts? What about color—we sell them in white, black, and blue. Are there then nine rows? Do we double each of these according to gender? This is an inefficient database design, and so this fault should call out to us that we are missing an idea—missing a part of our concept.

So seeing this disconnect we must create a new object: we create the idea of the *variant*. We now have created semantic space that allows these ideas of color, size, gender, and what-have-you to be full and rich in expression and be themselves extensible (if later we add one for men's and one for women's) but each have their integrity and maintain an efficient design.

It might seem counterintuitive after all these years of false conditioning to "keep it simple." But the smart designer enlarges the problem space. You create ideas that are semantically coherent with the overall design not to add complexity, but to make the inherent complexity of the world efficiently represented in your design. You see many contexts. You attempt to blow up and undermine your design the moment you see it leap to life, knowing it will be used many different ways, only some of which you intend.

Enlarging the problem space is about identifying multiple levels of causation. You have a problem: the user needs to do X. First, that might or might not be the problem. Ask why do they want to do that? In many cases, the user does not want to do at all the thing they are doing. They don't want to shop for that snazzy shirt and put it in their cart and buy it. They want to wear it. The shopping is a necessary evil to the wearing. This is an area in which Amazon simply excels.

You cannot solve all of these problems by continuing to trace things back in endless deferrals. But you can perhaps arrive at a different, more general solution. This often means that you can see many benefits, more than originally hoped for.

Often, it's just as easy to do it right as it is to settle for a lesser design because that will beget workarounds and compensations.

You can reduce the set later as needed to fit the timeline, budget, and other concerns.

Sets

As you saw in the previous example, design is about thinking in sets. In this view, we see the world as a collection of collections, each containing generally three element counts: zero, one, or many.

What belongs to this object necessarily and what doesn't? What does and doesn't belong together perhaps? What is optional to add on top?

Set theory is a rich and difficult study. For our purposes, two basic ideas will get us a long way:

Extension
> What belongs in this set? What is the name that puts these things in a group? For a retailer, the group might be "All the stores of Brand X," which is rather straightforward. Now you have something to call a stake in the ground. We continue, and posit "All the stores in Kalamazoo." But where is the border precisely, or is it a gerrymandering contorted border, a zip code, or set of them? What if they want to run a campaign that allows owners to set discounts for their own store, but Oscar owns several of them?

Essence
> Essence refers to that without which, not. That is, if you don't have some part of a thing, you can no longer say you still have that thing.

Determining essence is difficult, but essential in keeping the ambiguities at the margins to a minimum, which is what will undermine your design, and make it expensive and untoward to maintain.

If you take away your hand, are you still you? I think most people would agree that they are: they don't lose their identity because they lost their hand. They can still be found guilty of crimes and identified for tax purposes. How much of you can you lose before you are not you anymore? If you suffer early onset dementia with your body healthy and well intact, are you still you? These questions are difficult to determine. Luckily, software is not as complex as people are.

Naive Set Theory

For a good introduction to set theory, I encourage you to read the mathematics textbook *Naive Set Theory* by Paul Halmos from 1960. It's short and dense. For the truly impatient, make sure you're familiar with the concepts presented on the Wikipedia page (*https://en.wikipedia.org/wiki/Naive_set_theory*).

Relations

We already understand relations, the connections between objects. My aim is to formalize and problematize that understanding just a little bit so that you design with the edges in mind. Let's take a moment to consider these key terms:

The Axiom of Pairing
> It is the case that for any two sets there exists a set that they both belong to. When you assert a figure into the field, ask what other sets it also is a member of. Then determine validity and priority.

Domain
> We use this word regularly in software. It comes from set theory, and more formally refers to the set of input or argument values for which some function is defined.

Range
> The difference between the lowest and highest values in a set.

Intersection
> The intersection of *A* and *B* is the set of all objects that are both in *A* and in *B*.

Union
> The set consisting of all objects that are elements of *A* or of *B* or of both. For every collection of sets, there exists a set that contains all the elements that belong to at least one set of the given collection.

Complement
> The set of all objects that belong to *A* but *not* to *B*.

There are three ways to talk about equivalence:

Reflexive
> A relation is *reflexive* if all the members of a set have the same relation to the set. So equality is a reflexive relation. "Less than" is not reflexive.

Symmetric
> A relation is *symmetric* if, for all *A* and *B* in a set *X*, *A* is related to *B* if and only if *B* is related to *A*. Examples include:
>
> - Is married to
> - Is a sibling of

Transitive

A relation is *transitive* if it has the following property: if *A* is related to *B* and *B* is related to *C*, then *A* is also related to *C*. Examples include:

- Being a subset of
- Implies
- Divides

Even though we might be familiar with some of these terms from programming languages and databases, using this lens in your system analysis and design is sure to come in handy. The only point here is to encourage you to explore your concepts using this framework of how objects relate to one another.

Advantages of Semantic Design

On two occasions I have been asked, "Pray, Mr. Babbage, if you put into the machine wrong figures, will the right answers come out?" I am not able rightly to apprehend the kind of confusion of ideas that could provoke such a question.
—Charles Babbage

So we have thought of ourselves awkwardly as engineers and architects, and we've enjoyed none of the materials, methods, or tools, and that has meant we have misconceived of our field and misapplied a lot of square pegs into a lot of round holes. The only thing in our field that comes close, really, to the discourse of engineering is that the speed of light means we can enjoy an understanding of the limit and measurable rate of data transfer.

With the advent of user stories in Scrum and related Agile methods, we have lost a lot of our focus on communicating coherently and specifically. This leads to a culture in which there's never enough time to do it right, but somehow always enough time to do it over. This makes projects fail. The Semantic methodology offers a list of documents that together make it practicable and repeatable in your organization, capturing an incredibly rich and robust set of perspectives on the software, with various forms of communication. It focuses equally on the functional and nonfunctional requirements, which are often missing.

But if you think through your concept, you will purposely reveal more of the semantic field that is your representation of the world. As you work through the concept, the semantics evolve and are challenged and refined. Your resulting ideas and the language and logic overall will be more sound, more robust, more comprehensive, and more customer-centric, and your requirements, both functional and nonfunctional, will be far, far better than what you're used to. Your design will be fit to purpose, sturdy, harmonious, and beautiful. You will have expressed. You will have created the context in which fantastic software is born. That software will be reliable, maintainable, extensible, scalable, available, secure, and delightful to the user.

And that's the whole point.

There are a variety of other advantages in this method:

- It focuses the team and encourages them to be personally engaged and motivated.

- It unleashes more creativity.

- It offers informal methods for testing your logic and your biases at the point in the project where it will never be cheaper, quicker, or easier to change.

- It takes a comprehensive view. It's synthetic, from many sources, more open, less narrow and rigid. The ideas are native to software more so than engineering or architecture.

- It is failure-oriented, as much as success-oriented. By foregrounding opposites and contradictions and teasing them out, we predict more problems earlier and can work to prevent them.

- It encourages you to focus on not just dividing the existing cake, but on making more cakes because the only cost that matters in an innovative landscape is opportunity cost.

- It does not use metaphors that do not apply, which misguides our thinking. In software, that matters considerably given that logic and language are the only tools we have.

- Contrary to much of what we see in Agile, you insert the concept design as an upfront phase. This does not make it waterfall. And waterfall is not inherently bad. It is bad, however, to presume to spend years of dozens of people's time and millions of dollars of other people's money making software that you haven't thought through. Thinking it through as we outline here will make better requirements and make you far more likely to do it right the first time.

- The focus on setting the context helps developers be productive while owning— and being accountable for—the software they make.

- It's prescriptive in certain documents and very loose in other areas of the method. This allows for easy incorporation into the many other processes that you must or like to use, while retaining the flexibility of an Agile process.

- It underscores the multiplicity of "customers" of the software, which makes it more robust and usable to all the actual diverse users of your software.

- It sheds several false notions that lead us astray, such as a definition of "done." Software is almost never "done" the way a building gets done. One of the systems in my charge is nearly 20 years old, and yet 200 people still work on it every day.

They're not just doing operating system updates. An evolutionary approach works more naturally with how successful applications actually live in the real world. The semantic method establishes a framework for its further evolution by an array of teams and stakeholders.

- Because we foreground the concept and maximize context and extensibility, it is easier to adjust for changes, problems, or new ideas as they inevitably arise, minimizing churn. The abstractions will be at the optimal level across your design. Nonoptimal abstraction is often the way that lots of hacks and tacked-on additions begin to rise up like weeds or poorly executed additions to a house across your code, making it more difficult to maintain in the long run.

- Because a lack of timely, good decisions by the proper parties leads to failures, we include communication plans and clear semantic paths for working across teams in a complex environment. Decision making is an important part of the efficient flow.

- We foreground assumptions and list them along with requirements such that if they change, we can quickly plan for them.

- We thoughtfully align with the strategy and pave communication and decision routes between development teams and leadership. We do not assume, as other methods do, that software development teams exist in a vacuum, or only in some dark room decorated with *Star Trek* paraphernalia where executives never go except to slide pizza under the door. That isolation of the development teams is not one to maintain. When we foreground software design as a software problem instead of a semantic problem, we help build a wall that shouldn't exist. That wall creates divergence between the strategy and the local project and teams, which threatens the project. You can be "in the zone" when your alignment is clear.

Software projects fail because people don't know what they want, what they are making, why they're doing it, who makes what decisions about it, and what the abstractions and routes are to make those things clearer.

Our methods heretofore have improperly addressed these aspects, and they are the precise aspects of a software project that the semantic design method addresses. Let's dive deeper into what it is and how it works.

CHAPTER 3

Deconstruction and Design

Perhaps something has occurred in the history of the concept of structure that could be called an "event," if this loaded word did not entail a meaning which it is precisely the function of structural—structuralist—thought to reduce or suspect...

—Jacques Derrida, "Structure, Sign, and Play in the Discourse of the Human Sciences"

Introduction to Deconstruction

This section might appear "out there," marginal, even inconsequential, as some distracting oddity in a book on software design. It could feel external to our purpose, irrelevant, too unfamiliar, discomforting.

This section serves as critical context for the practical tools and strategies you will learn in Parts II and III of this text. Is this section the marginalia, or is it the thing itself?

***

Cut To:

INT. A CONFERENCE BALLROOM AT JOHNS HOPKINS UNIVER-SITY, BALTIMORE, MARYLAND, US, 1966 — NIGHT

The Scene: A conference for philosophy professors titled "The Language of Criticism and the Sciences of Man."

Action!

Enter French philosopher JACQUES DERRIDA. He is 36, French-Algerian, soft-spoken, dressed in a suit rumpled from his recent travel from Paris. He steps to the podium to deliver his paper. He takes a sip of water. He speaks.

> *(quietly)*
> Perhaps something has occurred in the
> history of the concept of structure
> that could be called an "event," if
> this loaded word did not entail a
> meaning which it is precisely the
> function of structural—structuralist—
> thought to reduce or to suspect...

As he continues, the room falls hushed. Then nervous. Then angry. Then astonished. His talk is called "Structure, Sign, and Play in the Discourse of the Human Sciences." After he delivers it, the attendees retire to a chamber to smoke and argue into the early hours of the next morning on its implications.

This paper would mark an origin of change, and advance, in the course of philosophy and the humanities for the next several decades. It is an astonishing piece of writing, and an incredibly erudite, fiery blast to his audience of assembled philosophy professors who, like those at the 1968 NATO conference, were searching for the path forward in their field.

Derrida had been invited to speak with the supposition that his work would elaborate and help popularize the idea of structuralism. Instead, he devoted his argument to illustrating how philosophers can only talk in the language they inherit, and that as a result, their concepts are limited: they rely on the patterns of previously established metaphysics and base their arguments on it, even as they denounce it. He exposed how the central theses and propositions of the structuralist philosophical endeavor were in contradiction and how, as a result, their field was in stasis.

Derrida gave this paper at a conference intended to promote structuralism, and in a sense, in a single evening, it ended the field. It is widely cited as the precipitating event, the rupture, that ignited post-structuralism in the United States, introducing new ways of thinking about writing, feminism, language, epistemology, ontology, aesthetics, social construction, ideology, and political theory, across philosophy, sociology, political science, the arts, and the humanities.

The Paper

You can read "Structure, Sign, and Play" here (*http://bit.ly/ 2kFSD5n*) in English translation. I highly encourage it. It's a (very) tough piece of writing, in part because the writing is *performative*. That is, the writing exhibits an acting out of the circling argument that Derrida is making. It is, purposefully, a triumph of structure.

In "Structure, Sign, and Play," Derrida begins with the idea that in an argument or analysis, terms (signs) are defined purely in relation to one another. Put simply, we only can conceive of "good" in relation to "bad," or "success" in relation to "failure," along a spectrum of nuance and differing meaning in contexts. Such structuralist systems thereby allow "play" in their terms because meaning is deferred; in a sense, the can is kicked down the road from one sign to another such that establishing a fixed and firm meaning in a sign is problematic because of this play.

The crux of Derrida's position is this: throughout the history of structuralist thought, we have relied on some *anchoring center*. This center is the term, sign, or idea that appears as fixed, immutable, assumed, given: metaphysical. As such, it is beyond the system of play that all the other signs operate within; it is incontrovertible, assumed and therefore unexamined, not held to the same standard or afforded the same interpretations. It is not subject to the same terms of the established system and as such is outside the system. "The center," he therefore concludes, "is not the center."

Derrida's philosophy, introduced in this talk and subsequently outlined in dozens of books across his formidable career, especially his key work *Of Grammatology*, is called *deconstruction*.

Deconstruction in Popular Culture

This is probably a term you've heard in popular culture, where it is typically misunderstood, diluted, misused. There's a movie, *Deconstructing Harry*. It is a term Derrida employed to mean destroy and create from within, at once. Before his death, he evolved this idea of deconstruction over decades in dozens of books. He was incredibly smart and learned, and his ideas are very complex, and are in no way intended for the layperson. Our aim here is to take up, in the manner of a *bricoleur*, the bits and pieces of these ideas available to us and apply them as tools to illuminate our endeavors in software design.

Derrida argues that when we examine semantic structure via deconstruction, we see that the structure of meaning rests upon a series of binary oppositions, sets of pairs that are opposed to each other in meaning, and from which they respectively derive their meaning. Such pairs, as we can see even in our loose conversation in our daily lives, might be good/bad, good/evil, presence/absence, speech/writing, man/beast, God/man, man/woman, being/nothingness, normal/abnormal, sane/insane, healing/hurting, primary/secondary, civilized/uncivilized or "savage," theory/practice, and so forth.

Binary Oppositions

The idea of binary oppositions is important to understand in semantic software design. You can read more about it here (*https://en.wikipedia.org/wiki/Binary_opposition*).

Assigning fixed meaning requires that we privilege one of the terms in a pair of binary oppositions that unwittingly are held up as unquestionable, beyond reproach. Derrida argues that the history of structuralism is the history of mere substitutions of one honored and indisputable center for another, whether the central idea is "God" or "Being" or "Man" or "presence." His point is that there is a contradiction inherent in structuralism such that it is rendered incoherent.

So what does all this mean in practice? The deconstructionist move is as follows:

1. Read the argument closely and carefully. For us, this means we consider our understanding of the domain, the semantic field, closely and carefully.

2. Find the sets of binary pairs that form the structure of the concept as given.

3. Determine which term in the binary pair the author privileges above the other.

4. This can lead us to the assumed anchoring center that escapes challenge and makes possible the rest of the discourse in which the terms can abound in meaning.

5. Expose this contradiction and overturn the binary oppositions such that the argument unravels and a new concept is created that properly can incorporate the terms in the system without the prior inconsistency and false privileging. It does this in a way that does not glibly reduce to "everything is everything," but rather marks the undecideability and interplay of the terms.

It's a Process

Pay careful attention to understand this method insofar as it's presented here. Deconstruction provides a critical means for gaining a true understanding for how a system operates, especially a system derived from a concept that is purely logical and linguistic, as any particular software system is. In this way, a method of deconstruction is a critical tool in better system design. These few steps in deconstruction represent a key, one might say "central," element in semantic software design as it unfolds throughout this book. We'll see how to apply it practically. For now, just don't lose this term.

In this talk, Derrida revealed the problems philosophy had at its core, how its internal contradictions abounded in ways that could no longer be ignored.

He closes his paper with the following:

> Here there is a sort of question, call it historical, of which we are only glimpsing today
> the conception, the formation, the gestation, the labor. I employ these words, I admit,
> with a glance toward the business of childbearing—but also with a glance toward those
> who, in a company from which I do not exclude myself, turn their eyes away in the face
> of the as-yet unnameable which is proclaiming itself and which can do so, as is neces-
> sary whenever a birth is in the offing, only under the species of the non-species, in the
> formless, mute, infant, and terrifying form of monstrosity.

It's interesting to note that building architecture, our sometime progenitor, has an entire school of deconstructionists who are among the best in their field. Included on this illustrious list are the Pritzker Prize–winning Zaha Hadid, whose opera houses, bridges, and cultural centers are among the most brilliant works of her generation; the Pritzker Prize–winning Rem Koolhaas, who has designed museums and Prada stores around the world while also holding a position as an architecture professor at Harvard; Frank Gehry, the architect of the practically perfect Disney Concert Hall; and Daniel Libeskind, whose work includes the very moving Jewish Museum in Berlin.

The power of deconstruction in philosophy over the years caused it to reach into farther-flung realms, including cuisine: the deconstructed Caesar salad introduced in California in the 1990s owes its existence to Derrida and his philosophy of decon-struction.

What does this have to do with software? Everything, in fact. Certainly as much as buildings and towns do.

After you define your concept and your semantic field, deconstruct it yourself in an analytical move to expose the inadvertent bad arguments and misunderstandings and contradictions and privileges introduced into the system. This is the step in which you really improve it for better flexibility, more accurate representation of the world, better resilience, scale, and more.

If it's not at all clear how exactly this is the case, not to worry. This is just an introduc-tion and we explore further what it means and how it works in the coming chapters.

Simplexity

We often are told, and sometimes cling to, the slogan to make systems simple. We hear, "Keep It Simple." We "know" that good design is simple. This is not the case. Or rather, while this statement passes for an idea, it isn't one.

The engine of a typical E-class Mercedes-Benz has three times as many parts than a typical Honda Accord. Which is the better engine? There's one answer if you want to go 180 mph. What are you hoping for from the car? Access to a greater number of mechanics with fewer specialized skills might be a design goal. That offers a different answer.

Is Google search "simple"? For the end user, amazingly so. It's estimated that Google contains two billion lines of code, or roughly 40 times the size of Microsoft Windows, estimated at 50 million lines.[1] This of course begs the question, What part of Google is "search," when it's used in web searches, Maps, Gmail, and many other products? Or is it more complex than that?

Your intent must not be a facile "simplicity." Nor can it be to design for its own sake. Nor, obviously, to overengineer because complexity is fun or because we're building our resumé, or we don't know when to stop or what we're designing or for whom.

We create accidental complexity when we focus improperly on simplicity.

Fred Brooks is the famous architect and manager of the IBM System/360, and the author of the book *The Mythical Man Month* in the 1970s. He thought to write it after his exit interview from IBM in which Thomas J. Watson asked him why it was so much harder to manage software projects than hardware projects. In his paper "No Silver Bullet," Brooks outlines two types of complexity:

Essential complexity
    This is the complexity inherent in the design problem. It cannot be reduced.

Accidental complexity
    This is the kind of complexity that is created by the developers themselves. It does not inhere in the concept itself. It is due to weak design, poor coding quality, or inattention to the problem.

Counterintuitively perhaps (and certainly counter to recent received ideas), your intent should be to embrace the complexity of the many users of different kinds with different needs. These include the many competing concerns of audit, attestation, accounting, the timeline, the budget, and so forth.

Right-size the complexity of your concepts according to the job.

More important, never mistake accidental, or potential complexity, for essential complexity.

---

1 See *https://bit.ly/2qo8mHB*.

(De)composition

The problem is not getting cool air to the engine, it's getting the hot air away.
—Dr. Ferry Porsche

When we go to design a software system for a Human Resources (HR) department to use, we ask what matters an HR department is concerned with. We decide they are concerned with *humans*: after all, it's in the name.

But, alas, they are not.

There are many humans that are not accounted for in an HR database—most of them, in fact. So we decide to cast the lasso that will demarcate our field, our ground, a bit more modestly. So we say: let an Employee (the kind of human the system is about) be a thing that exists in this world.

We quickly ascribe attributes to this class. We then consider what assumptions we have made, what we have left out. We realize there may be reasons to keep records of contractors who work for the company, but are not employees. So we must add an accounting for them, and their employers. Now we have extended the idea, and also realize we have room for some consolidation, because even though employees and contractors are different, they share many attributes that matter for these purposes.

So we say that a person exists, to hold these shared attributes, since both, for now at least until the robots come, are people. And so forth.

The point is not to review basic object-oriented analysis, an understanding of which is assumed. The point is to illustrate how this process might go well, how it might go wrong, and how we do best to quickly search out the boundaries of our field, the horizon beyond which we will not step, because that's where the ambiguities are found.

The second we cast any figure into the field, we ask what assumptions we're making.

To avoid oversimplifying, or early simplifying, both of which lead to accidental complexity or overengineering and poor design, is to understand the essence of a thing.

You do this by looking at the universe first and then zooming into your problem space. Then, after you have posited some figures onto the field, stop and zoom out further again, to ask what you might be assuming.

Focusing on making something simple will create unwanted complexity later.

Embracing complexity now will allow you to organize your work properly. The organization here is to reveal what functional, integral subsystems can work together to create the complete functional system (see Figure 3-1).

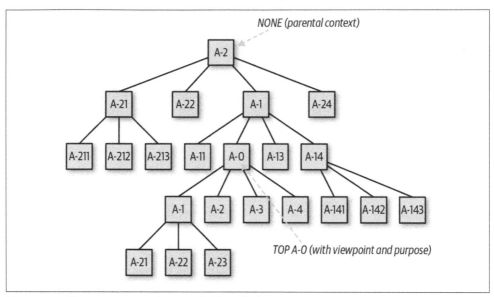

Figure 3-1. Decomposition (source: Wikipedia)

If you start from "simple," you will end up tacking things on to handle the burgeoning, competing concerns. This will create a design with less integrity and harmony and internal consistency.

Instead, start with the universe, and then narrow down subsystems.

With practice you can do this quickly, and then almost intuitively as a matter of course, so it doesn't take as long as it sounds.

If we think our problem is how to get cool air into the engine, we have made many assumptions, and started too late in the problem space. The problem is not that; it is how to keep the engine cool enough to function properly. These may casually sound the same, but they are entirely different.

These assumptions invite nonessential elements. They add unnecessary complexity to the design.

You might ask how to give more horsepower to a big engine that is already very powerful. That is a failure of analysis. Instead, ask whether the real problem is not that you want the car to go faster.

Look for the nonobvious places to start. We must take time to separate the categories of the problem space properly or assign relations properly.

To make a car go faster, increasing horsepower is an obvious place to start.

A Maserati Granturismo has a very large 4.7 liter V8 engine, which is made in partnership with Ferrari, at 454 horsepower. By contrast, the Lotus Evora 400 has a relatively modest 3.5 liter V6 engine made by Toyota, with only 400 horsepower. Which is the faster car?

Lotus did not ask how to make a bigger engine. They took a different view. Instead of focusing on changing the engine (the "figure"), as would be obvious, they turned their attention to the body (the "ground"). They threw out weight.

The Maserati weights 4,400 pounds. It needs that horsepower. The Lotus Evora weighs only 2,700 pounds. To the Evora, they added a supercharger that compresses air to make a bigger explosion in the same size engine. As a result both cars share the same top speed of 190 mph.

These are not trade-offs: these are design decisions.

First you are designing the concept, then designing the factory for making those concepts. The rest of the book is about how you create this concept realization factory. Then, the developers in the framework of your architecture go on within in it to make the thing.

> It's no longer all about horsepower, but more ideas per horsepower.
> —Porsche

Affordance

> Years ago when I was living very briefly with a stockbroker who had a very good cellar I asked him how I could learn about wine. "Drink it," he said.
> —Jeanette Winterson, Art [Objects]

The way you address ease of use is by considering *affordance*.

Norman doors got their name from the lovely book *The Design of Everyday Things* by Donald Norman. In the book, he recounts the design of a particular door he encountered: it had a handle on it, as doors do. But the way it was designed and installed meant it had to be *pushed* to open it. This is counterintuitive, and makes the door difficult to use. People see a handle and naturally pull, and their efforts to enter are thwarted, albeit temporarily. But the frustration is real and unnecessary. The handle, by its presence, affords pulling. It all but asks to be pulled. Pushing is not why we make handles. This is bad design and must be avoided.

We must ask in our empathy what the most intuitive thing would be, to a wide array of diverse people, with a wide array of aims, and design for what best affords, or suggests, how to use our system in the way they will want to.

This idea can be extended to include more: the keys of many cars today are electric and battery-operated. But the battery failing in the key should not mean you can't open your car. Then what is otherwise a very expensive and nonnecessary "convenience" becomes a nightmare of the tail wagging the dog: the key is supposed to serve the car. So these keys have a backup key: a small metal one inside the electric one that work when the battery fails.

Do not make two equally obvious ways to accomplish the goal. Make one obvious path and make the backup at once hidden and accessible.

You must also consider how you can afford from different perspectives.

Porsche has a rich heritage in track racing, and has won the Le Mans race more than any other manufacturer: 18 times to date. It used to be that drivers at Le Mans did not start in their cars: when the flag went down, they would sprint to their cars, get in, turn it on, and go. So the designers at Porsche realized that by placing the starter on the left of the steering wheel instead of the right, the driver could parallel process, by turning the ignition on with his left hand while getting into gear with his right hand. In a race like this, shaving off a few extra milliseconds matters. So to this day, even with the keys powered by Bluetooth and even with no racing requirements for the family getting into an SUV, every Porsche has its key on the left of the wheel.

Tying to their racing and design heritage and sense of tradition is important to Porsche owners, and this subtle reminder affords a desired pleasure and connection, even if it is silly or inconvenient for the 90% of people who are right-handed and are used to it being on the right side of the wheel like every other car in the world. It's a good design—from that perspective.

Give Intention and Use Value to Negative Space

Architecture is the thoughtful making of space.
—Louis Kahn

Whenever you make space, you are making two things: the space demarcated within the boundary, and the place outside it.

We demarcate a field in the raw space of thought. We then assert objects into this field, and pay them considerable attention. These are the systems we make, the applications, the databases, the products. We fret over the usability, the vendor, the cost, the performance, the maintainability, the ease of use of these objects. Much wringing of hands ensues. We are obsessed with the objects—the figures—that we assert.

But what of the negative space? The negative space is the field, or the *ground*, that which is not our asserted object, but the place in which it can obtain ontological status, appear on the horizon, come into existence.

The white chalk letters we draw on a blackboard are our figure, the blackboard is the ground. The charcoal letters we inscribe on brown butcher paper are the figure, the paper is the ground. The software is the figure. But what is its space?

We might say it is the infrastructure on which it can run. But is that not software? We might say it is the hardware, and software makers "abstract" this into a field—a public or private cloud—that we fancy simply exists. We don't have to bring it into existence. It is not part of the application. It is a supplement.

Similarly, we abstract away the "business." We narrow our scope to make our figure workable. We find binary oppositions (here/there, now/then, inside/outside) and assign one the status of priority.

You have likely encountered the image shown Figure 3-2 before.

Figure 3-2. Is it a vase, or two faces, or both? (Source: Wikipedia)

Figure-Ground theory states that the space that results from placing figures onto a place (asserting them into the field) should be as carefully considered as the figures themselves.

When you design, do not focus only on the figures, but look also to the ground. What negative space are you creating?

We first must create negative space because in software there is no "situation," no necessary context. We can outsource its creation, we can buy it, we can license it; at the outset we aren't sure what it will do or where it will run or exactly whom it will serve or how it will be used.

We create the negative space, the ground, every bit as much as we create the figure.

Our designs suffer, and our users suffer, when we do not recognize this. Because when we do not recognize it, we do not approach the design as purposively, as holistically, as intentionally, as thoughtfully.

The unattended space between the figure and the ground creates a zone of ambiguity, a tension, which, left unattended, creates an avenue of entry for uncertainty, uncoordination, chaos.

To improve the efficacy of the system, we recognize and closely observe the boundaries of the system, and attend to them with the same care we do our cherished figures. We must do this because by demarcating the field in the first place, as we must, we have invented that boundary, too. It is figure, too.

The Japanese word for this is "ma," meaning the space or pause between two structural elements, not created by the elements themselves, but in the perception of the human observer.

In a linguistic and conceptual failure, there is no corresponding word in English.

How can you give that negative space, the ground, an intention? How can you find for it a use value? How can it be incorporated so that there are not stars and extras, not masters and servants, not text and margins, not real and other?

The Cassandra distributed database has no masters and no servants. Each node is equal.

The Infrastructure as Code pattern inverts the old paradigm, and affords a way to version entire datacenters, allowing a rollback to a last known good state that is truly known, complete.

Zoom in, to contemplate the design of a single component of your application system, and recognize that now what was figure (the whole application) becomes ground, and that component must work within that ground, that field. And recognizing the haziness at the boundaries where the figure meets the field, find every opportunity to invert the logic, placing it outside.

The Eclipse IDE is the IDE for "everything and nothing." It is an IDE for making IDEs, and the Java assemblage just happens to be the first one, but it supports many other languages and tools through its empty space and its foregrounding of interfaces.

Make your software pan-pluggable, focus your work on the interfaces, the boundaries, making as few assumptions as possible about the business logic of the implementation. Do not make the application you're told to make. Make the frame on which it could be hung, as one route the data will take on its circulating journey through the world. Do not simply implement the requirements as given—not to ignore or devalue them, but to serve and realize them better. Instead, make a space where those requirements could spring to life. Then the implementation can be injected from the outside. Because we know that we don't know how things will change, what new constraints and possibilities will be introduced. Foreground the field, and make it the figure of your work.

The design that contemplates and sets in harmony the business, the application, the data, and the infrastructure is effective. The designer is effective when they recognize that during discovery, the executives are the users of the design, as they contemplate its budget and timeline and purpose and constraints; the developers are the users as they build it; the customers are the users as they wish it to disappear to gain the true value that lies behind it; and the monitors and maintainers are its subsequent users, who must navigate their way through consoles, documentation, tests, and code to find their avenue in.

What we assign to the margins, to the boundaries, to the field, will always leave its trace in the figure. Eventually, these traces will upend the figure. Perhaps nothing is destroyed entirely from the outside.

Give Design Decisions at Least Two Justifications

A stair is used for going up. And down. And also for congregating. Also for eavesdropping, for sitting, for enjoying the beauty of a grandeur, for showcasing adornment.

The quad at a university serves in organizing the buildings, studying, relaxing, meeting, playing Frisbee, graduations, protesting.

A theater is used for concerts, play productions, readings, assemblies.

We cook in a kitchen; we also gather, converse, prepare to leave, and eat.

Try to arrange the components of your design such that each has only one stated responsibility. But allow multiple "witnesses" standing to vouch for the component's justification for being in the system at all.

Do this, and you'll be able to get the most out of your components, maintain the "simplexity" of the system to best balance between what should be simple for the user and what is complex about the world, and see your best ideas win.

In software terms, you might envision a system that acts as a lookup registry to support service discovery. This system shields your application code from complexities of locating the right partition or shard where data is stored for geographically situated customers. You have data for Europe in Paris and data for APAC in Tokyo, but you don't want developers to have to know about or manage repeatedly finding the right database for the current runtime customer when what they want to be able to do is to just invoke the shopping function.

You might create an abstract "resource name" that knows how to find the appropriate database given the customer ID. Considering this as the service registry, it does only one thing and does it well: it maps the abstract service name to the proper location and metadata to create a connection. That's maintaining high cohesion, and the optimizations you make for your lookups will be inherited throughout the system, and the management of the cache and offload to resource bundles can all work the same. That's a worthy service.

But you can also consider that if you properly structure the resource names, this same system allows you to deploy multiple copies of your software in particular datacenters around the world, or allows one of the copies to span multiple datacenters, affording greater resilience.

So inserting that resource name has given you two justifications, though it performs its singular purpose very well.

By focusing on interfaces, which capture the idea and not the implementation, by focusing on factories, which embrace the result and not the means, your work will invite multiple justifications for utility while maintaining the sturdiness of its frame. You make your system fit to purpose when you contemplate many purposes while designing still for high cohesion. This is one hallmark of platforms, and truly usable and extensible systems, which are the ones that endure.

You know that you don't know all the uses. Your extreme users will find new ones. Embrace your extreme users.

Design from Multiple Perspectives

Think of your software as a three-dimensional object.

Do not design the entire application and then the entire infrastructure and then the entire data model. These are three subsystems, but consider the entire system at once, as well.

The data scientist might be concerned with choosing the proper neural network algorithm, but if the infrastructure architecture is not concomitantly thought of, you might miss a GPU-based server that would perform better.

Design it in "section," which to building architects means seeing the whole thing from the side top to bottom with the fourth wall cut out so you're seeing it from the side.

Then separately consider the floor plan, which is the view from the top with the roof cut out. Looking after only the floor plan might result in an undifferentiated box.

Design from multiple perspectives: a little section, then a little floor plan. Design from the view of the entire site, then do a detailed design of a specific minor detail in a corner, or a piece of furniture. Zoom in, and zoom out, and back again, repeatedly.

Consider how the software change would affect the organization. Consider how the infrastructure would change the software.

When the team at Google created the MapReduce algorithm, which resulted in the popular Hadoop implementation, it was specifically to perform with resilience even while running on cheap, commodity hardware that was presumed to regularly break.

A shift in perspective can create new constraints, which can be welcome design mates.

Create a Quarantine or Embassy

Consider the embassy. The geopolitical purpose of an embassy is, in part, to carve out a place for foreign government officials to work, free to abide by the laws of their own land, even while on foreign soil.

In software, when we want to do something innovative, but we are dealing with non-trivial legacy systems, we can create an embassy package, or more sharply, a quarantine package. We create space for the legacy mappings and adapters and business logic to work as they reliably have. But then you can have a standalone new system that is free from any such constraints within its many chambers.

This lets the new stay new and be different and allows one messy space for the legacy it must connect to, like the mudroom.

It's an underscoring and permutation of the Adapter pattern, not because the interfaces are incompatible and need to talk, but because the new interfaces don't exist yet, and you don't want them to be too compatible with the legacy. Otherwise, you won't innovate.

If you don't do this, it's very easy to unintentionally infect the new system and its design with the legacy's restrictions, received ideas, and ways of thinking. You will dumb everything down to the point where there's no point making a new system; it all looks just like the legacy.

Design for Failure

Design the system so that one part is the part you intend to fail or break. This allows the pressure to exert focus there, keeping other parts free from that pressure. That part can be swapped out readily. You can have service departments with a strong understanding of that area and parts ready to replace it.

You won't be able to anticipate where exactly it will fail. It won't fail conveniently where and how you want it to at just the right time when you're available and ready to fix it.

A corollary can be found in chaos engineering, which reveals to us the parts that break under different conditions and how they do so. This gives you feedback to understand how to make it more resilient.

With this scapegoat in the system, the rest of the system can stay more sturdy. You don't want to have to replace or update many little aspects across many areas in the system.

Design Language

One of Louis Kahn's many important contributions to architectural theory was to develop his distinction between "served" and "servant" spaces. For Kahn, "served" spaces are those spaces in a building that are actively used by people, with "servant" spaces being those spaces that serve the utilized: ventilation systems, furnace rooms, elevator shafts, and so forth. Those are primarily used by systems.

This sounds reasonable enough. We don't want to live in the stairway or the water closet. But we must be careful with this distinction, because as we've seen, it presents a privileged binary pair, which will inevitably become, one day, subject to a deconstruction, making the software very difficult, time-consuming, and expensive to work with.

Designing properly is about using words properly. The names demarcate the space. There should be truth in advertising in your API.

Naming

You define the semantic real estate when you name things.

This is very difficult for anyone to do. As stated earlier, we are forced to compromise in the language we use to describe our systems, and that creates problems.

Your system is a linguistic object.

Naming is one of the hardest things a designer will do—and one of the most important.

Name things as narrowly and as completely as their idea truly communicates. Do not "false advertise" in the name. If you write the Shopping service, by golly it better allow the user to shop All of The Things—hotels, houses, cruise ships, groceries, laptops, pencils, executive hoodies. What if your company wants to enter adjacent businesses, or new ventures? Are you really sure you want a "Shopping service"? If you have that, it is a good candidate to becomes a so-called God Object, which is the one gigantic, omnipotent class that is difficult to understand and change (let alone do so predictably and safely).

Are you sure it's not really the HotelShopping service? Then there's another one called the VacationRentalShopping service. Things that they can share can go in a library, or another service. But now they are allowed to be individuated and developed, maintained, tested, deployed, migrated, upgraded, retired, all on independent life cycles.

Name it properly and leave room for the other things and your user and help all your colleagues know what belongs where.

Additionally, consider the API for use in different contexts, whether that's Unix pipes and filters or in user interfaces such as Xbox, web, phone, and voice. The work the shopping service is doing in all those UIs should still be the same because it is about owning that idea. There might be separate components to handle what's distinctive about each of those platforms on which you expose the shopping capability.

After you have this arrangement, test whether they are *MECE*. You do this by forming the names at the same level into a single list and checking whether they are *Mutually Exclusive and Collectively Exhaustive.*[2]

Start Opposite the User

Do everything in thinking about the user, the personas, their needs. Then forget about them for a while and move to other users like the maintainers.

Design for the programmer first because they will become your factory for making designs. So start with what is most useful to them. The programmer is a big user and stakeholder in your design concept and the attendant guardrails you put in place to shape the system's possibilities. You are shaping work for the programmer, making their work friction-ful or easier, more pleasant, and clearer.

So, design the deployment pipeline first because the programmer will build and deploy their code a thousand times in the course of your project as they create it. Design framework interfaces. Design the monitoring so that you get used to understanding and interpreting and listening to your application more and more throughout the process so that by the time you launch, you have a well-understood repeatable process. Start with the fire escape, the furnace, the mundane parts that have little that seem specific about this business problem so that you create the best opportunity for repeatability, which begets predictability, which begets insight and understanding and reliability.

---

2 For much more on this important concept, see the companion book to this one, *Technology Strategy Patterns: Architect as Strategist* (O'Reilly, 2018).

Platforms

We know that we don't know how people will need or want to use our systems.

When making a product, consider the larger context (the chair in the room, the room in the house). Consider how it would work as a platform.

The platform is the unified ecosystem of services that enable products. Focus on creating the context, the place where the stated requirements could come to be true, not simply directly building the stated requirements themselves. Work with your partners in product management to set expectations properly, of course.

Tech blogger Jonathan Clarks (*http://bit.ly/2kPzVZ1*) helps build the argument here:

> Platforms are structures that allow multiple products to be built within the same technical framework. Companies invest in platforms in the hope that future products can be developed faster and cheaper than if they built them standalone. Today it is much more important to think of a platform as a business framework. By this I mean a framework that allows multiple business models to be built and supported. For instance, Amazon is an online retail framework. Amazon started by selling books. Over time they have expanded to selling all sorts of other things. Apple iTunes started by selling tracks and now uses the same framework to sell videos.

A platform could be your smartphone; that is, it has its own device form factor and its own ability to interconnect with other software streams, therefore it's a platform that you can do other things with that were not originally envisaged at the time of its initial design

Disappearing

Make the software or the system disappear as much as possible. Consider the progress of the web search engine: it has been on a path of disappearing.

In 1997, an early search engine, Hotbot (Figure 3-3), had an advanced "SuperSearch" that let you fill out many complex Boolean phrases, and its UI had many checkboxes. Over time, the web refined into directories with Yahoo and others, eventually tracing to Google's single field that lets you type anything. Now, even that is disappearing as intelligent digital assistants let you search with your voice. The aim is the same, the use case is the same.

Figure 3-3. The popular Hotbot search engine in 1997

It's more powerful than ever, but less present. Make your user the center of the power, and not your software.

Now in command of this theoretical frame, in the next part we explore the more practical application and artifacts involved in semantic software design.

PART II

Semantic Design in Practice

Philosophers have hitherto only interpreted the world in various ways; the point, however, is to change it.

   —Karl Marx

In software, ~~architects~~ have frequently dithered away their time classifying existing systems, often in arbitrary or irrelevant ways. We, as semantic designers, produce concepts, challenged by deconstruction, in order to make a meaningful difference in our organizations, to take action to create a new world of possibilities.

In this part, we explore the "ground" of action, and refine the archetypal concepts introduced in Part I into the material realm. It's filled with templates and practical guides to help you get your job done.

CHAPTER 4

Design Thinking

There exists a designerly way of thinking and communicating that is both different from scientific and scholarly ways of thinking and communicating, and as powerful...
—L. Bruce Archer, *Whatever Became of Design Methodology?*, 1979

Design Thinking is a method to help incite innovation, creativity, and purpose when you design solutions for customers. In this chapter, we transition to outline a repeatable process for applying Design Thinking within your organization as a semantic software designer (perhaps "creative director in technology").

Why Design Thinking?

When a customer approaches you for a technical solution, you need to start somewhere. Having a method for problem solving will help you map the territory in a repeatable way that gives customers and other stakeholders confidence and comfort as you guide them through a process. Using the tenets of Design Thinking specifically will help to improve your chances of coming up with the a creative, customer-focused solution.

We start with Design Thinking because we who have been called enterprise architects and have purview over the entire enterprise will see many problems as design problems. It helps encourage you to be focused on the customer, the solution, and a meaningful outcome, rather than focused on your own internal activities, classifications, and documents. This is the hallmark of the creative, effective semantic designer.

Further, we begin with Design Thinking because so many problems can be viewed as design problems. Consider these questions:

- If you deeply consider with empathy who will use this solution and how, and how it fits into their context, are you, in a sense, redefining the customer?

- What is the optimal organization to support the creation and ongoing maintenance of this solution? What process can be designed to optimize its delivery, before the solution gets to the user?
- How will you consider the schedule itself such that you align various competing factors for the creation, launch, and delivery to again optimize the experience?
- How will the solution be managed?

What these all suggest is that although we tend to consider only the technical solution as the object of design, there are many contributing aspects of our work that can benefit from approaching our problems as design problems. The organization, solution, production, delivery, and supporting infrastructure and maintenance all can be optimized by approaching them as design problems. With our purview across the enterprise in solving customer problems, we must consider the wide variety of stakeholders, the design of the business, the application, the data, and the infrastructure; you and your team must thoughtfully design all these areas of a technology solution and the supporting business.[1] Design Thinking offers a set of guidelines and practices to help you do this, which we examine now.

Exploring Design Thinking

In the 1950s, professors at MIT and Stanford began exploring creative methods for industrial design. The term "design thinking" originated in 1965 with L. Bruce Archer's book *Systematic Method for Designers*. This term and evolving related practices were later popularized by Palo Alto design consultancy company IDEO in the early 1990s, which based its early work on the Stanford curriculum. Given the breadth and long history of these concepts as they have routed through academe and industry, different adherents might not always agree on what Design Thinking precisely refers to. What we discuss here represents my particular take on it, as a curated collection of many of these different approaches to Design Thinking, refined over time with use in the field.

The primary steps in Design Thinking are illustrated in Figure 4-1.

---

1 A fun aside is that our approach to design can be expanded to help design your career, your life itself, if you shift to think of them as design problems.

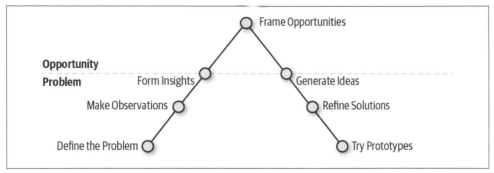

Figure 4-1. The Design Thinking process

Principles

Before we dive into each of these steps in the process, let's start with the principles that design thinkers can generally agree on:

Human-centricity

Design Thinking is perhaps first about empathy. It asserts that all designs exist to be used by a person to advance some human cause. Keeping the human user, their context and conditions, their different abilities, cultural differences, and their being situated in a social context is what makes great design relevant, useful, and delightful.

Showing, not telling

Instead of talking about the design, find creative ways to express it. Architects often present UML diagrams and written documents. These can be critical. What if you had to present your design on the back of a cereal box and make punchy illustrations of what its main features are and why it's exciting? If you had to present your architecture in the form of a story, how would you do that?

Clarification

One of my old mentors once told me, "leaders make the uncertain certain." How can you take the big, messy, wild-and-woolly problem space and clarify and refine it down to its key elements? How can you capture the essence of the solution and convey its impact succinctly?

Experimentation

Use a bias toward action. Even though it's called Design Thinking, it's really about *doing*. As in iterative software development, how can you start quickly making a prototype to get in front of people so that you can improve it with their feedback?

Collaboration

The orchestra wouldn't sound as good if it used only the horn section; by combining the wind instruments, the string instruments, and other types, you can do richer, more sophisticated things.

Diversions

If you search the web, you'll find other representations of Design Thinking principles, such as a focus on process. Process is very important to success, and much of this book is devoted to how you can turn your work into a repeatable (almost standard) process to make a compelling product with an architecture practice. However, I purposefully leave out the principle of "process" as stated by the d.school because to me, your own internal process, while important to know and follow as reality allows, is not interesting to the end user. There are no cookies for strict adherence to the dictates of a methodology as long as you understand it and employ it properly to achieve the desired aim. After all, it is about creativity, so it strikes me as a bit antithetical, especially given that there is no single, received, universal process here. Second, it is critically important to keep your eyes on the goal of creating something of use to someone else—overemphasizing process can result in finding yourself engaged in exciting-seeming, but ultimately fruitless, debates over schools of thought and niggling about your own internal activities in ways that don't benefit your customer.

Now that we understand the basic tenets of Design Thinking, let's walk through the process for how you can apply it as you approach architecture and software design.

The Method

The method is about following the path illustrated in Figure 4-1. We explore each of these steps and how to practically apply Design Thinking in your own architecture shop here.

 Design Thinking Is Context for Applied Architecting

The method outlined here is about viewing the world as a set of problems and opportunities and that designing your approach to both with the subsequent goal of designing a solution is broadly applicable. It is intended to be used as a context and foundational viewpoint for implementing the specific areas of "architecture" and design outlined in the remainder of this book.

Define the problem

The first step is to understand the problem that has been presented. Here, you clarify the need.

It's important, at least eventually, to refine the problem or challenge down to a single statement of need: one sentence that illustrates the purpose or goal. This will be useful later for internal marketing purposes, for getting others enlisted in your cause.

The second step is to define what success looks like. What are your acceptance criteria (to borrow the term from Agile) for having created something truly special that's an obvious improvement?

Make observations

This step is about discovery. After you know what the problem is that you're solving, and you know what success looks like at the end, you start your investigation.

Determine the users. The first question to ask yourself is, "Who are the stakeholders in this solution?" You might be surprised. Spend some time on this step to generate a real list. For example, if you're designing software for use in a hotel, it's easy to think of the front-desk person. But what about the concierge, housekeepers, groundskeepers, bellmen, doormen, managers, and so forth? Also consider the programmers who must maintain this software, your colleagues in the Network Operations Center monitoring its performance—are they not users, too? They might not be external paying customers, but they *will* use your software from a different point of view and for a different purpose. But deciding that they are part of your observation set or not will certainly modify your solution.

Defining *whom you're actually solving a problem for* is a potentially difficult exercise in set theory, but it is a critical first step to getting the scope right. If you leave out roles, you will have an inadequate observation set and leave things out. Push yourself to list as many roles of different user types as you can.

Observe users' actions. Now you can go about understanding their relation to this product or service or space. How do they try to accomplish the task today? What tools do they use? Why do they care about it? What parts are painful to use? What opportunities can you afford them to gain some new super power?

The primary way to do this is by observing them in action and then writing down what you see. Is there an existing tool they use to get their jobs done that you can watch them interact with? Try to shadow them during daily use. If you're designing a new cash register for a restaurant, can you follow a few different waiters to see where it works and doesn't work well for them?

Of course, it's important to talk with existing customers, too. They often will reveal things in conversation that are difficult to observe. You also want to note any disparity between what they say and what you observe.

Ask yourself the following questions:

- What do they say about their pains using the product? Is there a feature that they know they miss having?

- What workarounds do they have to implement to get past some inadequate aspect of the tool? A popular workaround in software is writing down passwords on a sticky note because they've become so complicated, and we all have so many of them that they can be difficult to remember. Newer computers allow you to login with a biometric feature such as a fingerprint, which is one way of making that problem go away.

- Are there aspects to its use that they never use? Why is that?

Jumping to Conclusions

At this stage, it's very tempting and easy to begin interpreting what you see and forming ideas immediately about the solution. You presumably have some familiarity with the problem space or you likely wouldn't be involved in designing the solution. You could design the whole thing in your head, perhaps. When that's the case, it's easy to bring your own biases and preconceived notions about the solution, which skips the entire point of Design Thinking.

To be more creative and innovative, you want to be free of those biases and be focused on the user. For now, simply observe people and record your observations, not what you think about them. We'll do that in a bit. For now, even though it doesn't feel like you're doing much, simply recording user interactions in the manner of a courtroom stenographer without judgment is actually an important step toward creating something innovative.

Consider at this stage different kinds of uses. When you watch customers actually using the product, does that match what they say about how they use it, or is there a cognitive disconnect? For example, do they say keyboard shortcuts are very important to them, but then they don't actually use them?

"I Use It Every Day"

So that you can record as many accurate observations as possible and create a comprehensive list, it's important to consider at this stage that sometimes "use value" can be a slippery subject. People don't always use a product as intended, or as we might expect them to. For example, once upon a time we had an architect at our house who was inquiring about how we used our space. He turned his attention to our swimming pool and asked with some skepticism if I ever actually used it. I quickly replied, "Yes, I use it every day: I look at it." Maybe I didn't swim in it very often (the obvious purpose of a pool, which implies it's not useful to me), but in a hot desert with a bright sun and lots of brown sand, it was very important to my sense of well being to see the cool, blue water. The idea is to be clear on the actual value users might derive, beyond a perceived or ostensible value.

Create personas. Now that you have your list of users, you can create *personas*. A persona is a fictional representation of a person who is a stakeholder or user of your solution. When you do this, you are essentially creating a character who is a composite of users that you interviewed and the observations you made about their goals and challenges.

One important trick here is to chose "extreme users." It's obvious and easier to focus on your mainstream or typical users. But this is a mistake. Extreme users are the experts, the people with a lot of knowledge about the problem space and existing solutions. They tend to have a lot at stake in their success using your product. They are highly knowledgeable on the subject and therefore very opinionated and vocal. They tend to be the ones who push the boundaries.

Early Adopters

Extreme users tend to have the most elaborate workarounds for things that aren't how they want them. In this way, in a sense, extreme users can become "early adopters" of a product or function that doesn't quite exist yet. Consider this example: in 1998, eBay was known mostly for selling regular household objects for a few dollars. The idea of selling a Ferrari for tens of thousands of dollars on the auction site then would have been flagged as suspicious behavior. But eBay took note, and instead of shutting it down, it launched a new division: eBay Motors.

Extreme users might also be people of very different ages. For example, Apple did well when making the iPad because it is usable not only by the initial obvious affluent market of technophiles, but also by three-year-old children. But Apple failed here when designing machine learning algorithms for facial recognition, which best worked only on white males (*https://nyti.ms/2H3QeaT*).

In listing your candidates to create as personas, you want to consider the typical activities they go about in a day. Then, write down their goals: what is it that they want to do. This is *not* about what they want to do *with your software*. It is guaranteed with 100% certainty that they do not want your software in any way. They want to do *something else* that your software helps them do. They don't want Photoshop and they don't want to "edit and crop photos": those are merely tasks they perform on the way to getting what they want. They don't want to "use" your music streaming software: they want to relax and be entertained after a long day. They don't want to arrange their web templates: they want to effectively market their products. No goal that is important to a person is about software. Sometimes, if we have a fun car and it's a beautiful day, we might take pleasure in driving just for driving's sake. There are many things pleasurable in their own right. But I submit that no human ever said: "I think I'm in the mood to use some software. Oh, any old application will do. I just want to use software for a bit."

As you see the list of activities and goals you've discovered, you can group them. These can potentially translate later into security roles as you do detailed architecture work.

A persona is a document that has the following attributes:

- A name. Create a name for this representative person.
- An age, occupation, and education.
- Fictional details. Create a few lines of personal details in order to bring the character to life and make them more vivid and real. Include their desires, interests, and limitations. Given the impression of a story behind this person, you can better focus on designing for real humans.
- A picture.

The document should likely fit on a single page and might look like Figure 4-2.

Be sure to include multiple personas, each representing a different set of user goals, cultural backgrounds, and ages.

Zoe, 26 Systems Analyst	Works for a hot-head fund manager. Has a CIS degree from State and has had three jobs since graduation. Worked for her mother's bakery since she was 11 and believes that rocks have feelings. Was trained as a Scrum Master but found it "silly". Studies online at night to become a Data Scientist.	Facing the challenge of creating a new financial product from scratch in a stretch assignment.

Figure 4-2. A sample persona template (icon via FlatIcon, Creative Commons)

Value Proposition Design

There's a wonderful book on the subject of determining the value proposition of your solution called *Value Proposition Design* (by Alexander Osterwalder et al). Although not strictly focused on Design Thinking, the book offers templates and a method to help you define and refine how to create products and services that matter to customers and help build your business.

Now you can use your collection of personas to form insights about what should be done to create your solution.

Form insights

An insight is an interpretation of your own, based on the facts. You "see into" the objective data and make refutable assertions about what might be the case about the situation. You can see patterns in the data and decide on some theme and notice correlations. You assign meanings among the interplay of signs that are beginning to form your semantic field.

An insight is nonobvious. It reveals something about the object that others might not have noticed or with which they might have an argument.

It is a moment that combines the raw data you've collected so far, and now you start to draw conclusions about what a solution looks like. You are not forming a design of the software. Resist that temptation. Yes, deadlines are tight, and we can be eager to skip steps and head right for the coding. But if we do that, we miss a lot.

You are simply making another list of your conclusions.

Now you can create a *Customer Journey Map.* This is a diagram that illustrates the steps your customers go through when they engage with your organization. It's a helpful tool for documenting a user's path through a service. You might think of it like a storyboard in films: the director creates a cartoon strip of drawings that makes sure everything is laid out properly and the sequences are right before they spend money doing expensive shots, particularly when there are limited opportunities, such as when failing daylight might affect the continuity of the shot.

These maps help you to identify the interactions that cause users most pain. (They also serve as a great starting point in building a process map later if you get into Business Process Modeling with BPMN to do business process reengineering using Lean Six Sigma. If that sounds fascinating, just wait until we get to Chapter 6.)

Mapping the Customer Journey

There's a great online tool at LucidChart that's easy to use and helps you make your own Customer Journey Maps (*http://bit.ly/2kEhre1*).

They allow us to visualize the emotional state of users and highlight the flow of the customer experience, including the good, the bad, and the ugly of their interactions. This helps us to focus our opportunities for improvement.

Frame opportunities

First, you need to transform those insights into opportunities. What are things you could do to creatively improve their interactions and experience?

Now you reflect on your collection of ideas, and pick one category to go with. For now, you can pick just one that you will pursue for prototyping. Of course, you still have this material if you want to return to it later.

Generate ideas and refine solutions

Your goal at this step is to transform the ideas into a solution. This is really a brainstorming phase. To brainstorm well, you must defer judgment, encourage wild ideas, build on the ideas of others, stay focused on the topic, be visual when possible, and go for quantity.

Now you can do a fun exercise. After you've picked your specific opportunity, you then draw the idea on some poster board. Draw four frames, or quadrants. Give it a name at the top and then a brief description and state what user need is addressed.

Then draw stick figure–type drawings into each of the four quadrants representing how people would use and benefit from your solution.

Try prototypes

Here you create named experiments.

When I visited the Google campus in Mountain View many years ago, I was given an early demonstration of Google Glass. I was fascinated to learn that in the Google X Labs, the first prototype was built in a single day, using a backpack, a laptop, a tiny projector and a piece of plexiglass with some hanger wire. The idea was that because the developers had started with thinking empathetically about the user, they quickly refined their priorities to conclude that it was a potential showstopper if people felt too awkward having the web projected into their glasses that way. So that's a boundary that they wanted to explore right away.

 A Prototype in a Day

You can read about the prototype development process for Google Glass at geek.com (*http://bit.ly/2lVZN5E*).

Build prototypes quickly that reflect a certain aspect of the product you know might be problematic or require an adjustment for your users.

To do this, ask yourself, what could be done for only $100 in just one day to test the *premise* of your solution? Remember, you're not testing anything like what a solution might be in the real world, you're testing the premise. In the case of Amazon Alexa, for example, the premise is that users would want to have a robotic assistant based primarily on voice interaction. You don't even need to build anything at all to play through a variety of scenarios with that idea; you just need to take regular interactions, such as playing music, checking the weather, or booking a hotel room with yourself and another person speaking the parts, with one of you playing "Alexa."

When you have landed upon the prototype that works best, the Design Thinking party is over, and you can then set about creating it as a full-fledged solution to move to production and delivery.

In the next section, we see how to put these ideas into practice with workshops to implement Design Thinking at your organization.

Implementing the Method

Much of the existing literature about Design Thinking assumes that you are designing a physical object for use out in the real world, or that if your realm is software, that it only would be of interest to user experience/user interface (UX/UI) designers. One assertion of this chapter is that the creative architect will find much here to fruitfully adopt and adapt, even when what you're focused on is not the UI, but the architecture for a data streaming application or cloud services or an API. Indeed, if many problems we face are design problems, I urge you to consider how to apply these concepts even without a UI or, indeed, even without software.

You should not consider the stages within Design Thinking as purely sequential. Your approach should be iterative, and the real world will end up necessitating that anyway. It's helpful to go back and revise or reconsider earlier decisions in light of new understandings.

Design Thinking as Fractal Within Your Structure

A *fractal* is a geometric figure in which each constituent part has the same structural or statistical dimensions as the whole. Because Design Thinking is a way of approaching design with an empathetic, collaborative, and iterative mindset, it is applicable whenever you are creating artifacts of ~~architecture~~ design. That is, it is not only to be considered in isolation regarding your software product, and I do not present it here as operating solely in the domain of user experience or user interface design.

In a larger project, use Design Thinking at each stage, not just once up front. You can employ an adaptation of the method when it's time to consider the business, application, data, and infrastructure aspects. The insights you generate can be incorporated entirely within each stage of a broader process while also observing how it operates at a higher level toward that broader goal of delivering the complete software product.

To begin your Design Thinking work, collect these tools:

- An easel with large conference room–sized paper
- Sticky notes
- Markers
- Dot-shaped stickers to vote with

Pull together a workshop, and depending on the scope of your challenge, you might need a couple of days or a few weeks.

First, frame the challenge. You do this by having everyone write on sticky notes what they think the problem might be. You should do this quickly, in a matter of five or seven minutes. Then put all of the sticky notes on a paper and discuss. People will typically see different emphases in the problem space, and you can use these to ensure that you have properly framed the problem.

Then, move on to focusing on the user, the customer. Determine who they are, and figure out how to make observations in the field. After you have this list, you'll likely break and then move on to scheduling how to make those observations with real people.

Now you have collected your data such that you can create personas.

Using the raw data from your field journal observing users as well as interview notes and personas, you are ready to form your insights. Time for another workshop!

Give people time to review the collected material. Then, in this workshop, try to get participants to start assertions with "I wonder...." This encourages them to exercise their thought process, to venture a thought that is perhaps incomplete but could be built upon, and to go beyond what they feel sure they already know. Otherwise, people tend to repeat their own entrenched views or to speak in platitudes so as to avoid conflict.

As they did before, have each person generate as many insights as they can, writing them down on sticky notes. Then, have the facilitator collect and place them altogether on the paper boards with markers so that everyone can see them together.

Now you can begin to see patterns in the insights. Eliminate true duplicates, being careful to discuss if any subtle differences in the apparent duplicates are relevant and shouldn't be lost. This is a consolidation step. Next, you can discuss and elaborate on what was meant. Ambiguity is just fine here and is in fact something to be encouraged. Be sure people are not designing the solution yet.

Group the insights into different categories.

Then, you can use the dot-shaped stickers to vote on the insights you've formed that make it to the posters. These are stickers of different colors that you can get at a hobby or office supply store. Each person voting has their own color so that everyone can trace back who voted for what in case further conversation is needed. The voting serves only to narrow down the focus on the most pressing concerns, setting the stage for the next step.

Now, you're ready to discuss what opportunities might be suggested by the insights. Again, you're not designing the solution (say, your software product) at this step. You are generating ideas on what could be new and how you might help your users mitigate the pains and realize the gains.

Now you can repeat the sticky-note voting process to again narrow toward a focus. You'll draw on your storyboard for your identified solution at this point.

At this point, you're ready to brainstorm solutions, describe them, and vote on them.

Now you leave the workshop with a slate of work, go build your prototype, and again go out into the field to test it with real people. This, of course, will be an iterative process of refining your prototypes until you have something buildable that you can deploy.

Throughout the process, be sure to honor the following principles:

- Focus on users' experiences with an emphasis on building empathy
- Allow, accept, and encourage ambiguity
- Tolerate mistakes or oversights
- Regularly reset expectations about what stage you're in throughout the process and restate the near-term goals

With all of this work, you will have come up with a terrific solution that has an excellent chance of being well designed for solving real people's problems and giving them usefulness and hopefully delight and maybe even joy. You'll have done that by seeing much of the world and experiences as design problems, by grounding your approach firmly in framing the problem properly, and by harboring strong empathy for your user.

Summary

This chapter introduced Design Thinking, the principles and practices, and how you as a creative architect can put it to work. If you'd like to learn more about Design Thinking, check out these additional resources:

- See this *Harvard Business Review* article (*http://bit.ly/2kEiFG9*).
- See this in-depth case study (*http://bit.ly/2kTXj7J*) on how Design Thinking was used to improve processes for veterans at the Bureau of Veteran Affairs.
- IDEO Design Kit. This website (*http://www.designkit.org/methods*) offers case studies and a wealth of practical resources to assist you in taking a Design Thinking approach in your next project. This includes a field guide and a variety of courses that you can take.
- The d.school at Stanford (*https://dschool.stanford.edu/*). The university's design school website offers some material about Design Thinking in broader application, such as designing space and furniture. Of course, that's the original purpose of Design Thinking anyway! Check out its Bootleg Toolkit to help support your process.

In the next chapter, we build on this Design Thinking approach. Keep it in your back pocket throughout the book: many problems and opportunities across the entire technology enterprise can be helped when framed as design problems with these tools.

CHAPTER 5

Semantic Design Practices and Artifacts

Building architects have blueprints, sections, physical models, software models, zoning codes, engineering codes, and other such received means with which to express their designs. Building architects have a known building envelope, beginning with the actual world. We in software are in a purely virtual semantic world.

You can express your design direction in conversation, as sometimes happens. But this is a recipe for disaster. All of the essential people aren't always in the same room all the time when the conversations are happening. People mishear, you forget to say things, the conference phone drops, and so forth. I wouldn't belabor the point, but I regularly see architects expressing their design in conversation, which quite pointedly I must say will fail. You must make the complex and abstract notions of your ~~architecture~~ design actionable, concrete, durable, precise.

Up to this point, you have worked to find the precise problem, frame the challenge and the solution properly, and create conceptual coherence in this space. Now, in this transitional stage, you must bring your ideas from being conceptually coherent to becoming material ready to record into architecture documents with specific, executable solutions and plans. You have the concept of your semantic field. Now you must define it in a way that software developers can understand and execute to create fantastic software.

In this chapter, we highlight some key practices of semantic software design and the accompanying artifacts that help you make it practicable. Some of these are intended to be used internally within your team, and some are more executive- and customer-facing.

Design Principles

Principles are propositions. They assert a set of beliefs about the world. They act as a substrate to a system of values. They serve to guide decision making across your entire organization.

Principles are important in architecture and design because they help to scale your team. They provide guidance to developers making a local decision. Many small local decisions made by the implementation teams will tend to add up over time to produce something that has imperceptibly skewed over a period of months to accrue toward a design result that looks little like you intended.

As propositions, principles are abstract, but they should precipitate actions on the part of your teams that support them. Presumably, the principles are subsets or decompositions of your overarching corporate vision or the strategy that you've identified. If they're not, your teams and department will suffer from a lack of alignment. You'll be doing stuff that doesn't matter. This is mistaking activity for progress.

Well-established principles will also allow you to negotiate with the product managers, executives, and other stakeholders. If you state your principles, and they follow logically from the stated business vision and strategy, you can more quickly resolve disputes as they arise in the project. If your CIO believes that they should be moving compute and storage to the cloud, and you believe that you must run your own data-centers, you have a mismatch of principles that must be reconciled to ensure that your project doesn't blow up.

On the other hand, if you state your principles and publish, circulate, and reference them in other architecture artifacts, you have a token for conversation with these stakeholders. If you can get them to agree on the principles, you can help guide the teams with confidence that you're all rowing the boat in the same direction. This makes decision making less fraught with friction; the answers become more obvious. They help you to gain alignment and clarity.

An obvious example of a set of principles is the Ten Commandments. Specifically, the commandment to "honor thy mother and father" works well here. You want your principles to be at this level. It is not certain what it means to "honor" a person; it is abstract. The discrete set of actions to carry out are not obvious or stated. You then must consider, when left to your own devices, how you should proceed in order to enact the concrete action of "honoring." Perhaps you decide that not blaming them for forgetting your birthday is the honorable thing to do. Perhaps you think it means that you must buy them a house. Because, like a parent, the architect cannot be there to direct when every local decision is being made. These are the sorts of things that will shape the overall quality and adherence to the timeline and budget, and the kinds of things developers decide all the time: whether to inline the stylesheet or not, or take an extra few minutes to code this to an interface instead of an implementation, or take the time to store the application's database passwords in a key management store instead of in plain text. If you have principles that they can consider, they will act more in accordance and the system will be closer to the desired image.

No Empty Slogans

Many so-called principles are stated as empty slogans. "Integrity" was, I believe, chiseled on the marble floor of the lobby of Enron as every day executives walked over the words in their Louboutin loafers while they ran the company into the ground with fraudulent accounting and valuation, taking the pensions of thousands of workers with it. When you state principles and don't turn them into action by making leaders accountable for them, they're empty slogans.

When you state principles that are so obvious that they are ignored, you must make finer distinctions to help them carry action. Similarly, many so-called principles are stated as ra-ra marketing slogans, like "Be the best." Maybe that works for some, but I don't see it helpful in driving action when two directors are disagreeing at an implementation meeting. You want to define principles such that some reasonable person could argue the *opposite* side. Would any company's principle be "Be the worst"? If not, better to move on.

There's an old adage I'm sure you're familiar with that states, "You can have it good, fast, cheap: pick two." That is applicable here. If the quality and craftsmanship are high and you deliver it inexpensively, it won't be done fast (and so on). It's OK to want it fast and cheap; this is the reason fast food restaurants exist. But stating what you value up front over other also desirable qualities is making an actual decision that can truly guide behavior.

The Open Group Architecture Framework (TOGAF), which was my architecture training and certification many years ago, publishes an in-depth way of approaching technology principles (*http://bit.ly/2Buottr*). You can also take a shortcut and read Digital Principles (*http://bit.ly/2BtQ5ib*) or IBM's old published principles (*https://ibm.co/2wbWoRG*).

Those sets of principles are in no way intended to be something to just copy. Take a look at them. They are just a sample so that you can see the level at which they're written. You can adopt them for use as a jumping-off point in creating your own.

Let's take one example: "Data is an asset." The opposite is "Data is not an asset." If you thought that your only job was to make applications for end users to accomplish tasks quickly and you wanted to keep costs, management, and liability down, that would be a reasonable conclusion. However, if you state that data is an asset for your organization, the applications might be window dressing over the data. You might spend considerable time gathering data, storing it, protecting it, organizing it, making it available to other applications, finding ways to market and sell it, finding new applications to build on top of it, foregrounding machine learning, and the like.

Your principles should be broad without being empty slogans. Guidelines (covered in an upcoming section) will be more local and specific. Your principles should be thoughtfully constructed, publicly stated, and often referred to. They will help guide your teams toward more efficient decision making, reduce churn, and create a sense of alignment.

Pair Designing

There are a few things you can do to help you capture the concept for the architecture that you have in your mind, which is still forming.

After you have an idea, you need to begin shaping it with others. When you're in the stage of forming the idea for what the software should be, what it can be, and what the general contours are, it's natural and important to express these in collaborative conversation.

To capture your ideas and test their validity, their boundaries, and their value, try *pair architecting*.

In 1999, the venerable Kent Beck, perhaps most famous for JUnit, wrote a book called *Extreme Programming Explained*. In it, he proposed the idea of pair programming, that two programmers should share one screen and one keyboard, each taking a different view into the partnership. Each could catch the other's bugs as they happen, learn the software, and think at different levels. It's mentally taxing to write software: you're essentially solving a logic puzzle in a foreign language. So when one programmer becomes tired, they could switch the keyboard to let the other drive and change roles.

I love the practice of pair programming, and it has served me and my teams quite well over the years. I don't see it used as much any more, because perhaps the people with the purse strings think it's a form of socializing. I've heard one executive complain that her pair programming teams were getting half as much done. I don't believe she was ever a programmer, because this is laughably far from the case.

As an ~~architect~~ designer, try carrying this practice forward. Set aside a time to solve a particular design challenge on some specific aspect of the system, especially at the idea stage. This does a variety of wonderful things:

- You'll get a clearer, more developed idea because your partner will prompt you to clarify what you mean. If you need to express it to someone else who is present, you'll be forced to shine a light on certain shadowy areas of your idea. You might not solve everything at that moment, but you'll know which areas you need to refine.

- Your partner will have better ideas than you about some things. Maybe they excel at hyperthreading models, whereas you're weaker, but you excel at design patterns. Together, your idea will take richer shape.

- Two people now understand the idea and can represent it. You're scaling the idea quickly. This provides better avenues into an eventual project planning session.

If you're not geolocated together, you might put this in practice by having a Webex or Hangout where one of you shares your screen, and you begin sketching your parti, your lookbook, subsystem components, and interface outlines. You might do this on a very specific piece of the puzzle. Then, you can zoom your camera out a bit and have a discussion about how this part relates to the broader concept and how it will support or shape related ideas.

Your work is to define the concept, agreeing on what populates this world, what their names are, how they interact, and where the boundaries are. I have used this technique a lot with my team; it results in more nuanced and thoughtful design, closer personal relationships, and more common understanding, and the best idea always wins.

The artifact result will be a few key sections of code that help clarify unknowns and reduce the risk to the project.

Murals

While you are in the archetypal and conceptual realm of design and are transitioning into the developmental stage, you might want to use a mural to help organize your design concepts into something you can begin to work on.

A mural can be a collage that might cover an entire conference room wall. Use the wall and sticky notes and pens to capture your ideas. The elements of your wall could include the following items that you would have created during Design Thinking:

Personas
Who will use this work?

Customer Journey Map
Why are they using this and how do they interact with it?

Pains
What about their current process is problematic? Where are they thwarted?

Gains
What new innovations can you offer them that might help them take a leap forward in productivity, delight, options, opportunities?

Outcomes

What is the change that would make a difference to your customers and other users? What gumdrop do they want at the end of the journey?

Metrics

How will your customers measure the difference that was made for them? How will they know they got great value from your system? Note that these should be rough and general at this stage.

Invite peers, executives, team members, and others to walk the wall with you. Guide them through how you are thinking about the project. This allows others to know where you're headed and to contribute their ideas before things are implemented. This is about ensuring that you're building the right thing.

Capturing the aforementioned items in the mural will help give you the shape of the work on which you will soon base your architecture definitions and your project plan.

You can make this a bit of a collage. It's OK, and even encouraged, to add elements to your collage that capture some of the extra-synthetic conceptual work you did in Chapter 4. What painting, image, piece of music, building, motto, sketch, fabric, sculpture, or texture is inspiring to you and helps brings your concept to life? You can capture these in your lookbook.

Consider the following example. When architect Frank Gehry was designing the tower at 8 Spruce Street in New York City, his inspiration for the building was the Bernini sculpture The Ecstasy of Saint Teresa (1652), shown in Figure 5-1.

Figure 5-1. Bernini's Ecstasy of Saint Teresa in Rome (photo by Alvesgaspar, Wikipedia CCA)

Notice how the building at 8 Spruce Street, depicted in Figure 5-2, incorporates and echoes the folds in Saint Teresa's robes.

Figure 5-2. The tower at 8 Spruce Street, New York City, incorporating Bernini's folds (photo by Jim.henderson, Wikipedia CCA)

Pushing yourself outside of what is comfortable and familiar to do this kind of work at this stage can mean the difference between making something mundane and forgettable and something truly special, useful, and exciting to your customers.

Digital Murals

If you are a geographically distributed team or prefer handling things digitally, you can use a tool like Mural (*https://mural.co/*). It comes with templates to capture many of these elements from Design Thinking, and you can invite team members to contribute.

It's one thing to see an example of how a marble sculptor inspired the lines for a steel building; even though one is art and one is architecture, both are in the realm of the physical, plastic arts. But what would this mean in our less tangible universe of software?

Is it a painting like Edward Hopper's "Automat," or Piet Mondrain's "Composition II"? A Volkswagen Beetle, a Bugatti, a Tesla, or a Mack truck? Is the system Glenn Gould's *Bach: The Goldberg Variations* or ABBA? Bootsy Collins of Parliament-Funkadelic is one kind of bass player, and Jaco Pastorius another. A sharp, classic Prada blue wool suit suggests one sense of style, whereas an Alexander McQueen patchwork paisley suit suggests another. Is the system more like a wild Jean Paul Gaultier or a buttoned-down Brooks Brothers? The venerable Chanel No. 5 perfume is appropriate for one kind of occasion, whereas Tom Ford's scent "Fucking Fabulous" represents another attitude altogether. Which informs your concept of your software? Add sketches.

After you feel you have the mural complete, you can invite stakeholders to visit it and vote on their level of confidence that it represents the correct direction and has the vital emphases.

The mural is a temporary, transitional artifact. It serves as an organizing mechanism for all of these disparate elements and eventually gives way into traces in other artifacts. Like a butterfly, it won't likely last more than a few weeks.

Vision Box

I will not deny, but possibly it might be reduced to a narrower Compass than it is; and that some Parts of it might be contracted.... But to confess the Truth, I am now too lazy, or too busy, to make it shorter.
—John Locke, *An Essay Concerning Human Understanding*

Making your concept expressable in a single sentence that represents it is the mark of a clear thinker and a clear concept. Allowing three to five phrases to further describe it will help advance your idea with executives and other stakeholders. You must be able to take your broad canvas and reduce it to the value proposition succinctly.

Software used to come in cardboard boxes that had disks in them. Although not as large, these boxes were colorful, featured images and slogans, and represented the product's promise. They told you what the name of the software was, what it was for, and what you could become by using it.

Even though software rarely comes in boxes anymore, you can adopt this idea to help create your executive summary and communicate quickly to stakeholders. The point is to work with your team in a couple of hours to produce the statement of value to customers and get away from the technical implementation underpinnings.

Jim Highsmith[1] introduced the idea of the *product vision box*, similar to a cereal box, which you can use to describe the main features of what you're building. The vision box acts as a kind of executive summary. The small space forces you to pare down the concept to the three to five most impactful things from your customer's view. Figure 5-3 shows a version of this.

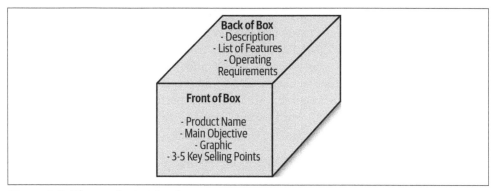

Figure 5-3. The product vision box

To structure this short activity with your team, ask of your system the standard reporter questions: who, what, when, where, why? Your answers to these should help you quickly put together your box.

Mind Maps

A *mind map* is a way to organize and classify ideas or information. You start with a single box in the middle and allow subtopics to branch out from it. In turn, these subtopics each have subtopics. In a sense, it's a visual representation of an outline. It acts as an aid in information architecture, and you should consider a mind map a necessary first step before any work is done on designing a user interface. It will act as a method for organizing the areas of functionality you will expose. It can serve as a method for determining the placement of your reveals (see Chapter 2 on the parti and reveals).

Mind maps are wonderful to create in collaboration with your team. Figure 5-4 shows an example.

Two great tools for making these are Lucidchart (*https://www.lucidchart.com/*) and XMind (*https://www.xmind.net/*). You can use both free of charge. Lucidchart is online and works well when you want to collaborate. XMind is locally installed, and the paid version allows many more advanced features, such as saving to PowerPoint.

---

1 For a bio, see *https://en.wikipedia.org/wiki/Jim_Highsmith*.

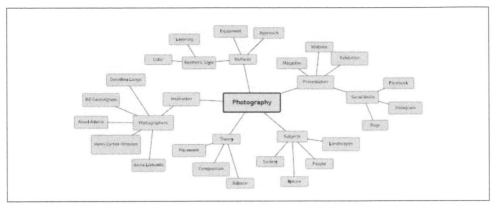

Figure 5-4. Mind map image from Lucidchart

Use Cases

At this point, you can use any mural, mind map, product vision box, and material generated in Design Thinking to begin to make your use cases. A use case captures a user role who performs an action to derive some clear value. These are captured two ways: in the form of a Unified Modeling Language (UML) diagram, and in a written list of steps.

Here is a template for use cases that you can use:

Overview

Provide a one-paragraph description of this use case.

Actors

Identify primary and supporting actors.

Relationship to Other Use Cases

This use case is related to the following use cases:

- *Extends Use Case 1 (link)*
- *Includes Use Case 2 (link)*

Preconditions

The following must be true for this use case to be started:

- *Condition 1*

Postconditions

Describe what will be true when this use case completes:

- *Condition 1*

Primary Flow

Describe the main flow of this use case, excluding error conditions:

1. *Step 1*
2. *Step 2*

Alternate Flows

Describe any desired alternative flows or error conditions. Identify step numbers where the alternative paths begin.

Special Requirements

Identify performance, scalability, availability, and internationalization requirements associated with this use case.

Capture all of your use cases together in a single list. These will become user stories or functional requirements. The Design Definition Document, which we cover in a moment, captures the nonfunctional requirements. Together, these are converged and refined into user stories, with acceptance criteria capturing both functional and nonfunctional requirements from these two sources.

Guidelines and Conventions

Principles are broad statements to guide decision making when no direct, specific guideline exists. Guidelines and conventions consist of a set of unambiguous directives for development teams to follow. So they are more specific and concrete direction on the management of certain processes, the use of certain tools, or the management of people than principles are.

You should publish *guidelines* on focused topics. They should state how you want people to use a particular tool, practice, methodology, or process. You might create guidelines on the Use of Security Groups in the Azure Cloud, how to use the Deployment Pipeline, best practices on writing integration tests, and so forth.

Publish *conventions* so that everyone does something the same way. You might have conventions on how to format source files to make them more readable and more readily understandable. The value in conventions is that your code is easier to maintain because it is quicker to read and understand, and tooling can be more predictable. It's not that camelCase is inherently better than InitialCaps for naming methods (as in Java versus .NET), but if everyone does it the same way, you can eschew obfuscation. When 80% of the cost of software is in the maintenance, making it easier to read and understand and find issues and fix them is a valuable long-term investment.

You don't need to invent many of these convention or style guides from whole cloth. For common languages and frameworks, first search to see whether someone has already written a convention guide that you can borrow. Here are some I've used, and you can, too:

Java
> Follow the Google Java coding guidelines (*http://bit.ly/2lX951m*).

JSON
> Follow the Google JSON coding guidelines (*http://bit.ly/2mlpnBa*).

React
> Follow the Airbnb coding standards for React (*http://bit.ly/2kSiVkR*).

These can often be checked as part of your automated build process.

You should create and publish guidelines and conventions for certain critical things in your project that you know must be correct and will make a material difference in the success of the architecture and strategy. For example, suppose that you have developers who don't get along and organize code differently in their own silos, and extensibility really matters in your project. You want to be sure to call out how to organize the codebase so that they can support your aim. You might write a guideline document stating the structure for the projects under the service, as shown in Example 5-1.

Example 5-1. Sample convention for a service project structure

```
+---<application name>
: +---<application name>-utils
: +---<application name>-domain
: +---<application name>-service-api
: +---<application name>-service-impl
: +---<application name>-service-client
: +---<application name>-web
```

Then, you can go the extra mile and explain the purpose of each of these subprojects, to help justify why you're asking people to do the extra work to separate them out. The subsections that follow provide some examples that can be used in any language type (but Java is assumed here).

Utils

This subproject provides common utility functions used throughout the application:

- It *should* contain utilities relative only to this application.
- It *must not* be dependent on any subproject.
- It *may* depend on libraries outside the project (e.g., Log4J).
- The artifact *must* be a JAR artifact.

Domain

This subproject provides common domain objects representing nouns (entities) used throughout the application:

- It *should* contain domain objects relative only to this application.
- It *may* depend on the Utilities project.
- It *may* depend on libraries outside the project.
- The artifact *must* be a JAR artifact.

service-api

This subproject provides interfaces to business functionality used in the application:

- It *must* contain only interfaces at the level of business functionality and capabilities relevant to this application.

- It *must* contain only interfaces and not implementing classes that belong in the service-impl project.
- It *may* depend on the Utilities project and/or the Domain objects project.
- It *may* depend on libraries outside the project.
- The artifact *must* be a JAR artifact.

service-impl

This subproject provides the implementation of the business service interfaces:

- It *must* only contain business service implementations.
- It *may* depend on the Utilities project and/or the Domain objects project.
- Dependencies outside of the project are allowed.
- The artifact *must* be a WAR artifact.

service-client

This subproject provides the client code necessary to call business functionality:

- It *must* contain only service client implementations; that is, the classes required to invoke the service, sharply distinct from any business logic.
- It *may* depend on the Utilities project and/or the Domain objects project. By definition, it depends on the service-impl project.
- Dependencies outside of the project are allowed.
- The artifact *must* be a JAR standalone or JAR built and added to classloader within a WAR artifact.

This is just an example of the sort of thing you might specify.

Approaches

Approaches are short versions of Design Definition Documents (discussed in the following chapters). These are perhaps 3 to 10 pages long and cover a specific engagement.

For example, we had a customer who wanted to integrate with our APIs in a certain unusual way because of constraints of their legacy system. So, the architect wrote an Approach document describing how the integration should be performed, the protocols to use, where to get certain data, the security implementation, and so forth.

Approaches have a loose structure, other than the expected front matter. The remainder has headers for the sections you need to draw attention to. Make sure they're MECE (Mutually Exclusive and Collectively Exhaustive).

Approaches are meant to be written quickly and focused on a specific local problem. They are not used when designing an entire new system or process or strategy.

When the development teams or sales teams come across one of the following situations, you have something of architectural significance on your hands and you should create an Approach:

- The requirement is associated with high business value and changes could break mission-critical/high-revenue components (such as Shopping), or there is a large new opportunity.

- Has high technical risk (our organization has little real experience with a proposed new technology).

- Has high business risk (could jeopardize our reputation, change intellectual property, mergers, and acquisitions).

- The requirement is "net new" or first-of-a-kind for us: none of the responsibilities of already existing components in the architecture addresses it.

- The requirement would cross service boundaries/create a new orchestration.

- The proposal requires crossing datacenter/cloud boundaries.

- The requirement is a concern/on the radar of a particularly important/influential stakeholder (big customer, President, etc.).

- The requirement has Quality of Service/Service-Level Agreement (SLA) characteristics that exceed current ones.

- The requirement has caused budget overruns or client dissatisfaction in a previous project with a similar context, suggesting that it needs more senior attention.

- The component breaks backward compatibility of an in-use production service

Design Definition Document

The *Design Definition Document* (or "D3") represents one of the crucial elements of a successful semantic design practice. This is a template that I have used with great success, and therefore little modification, for more than a decade. Here, I'll give you the basic outline of the template, which you can adopt and adapt for your purposes.

All of the work you have done in the conceptual stage has been captured in a variety of models, including your lookbook, parti, personas, use cases, guidelines, and more. These have helped you define your own terms and think about what you're doing, how you want to do it, and how it should be structured a bit. Some of these are internal, just for you. These help you to figure out where and what your semantic field is; they don't so much help others. It's not user-friendly to expect someone to sort through that collection of material, which is purposefully idiomatic.

But all of that concept work is not useful if it's not communicated to others in a way that is clearly executable. You must represent your concept in an act of translation in a way that is comprehensive in scope, captures the relevant elements in a single place, and is testable and measurable. The D3 is crucial to our practice because it acts as the translation of your concept into an executable, testable specification.

In this section, we present the template with the questions that you need to answer. In the next four chapters, we cover each of its main areas (business, application/services, data, and infrastructure) from a comprehensive view. Those chapters will help you formulate the content, the answers to the questions in this template.

Your audience for the D3 are the analysts who will write detailed requirements, developers who will write the code that realizes your design, testers, the operations or "run" team, compliance officers, "architects" in your organization, and the occasional executive who might need to understand how all of your quiet and contemplative concept work is going to help realize actual business value.

This is not a blueprint or specification exactly. It is at a technical and precise level. Its scope is the nonfunctional requirements of the system. The functional requirements are expected to be expressed elsewhere, say in the form of user stories derived from your use cases.

Here is the template:

Design Definition Document Template

Program Name Design Definition

Executive Summary
State the purpose of the program and what this document covers.

About this Document
This section contains metadata about the design document itself.

Authors
Names of people who did most of the writing.

Contributors
Names of people who contributed some writing or key ideas.

Reviewers
> Names of people who did some quality control on this document.

Document State
> Is this a draft, in review, or published?

Use of IETF Keywords
> This document employs a subset of the Internet Engineering Task Force keywords found in RFC 2119 (*https://www.ietf.org/rfc/rfc2119.txt*). These words are MUST, SHOULD, MAY, and their counterparts MUST NOT, SHOULD NOT, MAY NOT. They are capitalized throughout the document to draw attention to their special status as keywords used to indicate requirement levels.

Business Design

Describe the business objectives, drivers, and expected benefits for undertaking this program.

Capabilities
> Describe what capabilities the solution will have. What new benefits are provided in functional and nonfunctional terms? What new scalability, reliability, global distribution, performance, resilience, extensibility, manageability, portability, security, or other benefits are expected? Don't advertise or market to your audience; be concrete and concise.

Strategic Fit
> What element of the business and technology strategies does this help realize? How?

Business Drivers
> Why are we doing this? What priority is it among known others?

Assumptions
> What is expected to be in place for this solution approach to be successful? Refer to funding, availability of key resources, operations support, contracts, key processes, procurement, Global Network Operations Center (GNOC), regulations, stated standards and guidance or technology patterns from the leadership team, and so on.

Constraints

> *Applicable laws*
>> Does the Americans with Disabilities Act (ADA) apply?

> *Applicable regulations*
>> Reference need to maintain compliance with Payment Card Industry (PCI), Personally Identifiable Information (PII), General Data Protection Regulation (GDPR), and System and Organization Controls (SOC). Do not merely

state that these laws exist, state how your design specifically accounts for supporting them so that the developers can be sure to implement it accordingly.

Risks

List business risks in doing the project as envisioned, risks to the customer or existing business prospects or processes, how it can be maintained and operated properly, availability of staffing resources, securing funding, countries/markets, the inherent risks in trade-offs made, and so forth.

Impacts

What will this project or this architecture create in terms of organizational, training, and process needs that affect the business? How will the business need to change to best support this? Are there new processes that are expected to be adopted internally within product development to support a new technology or skillset? Should any roles and responsibilities change?

Stakeholders

List the organization, roles, and named individuals who stand to win or lose by a good or bad outcome on this program. Who must change to accommodate it? This will eventually feed your Responsible, Accountable, Consulted, Informed (RACI) document.

Governance

What is the framework you'll use to govern this project? Must you invent a new committee? Are there design review processes or cloud governance or financial governance processes to follow?

Application Design

Application overview and general strategy description.

Applicable Standards and Policies

List of links to published guidelines and conventions for development teams to follow. For example, any internal policies, industry-specific standards, PCI guidelines, ADA guidelines, and so forth that you expect teams to follow.

Guidelines and Conventions

Links to published guidelines and conventions for Dev teams to follow, such as published internal standards, Google Java coding guidelines, JavaScript conventions, code quality guidelines, and so forth.

Patterns

Diagrams, links, and descriptions of patterns for Dev teams to follow in the implementation. Reference any design patterns for designing and developing services as applicable.

Services

List services to be created or existing services to be reused, along with the owners of those services.

Security

Security requirements and design: how data will be secured, encrypted, authorized, authenticated at rest, in transmission, or in processing. Use of Open Web Application Security Project (OWASP) Top Ten and how those are addressed. What security groups are required? Highlight security requirements for development such as bastion hosts. List transport or Transport Layer Security (TLS)/ Secure Sockets Layer (SSL) requirements.

Availability

Target SLA in terms of 9's uptime and how specifically the architecture will support such numbers. How recoverability, disaster recovery, and the like is being supported. Consider these questions:

- What are the compensating actions taken in a failure?
- Will a circuit breaker be used?
- What redundancy is there?
- How is caching used to support certain failure events?
- Health-check page?
- Multideployments?
- How are specific key components particularly designed for resilience and high availability? Are you using multiple cloud zones?
- What is your service replacement and versioning strategy to support zero-downtime releases?

Scalability and Performance

What number of transactions per second at this latency and CPU utilization must the solution support? What is the unit of scale (container, virtual machine, cluster)? Use actual numbers and calculate the impact on server footprint that will have. What are the ways in which the application and services can scale through statelessness, Auto Scaling Groups (ASGs)? State the ASG threshold so developers aren't left to guess.

Extensibility

Will you use certain patterns in your services such as Strategy or Specification? How will APIs specifically support the ways that the application affords future change, how will the application support customizing per customer, and how are configurations afforded?

Testability

How will this be tested, what tools will be used, and what specific automation and targets will be in place? Include functional testing, regression testing, integration testing, and chaos/resilience testing. Load testing plan? How will this be automated? What specific toolset used in what process?

Maintainability

What software guidance for developers will help make the code base easier, cleaner, simple to maintain in the long term? Code repository needs or project needs? What is the maintenance schedule anticipated or downtime for upgrades strategy?

Monitorability and Metrics

What tools and dashboards are required, logging requirements, how the software itself must support event publishing to increase visibility. What are the specific metrics that will indicate system uptime, health, and proper performance? How will alerts be triggered at what threshold? Consider CPU, memory, drive/filesystem volumes, process monitoring, logs, event logs, and required procedures.

Data Design

Database Strategy

Overview the general data management strategy for this application. What special customer requirements should be called out for careful handling? What are the risks involved with this strategy? Expected benefits?

Standards and Guidelines

What is the applicable set of data technology standards, guidelines, and tools?

Technologies

What database technologies will be used for what purposes, what specific services? Are there any new database technologies being used, or new versions? Where can developers learn more? What guidance exists for them?

What instance types are being used? Are the available networking modes the proper type for that database? Have you used the cost calculator to size and price instances?

Import/Export

How will customers get data into your system?

If you're porting data, what are the source and target maps?

How will customers get their data back out of your system for their own use?

Replication, Backup, and Recovery

How is data replication supported? How will you distribute data globally?

What is the backup/recovery strategy? Will you store full or partial backups? For how long? On what systems, for what services?

What is the bulk data replication strategy? What is the multiregion strategy?

Data Versioning

How will your database be versioned? What about the data itself?

Database Automation

How will the database farm be automated and updated? What tools, pipelines, and processes are in place or should be developed?

Database Performance Considerations

What performance thresholds for transactions within the database are expected? Do you have a known level you must support?

Data Warehousing, Storage, and Management Requirements

What data volumes must be supported? Data movement policies and requirements. Reference how logs will be stored, managed, or forwarded.

Data Maintenance

How data will be maintained, data retention policies, scripting to offload, data restoration. How will data be populated for different environments for this application? Will data be truncated? At what interval? How will data be encrypted? Are there GDPR or PII/PCI requirements to be stated for development teams or infrastructure admins?

Data Migration

How will data get into the system? Is connecting to a legacy system required? Is Golden Gate or Kafka or Extract, Transform, and Load (ETL) or another tool in use? What time period is anticipated for this? Will data need to be synchronized over a certain period of time?

Data Volume

What is the expected starting volume of data? What size database is anticipated? Will there be multiple data stores? How many rows are anticipated to be added or removed daily for the key services?

Logging

What are your log rotation policies? Are there requirements for Splunk or another monitoring tool?

Reporting

How will we do reporting for customer use? For internal use?

Auditing

> How must the system audit user changes to track and report in case of a security breach or for compliance?

Security

> How is the database farm itself specifically secured? Will data be encrypted at rest, and how will that be managed? How will access to different environments be managed, including at the development level?

Analytics

> What data must be exposed by the application to support business analytics. How must that data be exposed to support analytics tools? Will you have a data lake? How will that be maintained, accessed, and used properly?

Caching Strategy

> Requirements for caching and the locations and technology to support caching. How distributed is it? Any guidance for application developers as applicable. Guidelines on caching for implementers and for developers subsequently using it.

Machine Learning

> What specific processes must be called out for machine learning? How will data pipelines be supported? What is that entire subsystem design? Feature engineering considerations.

Infrastructure Design

Infrastructure overview statement.

Infrastructure Strategy

> What are the patterns you employ? Are there deployment diagrams, component diagrams, other UML? Cloud infrastructure design? Do you need to include load balancers, DNS, application servers, networks, CIDR allowances, security, data servers, firewalls, storage, queues, and so on?

Latency and Performance

> How does your infrastructure support the specific application and customer-level SLAs described earlier?

Infrastructure Security

> How will the environments be secured?

Maintenance

> How will teams perform patching (hopefully no-patching)? Related policies such as operating system (OS) upgrades, replacements.

Standards, Guidelines, Conventions

> References or links to existing guidelines that you want the teams to follow.

Infrastructure as Code (IaC)
> References to templates, best practices, samples.

Environment Guidelines
> When/how to use reserve instances, autoscaling groups, VPN access to different environments by different teams, and so on.

Global Distribution
> How do we enable and maintain the ability to distribute our applications globally? Are there any particular concerns, such as regarding the Chinese firewall? Concerns associated with performance and security in globally distributing? Server replication processes and automation?

Immutable Infrastructure
> Describe how your infrastructure is immutable, including process automation.

Hybrid
> Are there any necessary strategies for hybrid architectures (solutions that span on-premise and cloud)?

SLAs
> State SLAs that you must meet. Put them in mathematically testable terms, from a customer perspective. Include the panoply of customers, not only the end user.

Considerations for Composing Your Design Definition

That's the template. Each section should liberally include UML diagrams, pictures, and other drawings to help illustrate your requirements. You are the owner of the nonfunctional requirements, and this is your opportunity to state them.

Your prose must be simple, directive, and testable in every statement. Do not allow yourself to write a sentence like, "Use caution when employing the thus-and-such feature of the new bleeding-edge database." That statement is problematic because it is impossible to test. How can a developer know whether they are "using caution"? An actual human cannot sit at an actual desk in front of an actual computer and "use caution." They can either flip the bit to turn that feature on or not. If you're tempted to write something like this, catch yourself and decompose it using the IETF keywords ("MUST," "MAY," "SHOULD," whose intended meaning in this context is clearly spelled out on the IETF's website (*https://www.ietf.org/rfc/rfc2119.txt*)).

Your document should vary based on the specific work you're doing. Just make sure to use the front matter as specified earlier, including the IETF keywords. This will encourage you to write very directive, unequivocating, testable statements. You want to do this such that there is no further question about what you're specifying and the programmer can read your document and go implement your design without a lot of confusion or pursuant clarifying emails. Also make sure to have sections for each of

Business, Application/Services, Data, and Infrastructure. This will encourage you to consider the comprehensive view.

Writing a really meaningful document like this can be grueling work. Enlist experts and colleagues. Do research. It takes considerable time, even if you're very knowledgeable and like writing a lot. Expect that your design document will be very long, 50 pages at a minimum, for a small system. Mine are typically 110 or 150 pages, sometimes hundreds of pages. I work with a chief architect, and together we will produce a 200-slide deck. It's basically like writing a Master's thesis for each system. If it's any shorter, you're not covering enough material, digging deep enough, being specific and directive enough, or you don't know the answers. You just need to do more work.

People might scoff that no one would read a document that long. I've certainly heard a few people say that to me. Here are a few thoughts on that:

- It doesn't need to be a single, giant monolithic document. It could mean here a dedicated wiki. The point is not to make something static and gigantic, it's to be sure you're capturing all of the relevant and necessary aspects

- It's the formalization of your concept as it evolved since the lookbook. It's closer to being an executable blueprint.

- Different people will read and focus on different parts of it. The operations team might get a lot more out of the Infrastructure section than the UI folks will.

- Teams read certain parts at different times. It's important that it's all in one place to have a coherent whole. The document itself is a system, too. It should be highly cohesive and loosely coupled so that it's easy to use parts of it as perspectives.

- When I start a big, mission-critical project, I give the team appropriate time to read it and ask questions, and we've even given mandatory tests on it before, with prizes for the winners.[2] You can't let it be an afterthought.

- This document is a cornerstone of understanding, communication, clarity, writing great requirements, setting expectations, making project plans, and making more predictable or accurate timelines. You can and should refer development teams to it often. As new people enter the project, they'll find it invaluable when the current teams have no time to stop and train up the new folks.

Here's another view on this: if people think it's silly or are unwilling or grumbling about reading 50 or 100 pages or 150 slides that inform them what they are supposed to build and why and how, why on earth would you allow them on your team? We

---

2 For that project, the team got to production on time and on budget with the initial milestone. The software went on to win industry innovation awards.

might equate this to the old adage that "if you think education is expensive, try ignorance."

The more you can automate into the software itself, the better. That is expected. The document is of no inherent value. It will be thrown away. But how will teams first know what to automate?

Building software of the kind of scope we're talking about here means that the company is spending maybe a year, maybe three to four years and millions (or tens of millions) of dollars of someone else's money. That's very serious business. If the developers or the engineering leaders don't recognize the gravity of that responsibility and still think such a document is a bad idea, I don't want them in my organization. Coding your heart out into the wide open sky with nothing but disconnected phrases contorted into the template of the user story represents mere tactics without strategy: "the noise before defeat." Those projects often fail, and it's dismally tiresome to see the defeat slouching ever closer toward us, especially when we can avoid it.

Of course, your project can still fail and have a thousand things go wrong with a good design document. And they will. This makes no guarantees. But it does give you a far better chance of success, especially when working with multiple, contentious, litigious stakeholders on a very complex project with many unknowns. This will help your project succeed.

Writing a hundred pages up front is *not* the answer. What *is* the answer is this:

- Creating a concept of the whole picture as well as it's understood and committing that to an external, formal format beyond the designer's internal thoughts and conversations that others can see, read, understand, and use.
- Performing a thorough and ongoing analysis and deconstruction of the concept based on its semantics. You don't need to complete the entire document up front. We just must make sure we do visit all of these concerns, understanding that they will evolve.
- Making a crisp, declarative, unambiguous, directive, testable set of design decisions that are clearly derived from the concept and record them formally in a public recording for the many diverse stakeholders.

That is, in a nutshell, the way of semantic design. That is the answer.

Things will undoubtedly change over the course of the project. That's expected. So having this record also helps inform "architecture sprints." Your architects can work a sprint ahead of the developers and get them short local designs. But don't do that without first having envisioned the entire thing, or expect a lot of churn. Churn means redoing stuff that's done, which takes time and money, which makes projects fail.

Of course, the document itself will serve a purpose and then fall away. Things will change. So it will eventually give way to smaller, local documents. That's a good thing. They'll be coherent with the concept. Alternatively, you can update the document, version it, and republish it depending on your project needs. Again, "document" here could mean evolving wiki pages or some other team site as long as its in a shareable and formal format.

Position Papers

These are comments that your architecture/design team makes on a particular tool, framework, style, or trend. When blockchain reached the common developer's minds recently, everyone wanted to make a proof of concept and look for places to implement it. When senior developers and development managers and directors stop you in the hall and ask you about a trendy new technology, you know it's time to write a *position paper*. You need to make a statement to the broad organization on your views on the value of this technology, and what applicability (if any) you see for it.

For example, when the Gartner hype cycle (*https://www.gartner.com/en/research/meth odologies/gartner-hype-cycle*) sees a technology (such as, say, blockchain) heading for the apex, it's probably time to write a position paper.

I've also had to do so in the past for warring internal factions: some thought we should use Python for machine learning, and others not; some thought we should use JavaSpaces, and others not; some thought we should use Hibernate, and others not; some thought we should always use stored procedures, and others never; and some thought we should use aspect-oriented programming; and so on. Or, consider a scenario where we all like a certain rules engine, but people do not know when or how to use it consistently.

Position papers tend to be oriented around a specific framework, and you're stating for the entire organization what your position is so that the organization can consider it further. Consider the objects of your position papers through the lens of people and process, as well as technology.

Position papers tend to be needed in two situations:

- When there is some emerging technology that people are excited about and you need to investigate to help keep entropy contained, lest developers begin randomly downloading some 0.01 version tool and marrying the organization to something that might be insecure, unsupported, inappropriately licensed, or wrong for some other reason. You want to state your reasons to help nurture the entire organization along.

- When there are two warring factions in your organization and you need to help clarify and set a direction for them.

You can use a ThoughtWorks Radar (*https://www.thoughtworks.com/radar*) here to help you see when things might be coming around in your own organizations as solutions looking for a problem or when a turf war or religious war is about to break out. Your position papers should go a long way to solving this.

RAID

The *RAID* document comes from the world of project management, and its name stands for Risks, Assumptions, Issues, Dependencies.

This is a document that will be owned and carried through the life of the project by the project or program manager. But you must start it off properly. You as the architect are the first person to be able to see and understand the risks, assumptions, issues, and dependencies that will matter most as you begin your project.

Let's define the words that make up the RAID.

Risks
Risks are something that could possibly occur in the course of your project, and if they did, they would have a detrimental impact. Consider risks across the areas of people, process, and technology. Second, characterize the likelihood of this event occurring as well as the anticipated impact or severity. Third, ensure you have metadata such as owner, status, and date raised.

Assumptions
This is a log of the factors that you anticipate will be in place to contribute to the success of your project. For example, you might assume that the CIO will accept your decision to deploy in the Microsoft Azure cloud, or that you will be able to hire three scrum teams. Or, you might assume that you will meet your first project milestone phase gate in order to unlock a new tranche of funding.

Include the date raised, a short name, and a description along with the reason for having made this assumption as well as the action to validate that the assumption is true. You can also include a necessary action or response to remediate, if the assumption proves false. Always include a status column with the values "open" or "closed."

Issues
An issue is something currently presenting a problem in the project. These must be logged, foregrounded, and actively managed. Your RAID document's issues tab will have columns for ID, short name, description, impact description, impact

---

level (high, medium, low), management priority (high, medium, low), mitigation plan, owner, and status. At the outset, you might not have any of these.

Dependencies

The columns include ID, date raised, short name, description, whether it is an internal or external dependency, the date it must be resolved, priority (high, medium, low), and status (open, closed).

This artifact is a spreadsheet, with four separate tabs, one for each letter. Each item should have its own ID for easy reference.

The RAID is a log, so you do not delete items as they are resolved; change their status to closed. This will help you in later projects to anticipate what kinds of concerns you will see. It will also help you in today's project to see how much progress you're making or whether you need to change your management: if you are opening as many new items as you're closing, your project is in churn and you need to get the management team together and evaluate what's going on, why information is not flowing or how you can better anticipate challenges, or how you can reduce areas of unknowns. Identify the source of the chaos.

RAID Template

You can download a simple and straightforward RAID template (*https://bit.ly/2DALXOH*). Also see the templates available for download at this book's companion website, *AletheaStudio.com*.

Perhaps it seems unusual to have this document started at this stage, before you've created the architecture document. But you already should be able to anticipate and identify many of the risks, assumptions, and dependencies at this point, even if there are no issues yet before the building work has begun.

Even if you are not the development manager or project manager, the creative architect is the spiritual leader of the endeavor. You help conceive and create it, and should assist in identifying in an actionable, formal manner what can go wrong so that you can help add effort and care in those areas.

Review the RAID regularly, such as at project status meetings, to ensure that you are actively managing the project toward success.

Presentations and Multiple Viewpoints

The building architect has the paying client for whom they are working. You have the same thing: the executives running the show. Perhaps you identified a need that no one else saw and are proposing some work. More often, someone in charge will ask you to do something that requires architecture work. Either way, someone is paying for it. Eventually, they will want to know how their money is being spent, and will expect the dots to be connected for them on how your proposal solves their problem.

 The Pitch Deck

For an extended and practical set of patterns for how to run the meetings and make the decks that will get your ideas across to executives and teams in a compelling way, see this book's companion text, *Technology Strategy Patterns (https://oreil.ly/YgqNc)* (O'Reilly, 2018).

Architecture changes by definition are not small, simple, local changes. You must have executive support at the highest level you can get: the COO, president, even the CEO for large projects.

To help you gain this support, put yourself in the executives' shoes and with empathy for their position, their context, and their charge, consider what pains them and what keeps them up at night. You must do two basic things:

- Map your ideas to their pains and concerns
- Illustrate these in a way that speaks their "love language"

I know one very senior executive who loves spreadsheets. He adores spreadsheets. I believe in the holiday cards he sends his friends and family, there's a stocking hung right next to those for children on his chimney reserved for Excel. Giving him a presentation that is something other than a decorated spreadsheet illustrating how you're managing costs gets you thrown out of the room and your project cancelled. He doesn't want to hear the ideas as much as read the numbers. He definitely doesn't want to see any text. Spreadsheets are his "love language." They are the way he sees, thinks, feels, understands, and interprets work.

He doesn't think in terms of project milestones, the points at which you ship along the way. He doesn't think in terms of quarters. He thinks only in terms of annual budget cycles.

Working for this client, you need to express the architecture in a way that maps to these concerns and speaks in this language.

You can't give them 200, or even 20, architecture slides. They won't read it. Then they won't have the right expectations about what you're doing or why. Confusion, frustration, and heartbreak ensues. Prepare a short-pitch deck that summarizes your project based on your Concept Canvas. It should include what you're doing, why, timeline and budget estimate, and what the state of the world will be (what value or new capabilities the executive gets) at the end of the project. Keep it to 4–8 slides. You'll be in good shape to earn their support for your project.

Summary

In this chapter, we reviewed the kinds of documents that you can create to represent architectural concepts and practical designs as well as how to present them. Following these will help your work be clear and actionable by many teams perhaps in a variety of time zones.

When you write these documents, keep the following tips in mind:

- Your design documents are systems, too. If you think of these written documents as you are structuring them as if they were systems, you then design the documents themselves just as you do the architecture itself.

- Make each section and each component highly cohesive (about one topic).

- Make each section loosely coupled so that readers can take a break and know where they left off and focus on just one section that they might refer back to for a specific answer. You can't make it one long Turing tape of interrelated ideas.

- The Design Definition Document must be MECE (Mutually Exclusive and Collectively Exhaustive). It must be comprehensive, and each part must not be repeated elsewhere. Keep the idea of a foreign key from relational databases in your mind to help with this as you write.

As you make your documents, prepare them in a way that they serve as a pool from which you can quickly and easily draw as you build the 5 or 10 or 15 decks for the presentations that you'll need to make to various executives, peers, teams, and other stakeholder groups.

In the coming chapters, we explore each of the major areas of traditional architecture, taking an enterprise view. Your work will vary between the enterprise and executive level, and also at the local application level. When you design one system, whether it's a new application or a modified business process, you must consider all the viewpoints of business, application and services, data, and infrastructure. For this reason, each of the next four chapters is devoted to those respective areas, and in some technical depth. We're switching gears.

CHAPTER 6

The Business Aspect

Allow me, dear reader, to state some propositions regarding the design of software, for your consideration:

Proposition 0

By definition, any purposive compound of objects and their relations is called a *system*. (Examples can include a software application, a datacenter, a business organization, a business process, a chemical compound, a written document, a play, a music composition, and so forth.)

Proposition 0a

These compounded elements and their relations are *not innate*, but are proposed, socially constructed, captured, augmented, determined, and filtered *by the designers* of that system.

Proposition 0b

Any system is either designed explicitly (purposively), or implicitly. If the design is implicit, its design is regarded and comprehended only after the fact, after the system is in place, as a result of a series of accidents, which is likely non-optimal.

Proposition 1

Certain principles apply to well-designed systems, and these *same principles* can be employed across the design of *any* system, though seemingly disparate.

Proposition 1a

The attributes of any well-designed system include, at a minimum:

Fitness to purpose

It must serve what it purports to serve, to help users achieve their goals efficiently.

Felicity

It must afford that purpose in a way that minimizes friction and noise, making it easy and delightful to use, consume, and participate in.

Flexibility

Given that the system operates in a world of frequent change, it should be designed in a way to allow modifications, updates, and extension according to future needs.

Proposition 1b

An additional set of attributes contemplated for a well-designed system (software or otherwise) include the following:

Maintainability

It should be easy to correct faults, improve performance, and adapt to a changed environment.

Manageability

You should be able to keep the system safe, secure, and operating smoothly.

Monitorability

You should be able to see into the system, to measure and understand how it is working.

Performance

It must excel at its purposes.

Portability

It should be able to operate in a variety of contexts.

Scalability

It should be able to operate at the same level, even under increased load.

Proposition 2

The software system you design will operate within a business context, and therefore, to be optimally designed, the software system must be designed to support and operate within this business context or a new business context the software, in its innovation, potentially requires the creation of.

Proposition 3

The business is a system of systems (these are business elements that are also systems: your service-oriented development organization, the sales delivery process, the architecture review board, the strategic funding process, local executive steering committee meetings, the joint venture strategy, the project execution plan, and so forth).

Proposition 4

The business therefore can be designed as systems; it operates according to these same principles.

Proposition 5

Because the semantic designer (creative architect) is foremost a designer of *systems*, the purview of the role includes the proper design of the software *as well as* the design of the business systems themselves.

Conclusion

The business is a system just like the application is, so you as the creative director must help design the business itself as a cohesive and coherent system according to these principles, to achieve a better overall business outcome. The resulting business, as a context in which software is developed, will help improve the software itself, and help you make it on time and on budget and according to user needs. They inform and help (or hurt) each other. This is shown in Figure 6-1.

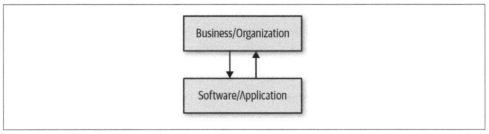

Figure 6-1. The business and application systems inform each other

So there are two points here:

- You might not have historically considered it part of your job, but to be especially effective, consider your purview to include the design of the organization itself and its processes according to received architecture and design principles.

- When you design especially effective software, you not only consider the application frameworks and software attributes, but consider the impact the business will have on your system, and the impact your system will have on the business.

Therefore, now we turn our attention to the business itself, to ask specifically:

- How can you see your organization and processes as *systems in themselves* to be understood and purposively designed?

- After you begin to see your organization through the lens of systems, how can you *optimize* the organization and processes toward maximum effectiveness?

- How can you determine the impact your burgeoning system might have on the business?

- How *aligned* is the business with the system you are creating? As you bring it to life, can it be properly supported?

By the end of this chapter, you will be able to answer these questions with the practical tools we'll introduce.

Capturing the Business Strategy

Business Architecture as we define it refers to the formal representation and active management of the design of the business. Any system that operates within a business will be heavily informed (for better or for worse) by this business context.

The business context includes the strategy, the organization design, business processes, culture, applicable laws and regulations, and other elements that we discuss shortly.

At this juncture, we are interested in a level of strategy in document form, usually a deck. Broader statements such as "establish our company as the leader in the sprinkled donut space" are not useful here. Such documents will perhaps delineate how the business leaders propose to answer three key questions:

- How will we *create* value? You need to understand your target markets, how the markets are expected to change, and how your products and services specifically address your markets' needs.

- How will we *capture* value? What are the ways you can effectively compete? How will you manage your technology to align with these objectives?

- How will we *deliver* value? What processes and capabilities do you need to bolster, streamline, expand, and improve to meet your customers in the market?

The Business Architecture Working Group of the Object Management Group (OMG) describes Business Architecture as "a blueprint of the enterprise that provides a common understanding of the organization and is used to align strategic objectives and tactical demands." I'm not a big fan of the "blueprint" metaphor, for reasons which should by now be obvious. But the OMG specifies many popular things in our industry, so let's build on that for a moment.

Provide a Common Understanding

It is important to know your company's org chart. For a startup, or a smaller organization, this might seem so obvious as to not bear stating. Everyone might know everyone else, and they all might have one job title: "Get Stuff Done."

But many larger, global conglomerates have thousands or tens of thousands of employees, including multiple CIOs for different geographic regions or different business units or functions. In such companies, it can be challenging to know who works on what and how.

Here's what you're doing:

- Gaining an understanding of the organization yourself
- Making it explicit in some documents that serve as a capture of that understanding
- Sharing that with others so that the understanding becomes common

To help design your organization explicitly, with purpose, and in accordance with the aforementioned system design principles, you must define "organization." It's a slippery term. For us, we would have an understanding of the organization if we knew the answer to all of the following questions:

- What functions does the organization perform? What are its capabilities?
- What organization performs each of those functions?
- Who works to support each function? What is the level of talent, the FTE-to-Contractor ratio, typical tenure of service?
- What software systems and services are used to aid each function?
- Which of these functions are *value creators* and which are *supporting* functions?
- For whom? Who are the key customers internally and externally? Who are the stakeholders along the value chain?
- How are they performed? That is, what are the business processes they engage in?
- Why do they perform them? What is the value they hope to generate? Do they generate that value efficiently?
- How does money come into the organization (revenue)?
- How does money leave the organization (costs)?
- Who is *ostensibly* in charge of making decisions over what areas?
- Who is *actually* a key contributor or influencer on those decisions?
- Are there overlaps or gaps, such that decision making is difficult or fraught with friction, slow, and inefficient?
- Where are there "accidental organizations"—those left over as ancillaries or misfits from various reorganizations over the years?
- What is the culture? What are the perks, the benefits, the attitudes among people? What do leaders say they value, and how real, well understood, and shared is that? How are people trained, developed, nurtured? How are people rewarded and promoted? When and why are they reprimanded or released?

- What is the geographic location of all the employees? What is the purpose behind that? Where are the dependencies across teams?

With these questions as the general backdrop, you aim to determine the following:

- The answer to these questions rather accurately for the *current state* of your business.
- What strategic objectives and tactical means the organization has for the *future* as it evolves.
- How you could help other leaders in your organization build an evolutionary map to that future.

Align Strategic Objectives and Tactical Demands

The second component of the OMG's definition of business architecture is the alignment between strategic objectives and tactical demands.

The job here is to take the set of strategic objectives, and create practices and processes that directly, efficiently support them. So let's begin with the business strategy.

To be clear, here we're talking about the strategy of the overall business, as outlined by the CEO and discussed by presidents and strategy officers. If you have a technology strategy, hopefully it lines up to this. But it might not. In that case, you might have two levels of work to do. But the first job is to get your hands on an approved strategy document, or two: at the business level and the technology level. This can be more difficult than it sounds.

Your business might have a strategy that is more or less explicit. For our purposes, let's characterize two kinds of companies: one in which the leader is new (say, installed in the past two years), and one in which the leader has been around a long time.

In companies where the leader is new, the board expects them to lay out a plan for how they will do things better,[1] and so it's an expectation that a new strategy, and typically accompanying new organizational model, will be rolled out. There can be a tremendous amount of change, eagerness for new ideas, excitement, and fear. The old guard leaves. Young Turks step up to gain the notice of the new boss. Some jockey for position, while others lose commitment, confidence, and conviction. New and odd alliances dissipate, form, and reform. Palace intrigue, politics, and chaos ensue. Eventually things settle—until the next time.

---

1 Note that "better" in this context typically means, "whatever is the opposite of what the last person did."

In companies where the leadership has not changed for a while, long-standing relationships have developed. The last strategy, created years ago, gave way to processes, habit, and culture among people with long-standing relationships. Those who like and understand one another communicate quickly, almost in code. Those who don't get along have figured out ways to work around one another. The strategy might not be written down. The expectations are more implicit. People hire for cultural fit. The once-explicit plans have settled into the roots of standard operating procedures where leaders don't feel quite the same urgency to document, publish, and circulate strategies, because people can get more done locally. In this case, you have a different kind of challenge.

If you find yourself in the former kind of organization, your work will be easier in some respects. For one thing, it's likely expected that things must be done differently now, and you might encounter less opposition and can ride a wave of change and get your new ideas across readily.

Depending on which of these kinds of environments you currently find yourself, you might modify your interpretation and adjust your use of the framework accordingly.

Either way, aligning strategic objectives with tactical demands in this case means that you must know what the strategy is in practical terms. If one is not immediately available, ask your manger or another leader so that you know what it is. Then any work you do can follow from it. If you are working in an organization that allows or expects it, you can even help drive the creation of the technology and/or business strategy yourself.[2]

The general approach for this alignment will be as follows:

- You must first discover and then examine the business strategy. What actions does it suggest?

- Then examine the current operating procedures, business process, and the way that work enters and leaves the organization. Refer to the questions in "Provide a Common Understanding" on page 120, and focus on who the work is for and how it is ordered and shipped. Within that, how is the work completed?

- Then prioritize where to aim your design sights.

Framework Introduction

To help improve your business, you can consider your business system as an object of design. There are a variety of practical tools I've found, borrowed, rerouted, or

---

2 To help create your strategy, see this book's companion text, *Technology Strategy Patterns* (O'Reilly, 2018).

invented over the years to aid in answering these questions, and then for doing something thoughtful about it. Together, these tools serve as your business system design framework.

Let's examine this framework now.

Scope of the Framework

You can use the tools in this chapter as a guide in two primary scopes:

- A broader business design
- A local business design

The first case has a very broad scope and is usually performed within the purview of very senior leaders. This can come about on a few occasions:

- In the event of a reorganization
- If you are considering acquiring a company
- If you are considering a major change in strategic direction, such as entering a new market
- After a new senior leader has come into the organization

Depending on how your organization is set up, you might find this business design works in the C-suite, strategy office, or enterprise architecture, or some combination of them.

In the second case, which will likely occur more frequently, you might be in one of these situations:

- You might have recognized the need to fine tune your own architecture department and processes, or some other single process.
- You might have been called on to assist or lead a process reengineering effort.
- Your department might be suffering in some regular, particular, acute way, such as with quality or on-time delivery, and you need to help repair this. Such repair will involve more than a manager standing behind the coders and beating them with a rubber hose while commanding them to work smarter; it will involve an examination of the organizational forces that have conspired to create this situation.

With your common set of documents describing the business organization, process, and capabilities, you will be able to share the common understanding to aid in all of these cases.

Create the Business Glossary

A *business glossary* is like any other glossary: it simply lists key terms relevant to your business and defines them. The purpose of doing this is because the words we use define the systems we create, and if the definitions are not both clear and shared, your systems, customers, and employees will suffer.

Every business has its own terms of art. A *term of art* is a word or phrase that has particular, specific meaning in a given industry, field, or company. For example, one such term in airlines is the "PNR," or "Passenger Name Record." In hospitality, they use "ARI" to refer to the availability, rates, and inventory of hotel rooms. In finance they use EBITDA. In each of these cases, there are loose ends exposed for deviating interpretations. It's difficult to trace, but starting from this innocent-seeming misunderstanding, many software projects are sent awry. Your glossary will help new people coming on board, but it will do wonders to help your analysts and those writing requirements and imagining and designing systems. It's amazing how few people have a clear and shared understanding of the most common terms in business.

Define your terms of art clearly and decisively. Do so in a single document, publish it in your architecture wiki, and link to it in your local documents. You won't need to update it very often.

Create the Organizational Map

You likely have an HR application such as WorkDay that allows you to view your organizational chart ("org chart") of who reports to whom and what everyone's titles are. You'll want to use this regularly in designing business systems.

Such an online tool is a great place to start, but you'll likely need to transfer this to a more pliable tool that you can use in your own related working documents in order to perform your analysis.

Export the Org Chart

See if your online tool will let you export the org chart to a comma-separated values (CSV) file or other usable format that will help you work with it as a system for analysis. This might save you some time.

You need to know the following:

- What are the primary business units?
- What departments are in each?

- What is the primary function of each, in a single sentence, in terms that would matter to a customer?
- Who is the leader of each of those?
- Who participates in each of the capabilities you mapped in the Capability Model?

You don't want to list the people working in each of these departments, just the key leaders and decision makers. This is less likely to change and is easier to update. At the level of the business process, business capability, and general effectiveness, you're not interested in the individual contributors here.

Also, don't only consider the technology-related departments. You're performing an enterprise-level analysis. Remember to include product management, development, training, support, delivery, account management, sales, strategy, and administrative and supporting functions.

Another reason to get the data out of your online tool is because you need a true and complete picture of how your capabilities are supported. Include any third parties, such as those managing your datacenters, and suppliers such as labor contracting companies. Map where those dependencies exist.

You'll be able to use this to determine stakeholders quickly in your local architecture documents.

Create a Business Capabilities Model

A business *capability* is something the business must be able to do successfully in order to execute its business model in creating and delivering value to customers. It does not represent the value (product or service) itself. Nor does it represent the business process that is carrying out creating or delivering that value. It's the set of stuff your company is good at doing (or needs to be good at doing) to achieve its goals.

Consider the example of writing a book: the book is the product. To create it you participate in the writing process with a publisher. But the capabilities involved might include subject matter expertise in a specific domain, ability to research and collect data, ability to create a concept, ability to write clearly, and so on. These are all then applied at various stages in the process of creating the book.

The Capability Model captures the complete set of business capabilities. After you have this catalog, you can use it to *assess the gaps* between the current state and desired future state. Consider how well they currently fulfill the creation and delivery of the products and services of value to your customers. You can also examine where they are redundant with other processes, and where gaps exist between them.

At this stage you can do a quick scoring to see what you're really good at and where you need to improve. This should suggest a list of actions that you can put in a project plan. It can also help you in your software architecture documents, to help you perform more accurate estimates and see what your architecture needs to take into account as you build software, move datacenters around, and do other technology work.

So you need to capture in a document the list of capabilities your business, organization, or department (depending on the scope of your current exercise) will expose to the market to create and deliver value.

Initially, I like to use a simple spreadsheet for this purpose. List the capabilities at the department level. This spreadsheet might have the columns shown in Table 6-1.

Table 6-1. Capabilities spreadsheet

ID	Department	Capability name	Description	Systems	Products	Services

This is not a complete database, but it serves as a simple and straightforward way to get started quickly.

Start by listing what you yourself know, because you can do that most easily. But expect that you'll have only a very incomplete picture, and interview others. Examine the org chart to see who might be involved in your established set of capabilities, and they will often refer to others that are part of their value chain.

Now you can continue this process for a bit. Don't do this exhaustively, because there is no "exhaustively." Not all stakeholders will agree on exactly what the discrete set is. So just do enough until you have reasonably covered it. The best way to do that is to start with the set of customers and customer segments that your business serves, and work inward by figuring out what products and services you provide them. Find the product managers in these areas and contact service delivery and other supporting organizations to see what they do.

 Capabilities Aren't Processes

Business capabilities are not business processes. Processes and applications support the *realization* of capabilities.

Now you can start another tab to do an analysis. Where are there gaps?

Score each of the capabilities according to the criteria for good systems design:

Performance

How efficient is it? What is the level of waste created? How quickly is it performed? What are the places where communications could be tightened? How clear are recommendation and decision responsibilities?

Scalability

Is this capability ready to serve 10 times the number of customers?

Stability

Is the capability delivered reliably and repeatably, with clear understanding of roles and clear expectations?

Monitorability

How well are the metrics aligned to measure the actual delivery of value in the eyes of the customer? Where are the "black boxes" in the system where no one seems to know what's going on, or what the current state is?

Extensibility

As the business changes, how ready is this capability to be augmented or adjusted without major disruptions?

Security

Is the data created in the production of this capability secure?

Score each capability against each of these criteria, on a scale of 1 to 5. Figure 6-2 shows a sample.

	Performance	Scalability	Stability	Monitorability	Extensibility	Security
Capability 1	4	4	3	5	5	2
Capability 2	5	2		2	2	3
Capability 3	2	2		2	3	4
Capability 4	2	1	3	1	4	2

Figure 6-2. Scoring your capabilities map

Now to improve it with an eye toward the future state, cross-reference the listed capabilities to the stated business objectives. For example, is your business strategy to expand in Europe? Do you need to create an outpost there? Do you need to move key team members to France for six months to develop key business contacts or work with important clients because your competition is well established there?

There is a more sophisticated analysis you are ready for at this stage. You can examine your capabilities map and consider how you can develop or capitalize on those capabilities that you're really good at. Can you create a new set of products or services around those? Can you create a new line of business around them? That analysis will consist of the following:

1. Looking at the high scorers.
2. Considering why you are good at them.
3. Imagining what products and services can you create by combining them in new ways or augmenting or bolstering them.
4. Having conversations with executives, strategists, and other leaders to see how they can contribute to your ideas and reshape them. Does anything look viable and interesting enough to carry forward into a more formal proposal?

This analysis should result in a list of actions you can put on a project plan to go improve those capabilities toward your stated objectives.

Create a Process Map

The basic structure of a process map is to define who does what, when. At a very rudimentary level, it's a set of boxes that each describe a discrete task, with arrows that lead to the next task, ultimately producing some meaningful result. Common high-level business processes include the sales process, product development, order to cash, the delivery and customer care process, and so forth.

First you must determine what process you're mapping. This exercise can eventually lead to other discoveries about related processes and subprocesses. At first, keep it focused by starting with an output: something of value that matters to someone. Start there, and then work backward to figure out the whole supply chain of events that lead up to that "gumball" result popping out of the machine. This is the best way to narrow the scope of your process to a workable size. It also is the best way to ensure that you're going to map a picture that you can work with to improve.

One typical aim of business process mapping is to discover how information flows through an organization. This provides a window into what systems are touched over the course of that flow, affording an opportunity to make that process more efficient (process reengineering) and to rationalize and simplify your set of systems.

Reengineer Processes

Often just mapping out a current state process to illustrate how things actually work today will be an enormous revelation. This alone can be enough of a conversation piece among executives to draw attention to how to improve the process. Sometimes the breakdowns, overlaps, gaps, and inefficiencies appear so obvious that they can be addressed in conversational direction.

In other cases, more formal or subtle work will be required to reengineer the process to make it more efficient. This takes time, and depending on the size and complexity of your organization, it can take weeks or months to determine the true current state process and to create an improved future state process. In this case, you will likely need to gain management approval to launch your reengineering effort as a full-fledged project.

As you interview stakeholders in the process, you'll find that people do not always agree. Each participant will have a different role, different levels of influence or inclusion, and different levels of self-understanding about their work, and therefore a different view into the overall system. People will have different understandings of how or why something is done as it is. They might not be sure who really contributes to a final product. Therefore, you will want to get as many different perspectives as you can regarding the same parts of the process. Don't just ask the sales person how the sales process works—they won't actually be able to communicate the whole picture. Getting many diverse perspectives will reveal the true process, as opposed to the socially acceptable or imagined process.

To improve the process, consider the power of the simplicity of Unix pipes and filters. Each program does one thing optimally, and has a clear interface for input and a clear format for output. Use this as a model for your processes.

We do not often see processes so well defined in business. For example, what is your customer defect intake process? In a typical large product organization, this will be poorly defined, depending primarily on personal relationships, threats to escalate to managers, and so on. Defects might go straight to development, which is also doing support. This creates problems because then product management will be left out of the loop, creating obscured resource availability and roadmap contention.

When selecting candidate processes for reengineering, ask about where the breakdowns are and where customers are unhappy. Pick one that is of clear value to a clear stakeholder so that you know you're working on something that matters and can be well defined. Trace it through as a flow.

You start by considering the value stream. A value stream (*http://bit.ly/2mnvaX4*) view defines the end-to-end set of activities that deliver value to external and internal stakeholders.

You can then represent the process using a modeling language called Business Process Modeling Notation (BPMN). This is an excellent way to represent all of your major processes consistently and without the confusion of communication that occurs when you create your own bespoke representation style. BPMN has standard types for swimlanes, starting tasks, ending tasks, forks/joins, decision points, timers, and all the basic tools you'll need to represent any process. Take the time to install a

BPMN plug-in if you're using Visio. If you're collaborating with others, you can use a tool like Lucidchart, which works great, too.

If you get really excited about process representation and reengineering, you can learn techniques from Six Sigma to help you do the work thoroughly. A great book with a comprehensive view is *The Six Sigma Handbook* by Pyzdek Keller.

Take Inventory of Systems

Surprisingly, many organizations do not know what systems they have. They see costs escalate and aren't sure why. They see confusion and poor design because they simply don't have a picture of actual inventory of systems. Some business system design work might benefit you here. It's a good idea for your team to know what you truly have. Take an inventory of your systems.

With this system inventory document, you list the systems you have, interviewing people in different roles. These should match entirely the list of systems in your process maps. If you imagine that some omniscient being in your organization had a perfect and complete view of all your processes, there would be no system unaccounted for: every system would have a place in at least one process.

In this list of systems, give them a name. Determine what capabilities each supports. Who is the named business or product-side owner of that system? Who is the named development or engineering-side owner? Who is the associated architect? Who is the enterprise operations side or infrastructure system owner?

You certainly have expiring items like certificates, vendor support contracts for databases, DNS, domains, functional account passwords, and other items that expire. These can be helpful to add to this inventory spreadsheet, too.

Knowing the answers to these questions will help you have a holistic and coordinated way to solve problems with development, enterprise operations and infrastructure, and even procurement. You can use this list to determine whether you have gaps or overlaps to help you rationalize your catalog, simplify governance and ownership, and reduce costs.

Define the Metrics

The saying goes that if you don't know where you're going, you'll never get there. Defining the metrics that will truly tell you whether your process is successful in the eyes of the key stakeholders is critical. Define these success metrics before you do any work reengineering your processes.

These can be determined in conversation with customers, peers, and executives. Here are some key considerations:

- Look at any existing scorecards and ask yourself if those are the best ones to reflect what makes a difference to customers. Do not merely use the existing set of metrics, taking them for granted. They might have been invented by someone working from the bottom up, or someone interested in showing their own constant activity rather than a meaningful customer outcome. But take them into account.

- You need to be able to *measure and communicate them definitively*. Words are slippery. Do you report uptime availability? Is that measured by total wall clock time because you have a lot of planned downtime that affects your customers? Do you measure it only in planned or also in unplanned downtime? Do you measure it based only on priority 1 or 2 incidents? If you state that the system was up and running fine, but that two-hour outage doesn't count against your uptime because even though the customer couldn't reach your system, it was a firewall problem, is that really appropriate? If your organization measures "customer caused" incidents, separates those out, and congratulates itself on not being the cause, are you sure that's what you want? That seems like the kind of reclassifying that I see bureaucrats do to make themselves look better. It means you are missing an opportunity to make your system more resilient by taking it into account and learning. Besides, if you give a customer enough rope to hang themselves, is that really their fault?

- Realize that *metrics drive behavior*. Ask yourself if you're picking the metrics that drive the behavior you want. In the development organizations I run, I ban any talk of user story points. Developers tend to get caught up in the idea that completing 13 points is better than 8, and it drives undesirable sandbagging. It is, to me, an unnecessary abstraction when people can estimate days just as well as meaningless numbers from the Fibonacci sequence, and they're likely to be equally as wrong, so why obscure things further?

Metrics matter. Define them such that teams can measure them accurately, consistently, and in a way that truly communicates customer success, not the team's own activities.

Institute Appropriate Governance

It's not enough to just capture the current state process and then do the analytical work on the value stream to determine what a more optimal future state process would be. It won't be successful without proper governance. Governance is a meta-process. In your value stream, ask how decisions are made, who the authorities are, what roles they have, and what relevant review boards are. Who can start a process? Who can stop it? What would occasion them to do those things? On what grounds can a product be rejected? At what points in the process? Who stands to gain by the successful completion of a process, and who could suffer if it's unsuccessful or late?

Process governance is a codified answer to these questions. Many times people intuit these, or know them because they've been at the company a long time, or they don't understand them and this wastes time. A little extra effort to help define a set of standards, guidelines, and a published process for the governance of a process will go a long way toward making it successful and creating more value in your reengineering effort.

A terrific way to ensure appropriate governance is through the Operational Scorecard, which we examine in detail in Chapter 10.

Business Architecture in Applications

To this point, we've talked about business architecture and business system design at the macro level: the process and organizational level. This is an area of the business that in my view is underserved by systems thinkers. My hope is that you can bring your design sensibilities and the practices we have covered here to improve the overall organization, with the business itself as your design target.

However, much of the time we are called on to architect or design a particular system, and the business aspects are commonly underserved by architects in this situation. In this section, we discuss what business architecture/design means at the system level.

When you are called on to provide an architecture for a new software product or project, your application or software product design should not only cover software-specific aspects, but to be truly effective, it should take into account the business aspects as well.

Your job with respect to business architecture at the single system/application level is to record a set of assumptions and requirements to create context for further technical decisions. This context that is often missing for development teams, but when they understand what they're doing and why it matters, they can be far more effective and engaged and have the pride of ownership of their work that really drives people to do great things. You don't need to try to explicitly motivate anyone here. You need to simply answer certain questions clearly and directly:

- What business strategy does this map to and support? Are there internal strategy documents you can cite to draw a line to certain strategic objectives and show how this fits in?
- Why does this project matter to the business? Why does it exist at all? What is the business trying to achieve? What will the anticipated state be at the end of the project?
- What new capabilities are you bringing to market?
- What are the major use cases the software must perform?

- Who are the audiences?

- When must the software be delivered? Do not get into project management specifics here, but only state this if there are certain large financial penalties for not delivering by a certain date, or rigid dates that matter for other reasons such as the holiday rush or tax day, and so forth.

In answering these questions, you might feel you're stating the obvious, but often developers or engineers are not aware of these answers. You'll have better software that is more fit for purpose if they are care about what they're doing. As a designer, you're creating the context for others to be successful, and the business architecture is a key part of doing that.

You are also setting the stage for the proper program management of your project. That means you must state your architecture requirements, known constraints, and guidance for effective execution of the project regarding the following aspects:

Organizational and business requirements

- Changes required to successfully execute the project. Are you introducing any new process that might affect other teams? The PM will need to know this to call it out: making it clear here in your document will make that more easily accomplished. For instance, you might be introducing DevSecOps or starting Chaos Engineering, or using containerization in a new way that could impact the enterprise operations or "run" teams. Often technical changes like this means someone else will likely need a heads up and ongoing coordination. Consider all the potential organizational impacts to existing processes because of the nature of this project.

- What "intake" documents are there that must be completed before you can go live? That is, your teams can type all the code correctly and brilliantly, but then not meet expectations of the run/enterprise operations organization and not be ready to release. Make sure that you have noted any such required documentation. It is part of the successful delivering of the complete solution: do not focus only on the software engineers. The truly effective architect is designing and helping manage the entire solution with all its interrelating parts.

- Finance: can part of this be capitalized? Can you take advantage of an R&D tax credit based on the work you're doing?

- Who are the stakeholders that help you manage the project going forward? These include product management, marketing, operations, procurement, known and relevant engineering leaders, the project executive sponsor, business stakeholders, the program management team, and so on. List them and their contact information here.

Team requirements
- What special business needs do you have because of some novelty in the project? Perhaps you're embarking on your first machine learning project and need special training, contractors with a particular skill set, or definition of a new department for data scientists.
- Will there be offshoring, nearshoring, or "insourcing" from other teams? What risks do those produce?
- What impacts or changes are required in the procurement department? Will you need them for any new team contract (such as if you plan to engage a specialized outside development firm) or software purchase?
- Does your project present any potential required changes to your business continuity plan that might require discussion with HR?

Legal and regulatory requirements
- The execution of particular contracts or legal dependencies. Do you need to consult the attorneys?
- Risks with respect to patents or impending/potential litigation.
- Risks with respect to General Data Protection Regulation (GDPR), data privacy, and business security. Do not plan to move data around in a cluster if the countries you are operating in do not allow it. Are you working with China or Russia, or do you have customers there? These countries will require knowledgeable handling and often a distinct solution, so state these considerations.
- Does your application need to comply with the Americans with Disabilities Act (ADA) laws? Ensuring that your UI complies with ADA standards is not only the law, it often makes for much better UI work. This can be a painful process to overhaul if you don't do it up front, but is often fairly straightforward to implement if you do. See the ADA Checker (*https://www.webaccessibility.com/*) tool, which works for public sites. Although a complete discussion is beyond our scope here, remember that the ADA can be required for internal applications as well, so be sure you are familiar with these regulations. Another tool I've used before called Pally (*http://pally.org/*) can be helpful here. There are attorneys who just troll for announcements of revamped websites, check them for compliance with a quick little tool, and send out form letters targeting failing companies in lawsuits. Part of your job as an architect/designer is ensuring you're making legally compliant software, no different than a building architect ensuring that the zoning laws are followed.
- What auditing is at work (SOC 2, SOX) that might require attestation, or the ability to efficiently show compliance? Making sure that developers track their time and mark their stories appropriately is important. Again, this might seem like project management work, and it is, but you should consult with the PMO and

state these matters up front in this handy single location of the architecture document. What you're doing is making it all visible so that estimates are better and all the work that people actually have to do is accounted for. Often the development itself is a small portion of the successful project (maybe 15%).

You might want to consider including in this section certain more specialized technical details that have a business impact.

For example, if you are moving to the cloud, or building a cloud-native system, you might record that you want to reserve instances so that you can get a better deal. Reserving instances can make a difference of 40% to 60% on your bill. It's a big deal. But left to their own devices, teams might just spin up servers and pay hourly at a much higher rate. With you noting it and directing them here, reserved instances become a nonfunctional requirement for the DevOps or pipeline team such that they're taking advantage of reserved instances and saving considerable money. This is a great example of the kind of real and meaningful impact you as a designer can have on both the business and the implementation that the technical teams create. It's the sweet spot for the effective enterprise architect.

The bottom line is that these myriad business considerations can seem remote from the work of developers. However, your job as the truly effective enterprise architect is to take all these matters into account, not simply police developers.

These business considerations can and should constrain software and application designs. Stating them explicitly and helping draw a path to how teams can support these requirements will make a difference in your project that people rarely concern themselves with, to their project's detriment. Considering and stating clear positions on the matters of business architecture can be a wonderful tool for you. This is often misunderstood or overlooked, and yet when it's employed, which is simple to do, it's powerful. In this way, you are helping architect or design the business aspects of the project itself so that it can be successful.

Summary

In this chapter, you learned how to consider the business aspects in designing your software systems, and how to consider the business itself as an object of design. You examined how to discover and engineer business processes, create a capabilities model, measure the success of the redesign with metrics, and consider governance.

For further consideration on this topic of business architecture, you can read up on the Business Process Framework (eTOM (*https://www.tmforum.org/business-process-framework/*)), published by the TM Forum, which describes the full scope of business processes required by a service provider in the telecommunications industry and defines key elements and how they interact.

The Process Classification Framework (PCF (*https://www.apqc.org/pcf*)), published by APQC, creates a common language for organizations to communicate and define work processes comprehensively and without redundancies. Organizations are using it to support benchmarking, manage content, and perform other important performance management activities.

CHAPTER 7

The Application Aspect

Most applications today are, or should be, service oriented. With the core of your software product or application built as services, you will gain clarity, high cohesion, the ability to scale, and improved portability, and provide the basis for a platform.

I tend not to be too zealous about following strict community dictates just because, say, the RESTafarians demand things be done a certain way. I rather try to find the true, concrete advantage in some dicta, and then, if there is a practical value to it, I'll choose to follow it. For example, it doesn't do you much good if I simply insist that you religiously follow the HATEOAS (Hypermedia as the Engine of Application State) creed because it's important, and you're not beholden to me in any regard. There are plenty of times when it makes considerable sense to use verbs and not nouns, or to use ProtoBuf or Avro over hypermedia. There is no silver bullet, and there is no one perfect way. There are the constraints, tools, knowledge, and goals that you and your team have, and that's the important thing to foreground. So please keep that in the back of your mind through this chapter.

In this chapter, we cover the fundamental guidelines for good service design that I use with engineering teams. Although there are certainly other helpful directions you can offer, these are what I find most pragmatic and useful. Doing just these will get you a very long way.

Embrace Constraints

It is not worth it to use marble for that which you don't believe in, but it is worth it to use cinder blocks for that which you do believe in.
—Louis Kahn

Frequently, the more that leaders express constraints to development teams, the more development teams complain. They don't have time to adhere to all these requirements, they say.

In my view, design constraints are like meetings. People say they don't like meetings and they want fewer meetings clogging up their day and wasting their time. I think what they really mean is that they don't like *ineffective* meetings, in which the goal or purpose is not clear, the wrong participants have been invited (or not invited), there is no agenda and no clear outcome, and the decision rights are not stated. If you do those things, your meetings will be effective, and people will enjoy them, because they will be useful, meaningful, move your project forward, and make things happen.

So by way of analogy, I think design constraints are similar. If you are policing developers, specifying where they should place every last semicolon, harping on things that don't truly make a material difference, and have not aligned the product organization around a shared voice for supporting the constraints you do state, no one is likely to appreciate that. But if you can express for teams the things that make a material difference, in a way that they can execute confidently, whether they like it or not, you'll be effective.

Constraints are actually positive, and something I actively seek in the early stages of design. They can ground you, give your work a boundary, kind of like filling out a puzzle by starting with the corner pieces and the edges: they give you something you can count on, that can orient you, and that can inform other design decisions over which you can exercise more judgment or taste.

Your constraints might come in the form of a deadline, or data privacy laws, or regulatory compliance, or a specific customer requirement. If you approach these with an open mind, you can use them to gain advantage in and improve your designs. For example, in one project I designed with my team, the executive sponsor imposed an arbitrary six-month constraint on us, stating, "You have to get to market with something usable in six months; I don't care what it is." (This has actually happened to me three times on major projects, so I've come to expect it).

This was very unwelcome news for the engineering team. The project was a three-year overall endeavor and represented the core of our system. We wanted to work on the foundational aspects and ensure that the structural underpinnings were absolutely solid before going through all the UI work and other things that customers required, and so this created considerable distraction in our eyes. We grumbled because we thought it meant that we would never get to come back to the key abstractions that made the system so powerful. So, we decided to interpret the constraint in a positive way, out of sheer cussedness more than anything else: we didn't want to give up our powerful abstraction for the deadline—so we didn't. We had to build the subsystem in a different way to accomplish our one chosen use case for a minimum viable product (MVP), but still make progress toward the overall substructure, which was the purpose of the project in the first place. In the end, we didn't compromise anything, and the deadline improved the design and tested it thoroughly. And being forced to test all the way through and build pipelines all the way through into production turned out to be terrific.

Use constraints to get the most out of everything.

Decouple User Interfaces

Your software products and applications should be thought of as thin user interfaces on top of collections of services.

Ensure that the user interfaces feature responsive designs; that is, you should not assume that you know the user interfaces that will be needed for your applications. Although today most UI JavaScript frameworks such as Angular, Ember, and React make this straightforward, be sure to design the web UI to work across mobile devices, tablets, and desktops at a minimum.

User interfaces can frustrate your users if they are not thoughtfully designed with user goals in mind. Therefore, applying Design Thinking and Concept Models, discussed in Chapter 4, is imperative. The trick, however, is that while considerable thought must go into making them easy and even delightful to use, you must also consider them disposable. In general, the UI will change more frequently than other parts of your application. Marketing will come up with a new color scheme, and the commercial officer will come up with new retailing and merchandising schemes and A/B testing. The product managers will create new business partnerships, which means that your business application might suddenly need to surface on a gaming console, a car console, a voice agent, a watch, an Internet of Things (IoT) product, and so forth. These are all very different ways of interacting with the same set of business services. Your business services should not need to change too much or too often, just because your UI does.

Therefore, you must be sure to keep your UI very separate from your business services. Do not assume that you know what the interface will be, and assume that there will be many of them. The UI should just do the work of displaying results, and not perform "work." This seems obvious, but it's amazing how frequently I see it violated.

UI Packages

Following our deconstructive method, you can create "UI Packages." At the start of your project design work, do not talk about "the UI" as if there were only one. This semantic misstep will lead you down a bad path. It closes down thinking, making an unconsidered, implicit assumption. It might be "mobile first" or "web" or whatever your thing is. Yes, of course you must settle on the one or three UIs realizations you will support for now. The point is to get to market. Just make sure that you are aware of implicit and unchallenged assumptions and decisions that aren't being made explicitly as decisions. Be aware of what you have anchored and privileged as the "central term," thereby casting the rest of the universe of possibilities as the secondary, ancillary, marginal, minor afterthoughts. You can do this in a matter of minutes. Just don't skip it.

At the beginning of your project, regardless of what the product managers state as the only "requirement," do right by them by considering the entire universe of UI possibilities that you are aware of. These might be web, table, mobile, gaming console, car console, headless, and a variety of IoT applications. Then, according to your current requirements, carve out the space for naming the UI package after only the ones your requirements call for. That is, instead of grouping "The UI Code" together (as if there were only one), you simply name it "web-mobile-xxx" for your responsive design for that UI as one channel among many possibilities. This leaves room in your concept for placeholders for other UI packages, such as "xbox-xxx," which would need to surface the UI in C# code, maybe written by another team with a different skill set.

Doing this creates the quickest time to market and the best ability to parallelize work and keeps things nice and tidy, preventing overlap with engineering teams. It also allows those UIs to be updated and retired on their own timelines, and leaves a path for the UI packages that you might not need today but that can open up new revenue streams if you have left semantic space for it.

Consider what elements are only display and interaction, and don't put anything else in the UI package. Then just use your UI to invoke your service APIs.

The other advantage of doing this is that you can create mock objects, demonstrate the UI in front of customers in a Design Thinking fashion, gain valuable feedback, and improve it quickly without a big lift.

On Platform Design

> *You keep using that word. I do not think it means what you think it means.*
> —Inigo Montoya, *The Princess Bride*

Many software people today cheerfully throw around the word "platform." A lot. In fact, it's hard to find a business today that isn't calling whatever it does a "platform" (which is often also "disruptive"). To me, the term "platform" is clear. It's something that someone stands on. Your software is a *platform* if someone else can build on top of it a new useful application that does something your original system doesn't. It's a *SaaS platform* if they can do that without calling you. Otherwise, it isn't: it's just an application. Amazon Web Services (AWS) is a platform. Google Cloud Platform (GCP) is a platform. SalesForce is a platform. Facebook is a platform. Platforms prevail. They create an incredible business opportunity. They create a great balance between offering something useful out of the box, something that can change with the quickly changing times, and something that can be customized without you hiring a bunch of Scrum teams to add a bunch of awful conditional logic for routing specific customer behavior into the main code base over the course of a six-month development project.

In a famous memo Jeff Bezos wrote to his teams in 2002, which you can readily find discussed online (*http://bit.ly/2kIxLul*), he basically said this: "Make sure everything you write is a service. Only communicate with any other teams' products through service APIs. I don't care what the implementation language is. If you don't do this, you're fired. Have a nice day." That presumably short memo is arguably the thing that enabled a storage engine to become the Amazon Simple Storage Service (Amazon S3) service and Dynamo to become a distributed data service, and indeed is arguably responsible for creating all the various building blocks for what would then become AWS three short years later. AWS went on to grow from $0 in revenue to $26 billion in revenue in just over a decade. To be clear, there are only about 400 companies in the world with more revenue than that, and many of them have taken an order of magnitude more time to create it. Services are the way to scale, and they're the way to create a platform.

Businesses, and the customers they serve, can realize the richest possibilities if you offer your software as a unified platform. The platform is not one corner of two or three services you expose to the outside world. It is the complete catalog of the services across your business, made available as APIs. Do not think, as some do, that "there is a services team, and they are the ones that build services and so I don't build them."

Like user interfaces, the core business services and the exposed external-facing services should be separated. Just like a UI, customer-facing services should do no work. In fact, these external APIs are just another UI, and should be designed and managed accordingly.

Your engineering teams must build services-first. Everything that might possibly be of use to anyone else should be considered as an API, and then exposed that way. One of the very first things your teams should do is consider in a list on the whiteboard or in Excel or whatever little tool the list of services that your application can and should be based around. It can't be an afterthought. For every team, for everything you build, build it as a service.

Some people get religious about the implementation language. This is not a mature view in businesses of any size or import. Now more than ever, the implementation language doesn't matter much, especially if you expose services. There are fun debates to be had over threading models and performance and scalability and portability, and how Java has become a teaching language, and something about Go, and so forth. I find these conversations insufferably boring. As a designer thinking like a business person, there is primarily one reason to care about the programming languages used in your platform work: human talent.

The protocol, too, is another element to consider in our deconstructed method. After doing this for more than 20 years, it becomes very apparent how much time we technologists spend rearranging the furniture for the flavor of the month. Everyone had to switch everything to SOAP. Then they hated SOAP and had to switch everything to XML. Then they hated that and had to switch everything to JSON. The clever minority touted ProtoBuf. Popular products like Cassandra used Avro, so a patch of proponents pop up around that. Soon something else will come along.

The point is that, like the UI, the API you expose via one or more protocols must be separate from the engine doing the work. Offering your services, at least as exposed to the external world, in a few protocols is a fine idea. At least expect that you will change them and put the seam of semantic separation in the right place. Consider the protocol, like the UI, as just a particular representation of how you get the message to the user; it's not the message itself and it certainly is not the worker engine that does math to make the message. I think of protocols the way I think of stories and their presentations in different venues. You might have a story of Cinderella. That could be read in a book, or performed as a Broadway play, or done in a cartoon movie. But the story is the same. The story is your engine service that does the work. These different venues are your protocol. If some executive says that you should be making services with RESTful interfaces that exchange JSON, that's fine. But just like the UI, it's free and only takes seconds to simply name the protocol package after its implementation ("rest-json-xxx") and then leave space in the code repository for "protobuf-xxx" and thereby remind yourself and everyone on your team to keep the separation of concerns (protocol as mere message delivery mechanism versus service doing the work).

Service Resources and Representations

It goes without saying that services must be thoughtfully designed. Because you have this basic structural idea of services in place, you need to consider how they will work together to orchestrate work flows, how they can scale and evolve independently, and how they can best support accomplishing user goals in a secure and fast manner.

With the basic idea that you're dividing your semantic real estate up into services, how shall you go about that division of neighborhoods?

Start with a simple word, usually a noun, that describes your idea. The idea might be "storage," "distributed database," "customer profile," "products," or other primary ideas in the system you're designing. Capture these key words from the conversations you have; the main aspects will come up all the time.

Then consider the verbs. What are the things that people want to do to or with those nouns? At this point, you're not coding anything or using some horrible heavy "enterprise architecture" software tool. Pencil and paper or a whiteboard is great here.

How you name things at this level is critically important. One of the most important things you will do in your design is to decide what to call things, and what ideas get names at all. Be certain you are not biting off too much semantic real estate with the name you give a concept. If you name your service HotelShopping, this means that a different service can be created to run VacationRentalShopping or MerchandiseShopping. Carefully consider these service names and talk with your colleagues to ensure that you are truly saying what you mean in the name, that the space the name takes up is actually supported by the service. Calling a service "Shopping" means it better allow the user to shop All The Things, which might not really be what you want.

Before you leave the pencil and paper stage, get inspiration and learn from the masters as a kind of test to see how your ideas look in comparison. Review popular APIs such as those at Twitter, AWS, Google, Microsoft, or Amazon Merchants, and see how they are constructed. A great resource to model your work after is the Google API explorer (*https://developers.google.com/apis-explorer/*), which lists the available APIs for many of its products such as Gmail, Cloud services, Android, and more. You can examine how it has set up the APIs in AWS (*https://amzn.to/2kQslgA*) for a great lesson. These have been incredibly popular, scalable, and successful for years.

Although REST teaches us to be oriented around resources and representations—which means the nouns in your application, such as Guest, Hotel, Flight Route, Product, or what have you—sometimes it services as functions. You might have a function that calculates the currency exchange rate, or a Shopping service. The challenge with a "Shopping" service is that it already combines a few ideas, such as Customer, Product, Cart, and so forth. So this can become a monolith, and a service in name only if you aren't careful.

But after you have considered the noun you're starting with, consider what it might do, what actions it might take, and what might be done to it. With the aforementioned AWS API, Amazon Elastic Compute Cloud (Amazon EC2) allows you to "reboot instance," or "create tags," and so forth.

With Twitter, the API includes functions to post a tweet, delete one, search and filter, upload media content, receive a stream of tweets, and so forth. The idea of tweets is one distinct idea and its API has the constellation of related actions. The idea of advertising is separate and distinct. We know this because in the conceptual universe, tweets can (and they did when it first started) exist without the idea of an ad, and vice versa. So they are distinct ideas and have different users. If you consider the stick figures in a use-case diagram, we have two now: the regular Twitter user and the Advertiser. They want, and do, different things. So we can expect that their product managers might evolve their businesses independently. Making these distinct APIs in the system takes advantage of Conway's Law, which is a great way to make sure your teams can work in parallel, efficiently, while minimizing the number of decision makers and communicators involved in any particular decision, allowing quicker movement.

Conway's Law

In 1967 Melvin Conway wrote a paper analyzing how committees work. He concluded that, "organizations which design systems...are constrained to produce designs which are copies of the communication structures of these organizations." Put simply, *your software is going to be structured they way your teams are structured*. I can attest to the veracity of Conway's Law across many different organizations. So it can make your life much easier, and your software cleaner, if you organize on purpose the way that you want your product to be. To make your architecture work easier, talk to your boss regularly about the way that your teams are organized, and how well that aligns with the product roadmap.

It is a tenet of REST that you separate the representation from the resource. In service APIs, this generally means the protocol is not thought to be fixed to the idea in the application code. You might have a Product API, in which case the product is the resource. But you could return to the end user a variety of different representations of that resource, such as XML, JSON, HTML, or an image collection. Be sure to keep the representation separate from the resource in your code to keep things flexible.

Domain Language

At this stage, you're not writing code, you're making lists of the basic categories to see how they interact. You're zoning the city: here's the airport, here's the train station, here's the park, here's the shopping center, here are the neighborhoods. Stay at that level for a moment to be sure you have the right ideas. This will prevent rework later.

The main thing is to be very clear on the words you use. The AWS API for EC2 features many "detach-" functions (such as "detach volume," "detach VPN gateway"). It also features many "disable-" and "disassociate-" functions. Define your terms very carefully, reuse them as much as you can, and be rigorously consistent about them.

Never say "find" in one part of your API and then "search" in another if they do roughly the same thing and it's not immediately obvious what that difference is.

Here you are settling on your domain language, and it's crucially important. Create a glossary of your key API words, whether they are "detach-," "disable-," or what have you. Do this from the point of view of an imagined new person on your team who has just joined as a new hire and needs to quickly get up to speed. Write out these key words, define them definitively, and prescribe their consistent use. For example, "get-" might always mean that you must pass a unique identifier in the request, and the operation is expected to return one or zero results. Then a "find-" operation might accept some search criteria and always return a collection.

API Guidelines

Some teams insist on making their own guidelines for engineers to follow when making an API. I would encourage you to make a short set of conventions that you want teams to follow across two vectors:

- What are the domain-specific names or ideas or terms of art that are particular to your business that you want to make sure people use in the same way?
- What are the specific guidelines you have regarding your internal use because of specific mechanisms your IT team has in place to handle cross-cutting concerns? These might include throttling based on customer tier, security gateways, and so forth. Those are not particular to your domain, but they are particular to your organization.

Beyond that, there is little point in re-creating the wheel. For general guidelines around developing services, someone else has already done it. There could be academic debates about the readability of code that puts its curly braces on a new line or not, but I recommend you save that for the pub, point people to well-considered API guidelines made by experts and publicly available, and get on with life. Here are a couple that you can review and then adopt:

- Microsoft for API design (*http://bit.ly/2miIQCt*)
- IBM Guidelines for Watson (*http://bit.ly/2ktn2nm*): this one is great because it includes multilingual conventions, coding, and repository guidelines

The point is not that one way of writing curly braces is blessed by a celestial omnipotent power; the important thing is that everyone does it more or less the same way, whichever way that is.

For cases in which having clear guidance does make a material difference to your business, such as how you illustrate versioning, following the guidelines is very important but is illustrated in the public ones that I just listed.

The main point of following these guidelines is this: as you consider your API contours, ask yourself if you have created cacheable URIs. If they are cacheable and don't violate out-of-band (like with using cookies) or create a split-brain scenario in which you have been sloppy about where certain required elements are implemented such that you need all of them to complete an action, you should be off to a better start than most.

Deconstructed Versioning

The proper versioning of your services is very important. Naive development teams state that the way to know a major change from a minor change is based around their personal volume of work: how many late nights they had or how much coffee they drank to get the release done. This is subjective, it's about you and not your customer, and it's far too slippery. Just because you had four teams working on something for six months, and that big effort is rewarded with cake and executive speeches at the end, does not make it a major version. It should be crystal clear what constitutes a major and minor version, because it has a big impact on your customers. As deconstructionist designers, we are always empathetically concerned with the customer view.

There's a strong argument for the idea that there is no such thing as a "version" in software, that a new major "version" must simply be a new and distinct deployable artifact. This is the deconstructed way of service versioning, and it's very simple and straightforward.

In general, you have a *minor version change* if your API has any of these changes, which should be considered (meaning, implemented and tested) as nonbreaking, backward-compatible changes:

- Addition of output fields.
- Addition of (optional) input parameters.
- Changes to underlying models and algorithms that may result in different results and values.
- Changes to string values, except string values that have special status as being structurally significant. A date is a structurally significant string; a name is not.
- Generally expansions, such as increasing a field size limit, but depending on your legacy systems, be careful with this.

Foursquare does this well, and IBM followed suit for Watson. Services should include a major version in the path (`/v1/`) and a minor version as a required query parameter that takes a date: `?version=2019-3-27`.

In general, you have a *major version change* if you will break clients. This means that you are not backward-compatible. This means that clients will need to update, which they cannot all do in the same magic instant when you cutover to the new API so that they can keep their businesses running. Therefore, you will need to run the current version and the new version at the same time, for some time (perhaps weeks, months, or even years). Therefore, a major version must be built and deployed separately, must run in a separate process from the prior version, and must be separately addressable. It must state explicitly in the URI what the major version number is. Therefore, it's just part of the name, it's just different software, and not really a "version" at all. But that's in a way academic, and the practical thing to do is to include the major version number in the path, to leave room for breaking changes in new versions later.

Breaking changes include these sorts of things:

- Deleting ideas/removing output fields
- Addition of a required input parameter
- Changes to parameter default values
- Change of field names
- Change of status codes

Even if certain fields are optional in your API, your clients building software on top of your API might consider them required for their use cases in their software, so deleting optional output fields is considered breaking. Changing structured data, which is used by clients for indexing and reporting and other built-around purposes, is a big deal, and so changes there mean a major version, too.

The obvious distinction here is that great teams consider what is major or minor from the customer's perspective; weaker practitioners consider what was major or minor in their own experience of doing the development.

It would be lovely if it could go without saying that it is imperative to communicate clearly and repeatedly any breaking and nonbreaking changes to your API well in advance of when you impose them on your customers, whether they are internal or external. Alas, it does not.

Cacheability and Idempotence

There is a simple test I like to use when designing services, to make sure they have proper separation of concerns. Here it is: be certain that your URIs are all accessible and usable as planned from the cUrl program. That's a good test to ensure that you are keeping business logic out of the UI, and that you aren't baking session logic and state assumptions into protocol mechanisms where they don't belong (such as in cookies—but you would never do that, would you?). I recognize that if you're using special protocols such as ProtoBuf or Avro, you won't be able to check it with cUrl, but that's then a completely different matter because you will have an entire client SDK.

If you're following that idea—that you always check if your services are properly accessible and usable from cUrl—you have good reason to believe that your service is cacheable by clients, which is a key tenet of REST.

If it's cacheable, it's also bookmarkable and easily readable, which comes in handy for clients, helps drive traffic, and makes working with your API easier and clearer. If it's bookmarkable by clients, you can bookmark it yourself and make a "saved search" type feature very easily. You can also then easily perform producer-side caching to relieve pressure on your database and offer fast performance.

The cUrl test doesn't prove it, but you want to make sure your services are *idempotent*. A function is idempotent if invoking it repeatedly produces the same result as invoking it once, without side effects. Except for "creationary" functions, they should be idempotent. That is, a `PUT` operation is not idempotent. You create a Customer row and that returns a `200 OK`, and then attempting to create the same customer should return an error status that the resource already exists. Otherwise, the `GET`, `PUT`, `DELETE`, `HEAD`, `OPTIONS`, and `TRACE` invocations are idempotent in HTTP and should be in your APIs, too.

This is easily done. Again, with the plurality that our deconstructionist design highlights, never invoke your noncreationary services once in regression testing, but always at least twice with the same parameters. This makes sure that you are designing in a way that affords you the most flexibility with future clients, makes you most resilient to changes, and puts your dependencies where they belong without creating a split brain.

Make sure that your REST APIs are hypermedia-driven, such that they observe the HATEOAS principle.

Hypermedia as the Engine...

For a good overview of the RESTful HATEOAS principle, see the Spring page (*http://bit.ly/2lWkzC8*) on the topic, or read Roy T. Fielding's original dissertation (*http://bit.ly/2lUEphg*), which I highly recommend.

This principle of REST is the one I see violated most often, and what then creates a variety of artificial constraints that make later extensibility, flexibility, reuse, change, or porting very difficult.

Independently Buildable

You should be able to build, test, and deploy each service independently from others. Building a service should be an automated job through a tool such as Jenkins, and the result should be a deployable artifact.

Rebuilding a client application, or UI package application, should not require that your services are rebuilt. Otherwise, they aren't really services; they are part of your application monolith.

If you make a breaking change, it is likely that you will need to rebuild both your UI application and one or more services, but that job should be a separately defined job from the overall housing application's build.

Give yourself the option to always be able to do the following:

- Rebuild everything all at once
- Rebuild only one specific aspect (UI packager aspect, service, orchestration, etc.).

That allows you to define an arbitrary collection of services and UI packagers to rebuild as necessary for whatever update you've made. This is the best intersection of keeping things quick and understandable. If you have to rebuild a lot of things because you changed one thing, you're not getting much advantage. Part of what's great about services that isn't often mentioned is that rebuilding and subsequently redeploying only a small percentage of your application's overall footprint means that a lot of things go much faster: building, testing, deploying, replicating. And it means that any new problems that you might have introduced are likely to have a very confined scope, or at least be more quickly identified.

Strategies and Configurable Services

Sometimes teams try to envision everything a user will need and create the service that includes all of those features. But this is pretty tough to do. And of course, you already know that some customers will need to set up some features differently. Allowing users to do this through a UI or an API is configuration. Users are not changing the behavior of the service; they are specifying certain things they want to see done in a certain way, and you have already afforded them the exact dials they will be able to twist.

Configurability in this way is great, but it still requires that you are able to sharply anticipate all of the things your users will need to be able to change in fairly fine-grained ways.

You might also consider configurability in another way. The traditional Gang of Four Strategy pattern should be your default, go-to solution for implementing any business logic. As a refresher, let's quickly examine the Strategy pattern.

Deconstructionist designers assume that their current way of implementing is just one of many possible ways, and so they don't just directly implement exactly what the requirements are. They pave a path forward for change and concurrent differences in behavior based on the channel, the client type, the customer, or anything.

The Strategy pattern allows you to define a family of algorithms that can achieve a result differently and allow clients to select the algorithm they want to use at runtime. This produces more flexible and reusable software. As a simple example, imagine that you have a sorting function. Computer scientists have written several different sorting algorithms to sort a list that each have different advantages, such as BubbleSort, MergeSort, and QuickSort. Instead of designing your sorting function by trying to know in advance what the best one to use must be and then giving up all the others, the Strategy pattern would always produce a sorted list, but allow clients to specify how to sort it themselves, as demonstrated in Figure 7-1.

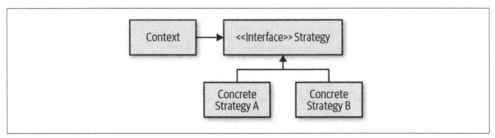

Figure 7-1. The Gang of Four Strategy pattern

This is an important pattern in deconstruction and semantic design, and it serves as a kind of paradigm or kernel of this entire approach to system design. You first define a context, which calls the strategy interface to get its result, and the context is independent of the particular strategy employed in achieving the result.

The Strategy pattern represents the object-oriented tenet of composition over inheritance. Inheritance is frequently antithetical to deconstructed software designs. Inheritance in software creates rigid hierarchies, which are almost always reducable to arbitrary distinctions that fall apart when challenged, creating brittle and unmaintainable software. There are times when your domain is specifically about hierarchies, such as in a genealogy model or a military chain of command perhaps, and then it's less cumbersome and a more natural fit. But in general, I try to avoid designing categories of assumed hierarchies in my data model, because too many times I have seen how difficult and expensive and time consuming it is to change them later. Instead of hierarchies, try compositions with associations such as tagging. Arranging your list of products via tags as opposed to categories can usually achieve the same apparent result and functionality, and it saves you the time it takes to design something in a false representation of the world.

The Strategy pattern is very simple and yet very powerful. As a rule, your services should implement their business logic as strategies. Even if the first Strategy you define is the only one you ever really use, you added only about five minutes of coding time to make the separation. But if someone within or outside your organization were ever to change their mind or have a different need at the same time, you'd have saved untold hours of development time and kept the code very neat, tidy, communicative, and easy to read and understand.

Another great way to support configuration is through a library such as Lightbend (*https://github.com/lightbend/config*). It allows you to read from a local file or URL to get configuration settings. If you set this up from the beginning to allow many of your application features to be configurable, you can have different clients load their own settings, creating a very dynamic platform.

Application-Specific Services

In general, disallow the idea of "application-specific" services to creep into your vocabulary or engineering organization. I've seen teams far too many times assume that a service will only ever be used by the application or product whose inception first caused it to be written.

There is no real advantage other than the illusion of immediate convenience to defining something like an application-specific service. There is a certain hotel in Paris, the beautiful and artful Molitor, which actually started life as a community pool and not a hotel at all. The hotel was built around it later, and yet the community continues to use the pool today with no intention of staying at the hotel. Because the two services of the hotel and the pool are conceived independently, they can be managed separately with revenue recognized separately, or rolled up together, and the business model is more flexible. This is one way of seeing how the world reflects the advantages of not making too many assumptions.

A central tenet of deconstructive design is that we know that we don't know how things will change and how people will want to use them in a changing world. The easiest way to make flexible, reusable, and easily maintained software is to not make any unnecessary assumptions about how things are yolked together. When you hear someone saying, "we know that no one will ever want to invoke this function outside of the context of this particular application," that should send up red flags for you. Honestly, I don't understand why people sometimes cling to this idea of "application-specific services." It seems a necessarily arbitrary and unhelpful distinction.

If you think more generally, honoring the precepts discussed earlier, you'll find that your product team is very happy with the many options for business capabilities you readily afford them.

Communicate Through Services

As in the famous Bezos memo of 2002, the way to achieve a fantastic platform is to ensure that all communication is done only through service interfaces. Services must own their own data. Other applications or services must not go through the "back door." No team must ever read directly from another team (service)'s data store. Instead, they should go through the service interface. Do not allow teams to get another service's data via direct linking, extended queries directly at the database level, shared memory, or vendor-specific data emulsion extensions.

Services own, and are responsible for, the data they have—the noun or function they represent in our domain. When a service is ready, all other applications should reuse it and not build their own that does the same thing, or with a slight variation.

This means that no two services in our domain should overlap and do the same job.

Expect Externalization

Throughout this book, I've begged for us to assume *less* in order to make better software. There is one case, however, for which making an assumption, or at least having a vague expectation, will do wonders for the robust resilience, performance, and scalability of your design. That is to expect that any service you write will be publicly available, externalized from your own organization and applications and used by other business units, and exposed out on the open internet.

Now there is a balance here of course. If for the near-term roadmap you have no reason to suppose that your service would be externalized, and you have a tight and hard deadline, it's perhaps inappropriate to take the extra time to create a new public interface for your service, which would (as we discussed earlier) need to be separately built and deployed, and go through a perhaps cumbersome change request process and set up space in the DMZ and incur the cost of that compute and storage if no one is going to use it. The point is not to do all that, but do imagine that someone soon will ask you to do that, and that would cause you to do a few precautionary things first:

- Ensure that you have a full set of security scans such as with a tool like Veracode. Running static scans and gaining insight from the reports on how you might accidentally be violating Open Web Application Security Project (OWASP) constraints is a rich source of data to help you prioritize security bugs lurking in your software and fix them now.

- Ensure that you have properly designed your software to be scalable. Gaining data now by running load tests in automation regularly will give you a clear path for how far you would have to go make your service publicly available. If you imagine this scenario up front, you might take the time to design it more thoughtfully. Using just a few basic scaling techniques, such as asynchronous invocations, eventing, loose coupling, statelessness, and horizontal scalability up front can literally save your business and can help it prosper. Scaling means that the business can scale, too. It can become very expensive if you neglect to consider public-level scale. I have seen businesses that actually lost more money the more large customers they added because the services weren't designed with big scale in mind, by which time it is too difficult to change. That's the opposite of scaling a business. You don't need to do more than is necessary; just consider these scalability techniques from the beginning, and then public or even global scale is much easier later. It's mostly a matter of considering carefully how you manage state.
- Carefully select how you address functions on the network.

Mostly what this means, though, is that you design for resilience.

Design for Resilience

Often when designing services, we consider only the Happy Path. That's natural because the product team has described what it wants it to do, and so we go implement that. But we know things sometimes go awry, so we do logging and exception handling and monitoring.

The problem with doing only these things is that they don't help the caller. In the case of logging and monitoring, we learn only after something blows up that it's happened, and we rush onto a crit-sit call (or if it's less severe, we put it on a priority list for later bug fixes). But we can do better and provide an answer to the customer now. We're all accustomed to seeing 404 pages if we type a wrong URL. That's better than nothing. But a 404 page that offers a search bar in it and a list of help topics is even better. In the event of a 500 Internal Server Error, a Bad Gateway error, a request timeout, or a rate limit violation, the improved response is not quite so clear. But we must consider those possible errors and design for them, just as we design the Happy Path.

A second point is that there is a spectrum here: things are not, in my mind anyway, totally up or totally down as much as they are functioning along a spectrum, across many different aspects of the system. We're used to jumping if things are hard down. But many users experience very frustrating engagements with our software for a variety of reasons, including very long response times, or haphazard behavior, things that are not quite so readily identifiable as someone running through the halls screaming because the entire site is "hard down."

Consider graceful degradation in your services up front, and throughout their life. Hystrix is a tool that was open-sourced by Netflix a few years ago and has been a good way to handle resilience features. But it required a lot of up-front configuration, which violates the deconstruction tenet of not trying to use a crystal ball to imagine every kind of failure and how it will happen and what the impact will be. So Hystrix is just in maintenance mode and no longer under active development. At the time of this writing, Netflix itself is moving toward a newer, more dynamic and lighter-weight framework suitable for functional programming called Resilience4j.

You can use a library like one of these, or roll your own, but either way, you must design for resilience, which means graceful degradation, compensation, and recovery. Your service functions and engineering team should have an answer for each one of these items in your services:

- Where you will employ circuit breaking and how you will implement it? At heart, a Circuit Breaker pattern is essentially an implementation of the old Gang of Four Decorator pattern working with an Observable. The trick is not implementing the circuit breaker as much as it is determining the next-best state for your function to delegate to.

- How you will allow rate limiting? This allows you to restrict the calling rate of some method to be not higher than two requests per second, for example. This is an important element in any service. If you think that your service is just to be used by internal customers and so you don't need to consider rate limiting, I urge you to think again. Well-intentioned junior colleagues two cubicles over can accidentally launch a Denial of Service attack with a little improper loop logic that can flood or bring down your service. You won't be able to responsibly plan for regular usage and future provisioning and costing if you don't have a rate limiter in place for your services.

- Bulkheading. This is related to rate limiting, but specifically restricts how many parallel invocations you will allow on a function at once.

- Automatic retrying. If this request fails, can you automatically try again?

- Compensation. Can you perform a different action?

- Response caching. We tend to think of caching strictly as a mechanism to improve performance. But it also can improve resilience. Caching in order to reuse a previous response for the same request is a great performance improvement and relieves pressure on the database, reduces network calls, and so forth. Caching responses as a resilience consideration is a powerful way to allow graceful degradation: think of how your application might answer user queries starting with "No, but...," as in, "I can't do exactly that right now because something is broken, but I can give you a related response to a similar question."

- Notification. Some companies have implemented a nice service wherein if you call into customer service and there are currently long wait times to speak with a representative, they can record your number in the system and call you back. Since HTTP/2 and WebSockets and push notifications and other advances in technology, websites and mobile apps can now do this, too. You can can implement a feature whereby there is no good cache and no good circuit breaker, but you can automatically call back the client later when you're back up again. It's not ideal of course, but it makes the customer feel more cared for than just blowing up in their lap with no clear next step.

The deconstruction tenet here is that exceptions are not exceptions. They happen all the time and the results of failures can obviously range from irritating to disastrous. If you treat the Happy Path as the privileged term and focus all your implementation effort there, and treat exceptions and failures as marginalized second-class citizens, they will eventually undermine you.

Adding these with a library such as Resilience4J will make your life, and your customers' lives, so much easier.

Interactive Documentation

If you're using RESTful services, publish Open API documentation (Swagger (*https://swagger.io/*)). The OpenAPI Specification was donated to the Linux Foundation in 2015. The specification creates a RESTful interface for easily developing and consuming an API by mapping all the resources and operations associated with it.

Doing this provides a variety of advantages:

- It allows you to write a complete specification before you write any code.
- It lets you visualize the operations in your APIs and allows internal developers and external consumers to quickly and confidently adopt your API.
- It provides SDK and scaffolding generation.
- It promotes test case automation by supporting response generation.

Also publish *documentation guidance* with your service so that others can use it without talking to you. We use services all the time on the web, and then when we turn around to make them, we forget our own personal experience and think we're done when the code for the function is done.

Think of how you use something like Amazon S3. You don't call Amazon and have meetings with them when you want to use Amazon S3; you just call the API. You can do that because AWS provides the documentation, examples, automated API keys and credential management, and other necessary functions to make this possible. That's why it's called a service. If you go to a taco stand and place your order and the guy at the counter invites you back into the kitchen to cook it yourself, that's not food service, that's outsourcing your kitchen.

As a rule, you should automatically add Swagger documentation to your services and publish them to a demo environment so that users can try them out interactively and see how to use them without hurting themselves or you. This will also help ensure strong contracts and efficient communications between your internal teams. Minimize the communication necessary to achieve this by automatically publishing the documentation at build time and deploying it as a step in your pipeline.

At a minimum, use GitHub as a model and publish Markdown describing your service with the service (not on some remote wiki). If you use Java and Maven, it's a step up to use the Maven HTML site generator for each service with the Site Plugin. This will just put the documentation in the site folder, so make sure to include Wagon or another tool to then post your documentation to the proper public repository. This should be automated and easy given that your services are independently buildable and deployable.

Anatomy of a Service

There are a few basic kinds of services my teams and I find helpful.

The overarching rule is that services must have *high cohesion*, so each one represents one important noun in the domain or performs only one meaningful action. A service API can have many functions, but they should all be related around a single idea from the domain perspective.

UI Packages

The UI package is a service with the single job of displaying information to users and providing a means of input and user interaction. These services can be put together with building blocks of UI widgets or reusable UI components that can invoke orchestration services in their own process. For example, if you have a shopping service that returns a list of offers that a customer can pick from, you might want a corresponding Shopping UI widget in your JavaScript framework so that you can reuse it across various channels such as your public website or your onsite application for store employees as well as your voice agent call-in channel application. Your UI package service then becomes a collection of such reusable widgets.

Orchestrations

The UI package widgets will likely invoke the second layer of services, which are orchestrations. Orchestrations have the single purpose of representing a workflow and managing state for the end user. They should be designed from a business perspective. These services are called orchestrations because they are like the conductor in an orchestra who doesn't play an instrument but pulls together all the different individual players to make a coherent whole. Orchestrations just perform the job of combining others that actually do the work (these we call engines, which we look at in a moment).

If you have a user experience (UX) team or knowledgeable product managers, work closely with them to determine the best workflow for a particular use case and map it out on a whiteboard or with a tool like Balsamiq so that it's easy to change. Using Design Thinking techniques discussed earlier will help ensure that your workflow makes the most sense to your users: it's very important to design workflows from the outside in or top down. Resist the temptation to start from code (bottom up). This will have the effect of dumping the database out onto your user. You want to be user-goal-oriented here, constantly asking yourself what the thing of value that the user is trying to do is, and how you help them achieve it most effortlessly.

Here are some guidelines for considering how to create your orchestration services:

- Start with a clear definition of the user goal.
- Consider this particular workflow at the same time that you consider a variety of related workflows so that you're taking the holistic view and placing tasks where they best belong, not only for this particular goal, but in relation to all the things a user will want to do in your application. It's crucial here to recall our theme of the importance of naming and the importance of picking the right levels of abstraction as you work with your concept. For example, you could decide that you have one user goal to Add Products and a second one to Edit Products and then create two workflows. This would be obvious and seems reasonable enough. But if you decided that, at a higher level of abstraction, the user wants to "Work with Products," you might have a single display that lets them do both of those things that is more convenient, obvious, and less mentally taxing and time consuming for your user. This might make your design work more complex, but again the point is to keep it simple for your user, not necessarily for yourself.
- Orchestrations might be step by step or rules driven. It's probably easiest to start with the step-by-step process, but then to use that only as a starting point or input to a second round of refinements to discover if and how you should combine workflows. This will also reveal some complexities that might suggest to you that a rules-driven workflow approach makes the most sense here. Consider the tax application TurboTax. This is a rules-driven workflow. Although the goal is to get your taxes filed, it's great software because the user input values might trigger different rules that show different screens. It's nonlinear. It's convenient for engineers to think in simple, linear, step-by-step processes, but this is rarely what's best for a user.

- Do not start with UI design here. This is a common mistake. You define your end goal, and a logical starting place based on the minimum amount of information a user needs to have to start achieving that goal. Then, fill in the necessary steps in between. The naive, or hasty, approach is to then make each one of those steps a screen. If your goal is to minimize friction or time-on-task for the user, they will be happier. So you have a prior step of conceptualizing the best way to design the UX after you have the clear goal and set of steps.

- Mark clearly which steps are required and which are optional. Ask yourself how you can make the easy things easy and the difficult things possible. This is a hallmark of good workflow design. Doing this requires that you consider, as we do in deconstruction, the multitude of user personas: there is no such thing as "the user." There are users in extremes: the three year old and the grandmother; the casual user and the one for whom it is mission critical; novices and power users; and users who need it heavily for a short period of time and then might not come back to it for several months. Look at your workflow through all of these lenses in order to determine the best way to conceive of the steps and screens (or voice commands).

- Highlight any dependencies: what steps can be done at any point, and what steps absolutely require something prior to be done?

- In deconstruction design, we always consider the opposite as early as possible, to free ourselves from unwarranted assumptions and do something delightful and innovative. Ask yourself what the world would look like if you didn't have this workflow at all. Is that possible? How can you eliminate it altogether? What would have to be the case for you to do that and save your user all the time? Perhaps you can't eliminate it altogether, but putting your team through this exercise will likely help you come up with ways in which you can simplify things for them. An obvious answer is how you can use automation, previously collected data, or a machine learning recommender engine to prepopulate as much as possible by guessing what the user would want to do. Then, if 7 times out of 10 they are just approving and going to the next step, you've saved them a lot of time.

- Make sure that every task is rigorously defined in this one structure: verb/noun. The user is doing something to or with something. The task might be "Search Songs" or "Pick Room."

- Be sure to include the exceptions in your workflows, and not only the Happy Path.

As you draw out your workflow, you can use a tool such as SmartDraw to make sure you are defining the flow based around user goals and tasks before jumping into the UI design; they're separate matters.

Engines

A third type of service we might call the engine. These are the services that do the work. They perform calculations, execute algorithms on data, run searches, invoke data services to persist changes, and save state.

When you design your engines, make sure they do one thing only. The engine might represent the Profile Persona service, the Offers service, the Cart service, or the Ordering service. Shopping and ordering are two different things, which we can know for certain by observing the world. Out walking around in the world, we can shop without buying anything. We might shop, take a rain check, and save this and submit it for ordering later without shopping again. Therefore, we know for certain that these are two distinct ideas, and should be two different services.

Separating ideas like this encourages you to make strong interfaces. We can see in that previous example that if we can place an order without shopping, as long as we have a well-formed order slip, that input to the Ordering service can be generated by a variety of possible other services or systems. The message can be created from the Cart service during checkout for a typical ecommerce flow, or generated by a third-party business partner channel, or by a voice agent. Keeping things well defined in this way is the best thing you can do to make your services portable. Because we know that we don't know what the new business direction will be, portability is important. New executives come in and change direction, the cloud gets invented, car consoles get invented, NoSQL databases come on the scene and are initially fantastic and then get taken over by corporations that squeeze you for money and there's pressure to switch. We know how this all goes. Making sure your services feature high cohesion and loose coupling is the best thing you can do to keep your business nimble and cost efficient.

Make engines stateless

As much as possible, engines should be stateless. This is generally an impossible goal given that the whole point of any software is to modify the state of some representation.

What you can do is to disallow developers from writing to a server's local filesystem. Application developers should not implement code that allows users or systems to upload or transfer objects for storage on any server's local filesystem. Doing so would create servers that hold state and are not automatically replicated. State MUST be held only by databases or specified object storage systems. Otherwise, the overall system's resilience would be compromised.

System designers and developers should make local choices that support stateless interactions across use cases, anticipating that web and application servers will randomly fail partially or completely at any time; the system's resilience design should support this.

Scaling engines

A primary goal in designing engines should be their scalability. The most inexpensive and quickest way to scale is *horizontally*, which means that you can replicate, as if off a conveyor belt, many exact duplicates of your services and deploy them alongside one another. These nodes are just some drone army that are indistinguishable from one another. You then have a set of load balancers send requests to servers with available capacity to do the work. Cloud providers let us define autoscaling groups, so that we can define triggers for specific thresholds to deploy a new copy of the service, add it to the load-balancer pool, and let it begin accepting requests. Then they can automatically scale back down again when demand is reduced in order to save costs.

You can't do that when *vertically scaling*—adding more hardware capacity in terms of memory or processor power to the same service instance. This often requires approvals in a lengthy provisioning process, ordering new hardware, adding it to the available capacity, and making many potentially dangerous network changes. You therefore need to vertically scale months in advance of when you might actually need the additional capacity. In short, vertical scaling is not transparent and as fluid with your business in the way that horizontal scaling is. So horizontal scaling is far more preferable. It requires that you design your services thoughtfully around how you hold state, how much work you make each service do, and at what point in your design you do what work.

You must design your services to horizontally scale at the service level. That is, you don't scale your entire application set at once. You might have a web server farm that is performing just fine, but the shopping engine services running your .NET code are performing complex calculations that take 200 ms and so you need to scale out only those nodes without adding any more web server nodes.

You can then allow your load balancers to execute the simplest round-robin algorithm to select which service it directs the request to. Of course depending on your load-balancing hardware or software, you can select more sophisticated algorithms that direct requests based on actual server capacity at that moment.

Every engine must have defined scale goals and clear current scale ceilings. These metrics should be expressed only in math and never in any other way. I have heard very senior folks in different organizations talk about whether the service is "scalable," or claim that their service is "scalable." This is nonsense, absolute fiddlesticks. It doesn't even mean anything at all to say that. In the case of expressing scalability, there is only math representing the current ceiling, and the math structured the same way that represents the scalability goal (if they're different). Scalability means that you can perform the same under additional load. This obviously means that you need to know what acceptable performance is, stated in terms of response time to the user, and then under what load. It's obvious then how to represent scalability; state it like this in your design documents:

> For 500 concurrent users, the response time to the end user agent will be under 2 seconds 80% of the time, 2 to 4 seconds 19% of the time, and 4 seconds or greater 1% of the time.

Change the numbers, of course, as you need for your business, but the structure of the sentence should be the same. But let's unpack this a bit more. Notice that we state "to the end user agent." That could mean the browser. This is differentiating because first, it's user oriented, which we love; second, it's clear. I have seen vice presidents argue vehemently over this because they weren't clear on this precise point: response time to *where*? The engineering guy would proclaim he was within his SLA because the service responded to the load balancer in under two seconds, and the product guy would proclaim that doesn't matter to the end user because they see the result several seconds later. Then, engineering claims that's the network and the Wild West of the internet over which they have no control, and so forth. You can see where that goes: nowhere good. So if you do elect to define "at the end user agent," you need to know how you will measure that consistently and store that data to track it, which is a great idea. It also means that you would need to carefully consider holistically all of the components in the stack for that service request, including the load balancer, the edge cache, the network, and your datacenter regions. You might then restate your goal as "in Europe" and have a different goal for "in the US."

The best thing here is to, within your budget and timeline as appropriate, do the best job by your users. Don't use this scalability sentence structure to "game the system" and look good in your metrics because of the fine print. People see through that pretty quickly and it doesn't truly help your business. Instead, make aggressive goals and use them as a statement of work for yourself to examine and improve the different parts of your stack.

First, you need to have an understanding of your customer base. How many people are using it concurrently? What is the response time they require? What response time would delight them while still being cost effective for your business?

You then would need to have in place a good load test using a tool such as Selenium. But then you also would need to run that load test regularly, which would mean that you need to automate the execution and reporting of the load test results. You want to do this throughout development so that you can quickly spot which additional features or implementations affected your results. This means that you want to set up your load testing as early as possible and launch it even against your initial hello world engines. It's a lot of effort to define and run and report load tests, and so putting this work up front instead of at the end means that you will get to do it many,

many times before you actually go live, and so you'll have a very clear understanding of your application when you need to most.

To state your scalability goals, you follow the same structure, but using the future tense. Now, you have a goal that's measurable and testable, and you can show your success and be prepared if things begin trending downward.

High-Scalability Case Studies

There's a website that's been around for many years now that hosts case studies by different companies on how they scaled their systems. It's called HighScalability.com and it hosts a section on "Real Life Architectures," featuring articles about how the usual suspect companies like Netflix, Amazon, Twitter, and Uber faced certain scaling challenges and how they designed to scale better.

Another good way to scale engines is to consider where you can do work asynchronously (discussed in a moment). Again, this is more difficult for us because it makes things more complex, but it's better for the end user in terms of performance.

Serverless

Serverless functions such as AWS Lambda, Microsoft Azure Functions, and Google Functions can also serve as a backbone for some of your engines, but you should employ these with caution. Recall that the person who invented the ship also invented the shipwreck. No benefit is free, and the cost of the convenience and scalability that serverless provides comes in the form of challenges in monitoring and permissions management, general confusion, and difficulties for team development.

Teams need to experiment, to try to test things. This is very easy to do with serverless. But you must make sure that testing a function in this way does not inadvertently cause you to forego the design process of considering whether serverless is really the best place for that function in your overall design.

The confusion comes in because until serverless matures, it remains a rather opaque part of your stack. You can use tools such as XRay in AWS to help understand the general metrics, but it can be difficult to integrate these with other monitoring tools your organization might have as standards, making it difficult to trace and piece together the overall behavior. There are other tools that you can employ such as IOPipe and Epsagon that might be of use in improving your observability.

The takeaway on serverless for now is that it will add considerable complexity to your architecture: everything is a trade-off and there are no silver bullets. So as you grow your serverless footprint, you will find a proliferation of satellite tools creeping into your stack like weeds, accidentally changing the landscape of your architecture. No tool solves everything for you. Considering up front how you are going to handle all the good old-fashioned concerns that you will always need to account for, including availability, monitorability, manageability, scalability, performance, cost, and security, is paramount.

Any time you go to use a new tool, remember that you still have all those concerns to account for, and imagine a kind of scorecard. Where one tool succeeds, another might stumble. This will help you to make the requisite trade-offs more purposefully.

Data Accessors

All data access must be through service APIs. These services are called Data Accessors. Data Accessor services are invoked by engines and interact with the data store for the engines to do the work.

We examine those more in detail in Chapter 8 because they're a big topic on their own. I mentioned them here solely for completeness. For now, just know that there are services called Data Accessors and they are distinct services from engines.

Eventing

The most basic form of asynchronous processing is publisher/subscriber, or pub/sub. One component, the event producer, publishes an event to a queue or topic. A queue, here, stores that event and allows it to be read asynchronously by a single separate second component (the subscriber). A topic is like a queue that allows multiple subscribers to pick up the event.

The idea of publishing events to topics is a crucial one in deconstructed design. Fundamentally, the fact that there are multiple event subscribers, and they are free to come and go (subscribe and unsubscribe), free to process the event in their own time, in some way unbeknownst to the event producer, is a perfect vehicle for many of the concepts we're working with. Because we know that we don't know what something will mean, because we know that we don't know the "correct" response (or assume that there is only one of them), and because we want to design systems to be incredibly scalable, pub/sub eventing fits the bill perfectly. It's the architectural choice that makes the fewest assumptions about the world. It allows you the most scalability, flexibility, extensibility, loose coupling, and portability.

At the heart of this pattern is the event. Every event should be represented with the same idea: that there is a state change that just happened to this noun in the immediate past. In the hotel domain, for instance, you could conceive that "Guest Checked Out" is an important event. Others might be "Order Placed" or "Reservation Cancelled." Notice that any human being who has ever stayed in a hotel is likely aware of these events. That's the appropriate level for now: nontechnical, business oriented. Just take a few minutes to list out what some of the major and obvious events are in your domain.

When performing your domain analysis and representing your set of services as we discussed earlier in this chapter, take another pass through that work, viewing it through the lens of events. Examine each of your services and the ideas in your domain model and ask which of them can benefit from an event pattern. Just as you examined the domain model to ask how the verbs and nouns interact, consider too which services have strong associations with the events you have listed. This will lead you to some clear places where you can take advantage of events for the things they're best at: loose coupling, perceived performance, scalability, extensibility, and portability.

Because managers run the orchestration of services, it is best to have the manager emit the significant events. The manager service places an event on a pub/sub topic so that multiple subscribers can respond, as shown in Figure 7-2.

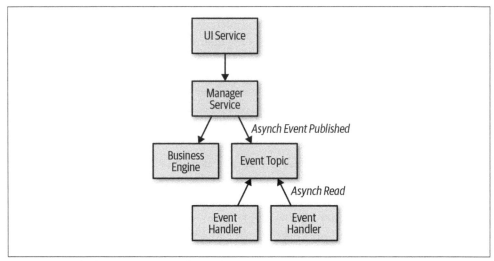

Figure 7-2. The basic anatomy of asynchronous service components

Managers should own their events, such that no other manager or subsystem should produce the same type of event. The Event Handler is an interface that listens to a topic to read events it subscribes to, performing filtering as necessary.

For all the benefits in perceived performance and scalability that pub/sub brings, after you have created a number of event producers and subscribers, it can be confusing to know exactly how your system is working. Before you create too many of these, it is therefore a good idea to create a master index file of all known event types and which orchestration services publish them. This is documentation, and not necessarily a central online registry. This will help teams know which events are already being generated, such that you might be able to easily add extensibility and customer customizations to your system by adding another subscriber to an existing event. This is one reason why it is best to start out with what in JMS is called a Topic (which allows multiple subscribers) rather than a Queue, which is a one-to-one publisher/subscriber mechanism.

Events should be lightweight messages that should not contain a copy of the complete current state. Instead, events should contain their header or metadata information and a reference ID that they can use to access a copy of the complete information should they require it. The Claim Check pattern (*http://bit.ly/2kmeoXy*) is helpful here to get the current state from the system of record. Using this pattern prevents you from inadvertently "leaking" the system of record out into the many provinces of a complex system, maintaining the integrity of each service. It also means that you can maintain a tighter security boundary to help maintain compliance with the General Data Protection Regulation (GDPR) as well as Payment Card Industry (PCI), Personally Identifiable Information (PII), Service Organization Control 2 (SOC 2), and other important data privacy and security restrictions.

Enterprise Integration Patterns

A very helpful and informative book on integration patterns is Gregor Hohpe and Bobby Woolf's *Enterprise Integration Patterns* (*https://www.enterpriseintegrationpatterns.com*). For more sophisticated interactions, you will find places to perform a Scatter-Gather or use Claim Check (these are patterns in the book that are overviewed on the website). It's many years old now, and newer tools such as Apache Camel have been built using the patterns so you don't need to implement them all from scratch. But much of the book is still quite relevant. It's an excellent reference.

Asynchronous calls are wonderful, but use them wisely. You do not want to use asynchronous calls every place possible, for a few reasons:

- First, they come with a cost of complexity. You need to create more infrastructure to support asynchronous systems like pub/sub.
- More infrastructure can mean more cost.
- You also will have a harder time monitoring and tracing requests through those systems after they are in place.

Many teams will default to simply assuming everything is synchronous because that's by far the easier thing to implement. Be thoughtful and specific about where to use synchronous calls given the use case and your scalability needs. If your use case allows for a short time between interactions, you should almost certainly use asynchronous processing. For example, if the user places an order and then an email confirmation is required, the notification to the email system and then the sending of the email itself should occur in separate processes. Some use cases, such as this one, are obvious, to make the point.

There are some that are less obvious. If you need to scale to many thousands of requests per second, you might find even asynchronous queues for shopping read requests are valuable.

Structure of an Event Message

Every single event in your system should be structured in the same way to ensure that you capture everything consistently for processing. Table 7-1 shows an example.

Table 7-1. Structure of an event message

Attribute	Data type	Req'd	Description	Example
EventType	String	Y	Code that identifies the type of event	ProfileModified, OrderCreated
EventID	String	Y	Unique identifier for every event	[UUID]
Correlation ID	String	N	Identifier for finding relation to another event ID	[UUID]
Timestamp	TS	Y	When the event was created	03/27/2020 17:15:00Z00
Event Context	Map	N	Set of key/value pairs with context data specific to the event type	ProfileID:1148652 StartDate: … EndDate: …
EventName	Structured String	Y	The resource name, fully qualified and discoverable	[discoverable address name]

Make the UUIDs strings instead of native language UUID types for interoperability between services. After the translations happen in and out of the database and across service implementations in .NET, Java, and Python, you will wish they were strings.

In conclusion, use eventing liberally, but of course thoughtfully. We default to synchronous request/response models, as if we know the meaning, we know what should always happen. Instead, foreground asynchronous. This improves scalability and description of the system. But it also does something for you where you don't need to decide the meaning: you allow the "import" of the event to be deferred. This is powerful because the business changes its mind frequently, the system evolves, different customers need different things, and things means something different to diverse audiences. Any reaction in your application should not be hardcoded. Use event handlers instead. This helps you model services as contextual agents, not static and predetermined and fixed essences. It's a key tenet of deconstructed design.

Contextual Services and Service Mixins

When you design with eventing foremost in your mind, we tend to make things far more flexible and yet more solid. It pulls you away from obvious and wrong ideas, such that there could be the One True "Customer Profile" service to rule them all.

Customers, products, all the things in this glorious and rich world are multi-dimensional and varied. When we try to lock them down we quickly are forced to make false statements about them in how we represent them in our classes, and this is where the trouble begins.

Consider the traveler. You have likely traveled many places for many reasons in your life. We can consider that we might go on a leisure trip with our sweethearts, and also go on a business trip with our colleagues. If we as service designers decide that there is a single profile for a person, we will be painted into a corner. For instance, if you book a room for two nights on a Tuesday for one person, we can assume that is business travel, whereas we might well assume that a booking for two people on a Friday is leisure. And perhaps they are. But the context here is king. The same traveler could (and frequently does) book both these trips, but have entirely different reasons for them.

The temptation, of course, is to continuously add to the same one Traveler or Customer table or the same one Product table, with their encompassing services becoming ever larger and more complex Swiss Army knives to try to support all these different use cases. In this model, different services will all put pressure on the same one bottleneck, and find it confusing to wade through dozens of optional input and output fields that only make sense in certain use cases. You eventually need to have a very complex rubric to understand how to make proper requests of such services. Instead, we want to take that rubric as metadata or documentation and break it out into actual functions on separate service implementations. To embrace this concept, we might call this manner of writing services "service mixins" or "contextual services."

We do not define services in accordance with a unifying idea of the single Grand Narrative (*https://en.wikipedia.org/wiki/Metanarrative*). Doing so would mean participating in perhaps not quite a fantasy, but a limited view that will have serious and costly ramifications for extensibility, and portability.

Instead, we ask what use cases this entity participates in, and in what contexts the entity might be required to store or share information. We might discover smaller, more specific related Personae services, wherein the single person with one tax ID has many different relevant modes of being in the world, and appears differently in your system in different contexts. Designing for that multiplicity will aggregate nuances that improve the richness of the system.

For example, instead of storing one single unified Traveler service, you might have a Business Traveler and a Leisure Traveler and a Bleisure Traveler service, all relating to the same unique identifier for the same individual actual human, but capable of recognizing that in different contexts the same person will have different needs and desires for communication, notifications, recommendations, and the relevant attributes that support those.

You might have a variety of brands in your company portfolio that cater to the economy segment and the luxury segment. You might have customers that plot against a 2x2 matrix of income level (low to high) and spend level (low to high).

Consider the way that, say, an unsupervised machine learning system will determine customer clusters based on runtime or historical behavior. You can use these ideas, or even the actual cluster results to help inform if not drive the design of your services.

Clustering

Clustering is an unsupervised machine learning technique. There are no defined dependent and independent variables that anchor the data. Instead, the patterns observed in the data are used to identify and then group similar data points into clusters.

In this way, we can design much richer, more targeted and helpful business systems. If you are in a modernization or digital transformation effort, in which you have the luxury of a strong historical understanding of your business, your customers, and your systems, consider using machine learning principles such as these to actually help define your modernized system. You might call this machine learning–driven design.

Performance Improvement Checklist

There are a few simple things that you can do to improve performance in your web applications. Hopefully, you do all this already and it's obvious to everyone. I wish it were. I list them here for you as a kind of helpful checklist. They are general rules of thumb that you should always tick through; make sure they find their way into the Acceptance Criteria of your user stories.

1. On web APIs, collections must provide filtering, sorting, field selection, and paging to keep performance tight.

2. Use GZip compression. Add this configuration to your web server to enable it, and browsers that advertise that they accept GZip encoding in the request header will be sent the compressed version. This can save up to 70% of the response file size, reducing the time to return the response and reducing your network bill.

3. Combine and minify both CSS and JavaScript files. Instead of forcing the browser to make multiple network requests to many CSS files and many JavaScript files, use a tool to combine your JavaScript into one file and then minify it. Check out JSCompress, Gulp, Webpack, Blendid (*https://github.com/vigetlabs/ blendid*), or any others that might serve your purposes best.

4. Ensure that your image files are the same size as your <div> display containers. Do not rely on the browser to crop large images while needlessly sending and processing a lot of bytes that it will just throw away.

5. Tune your database. First, use indexes. If you are using a relational database and have columns listed in a WHERE, ORDER BY, or GROUP BY query, they should all be indexed and those indexes should be regularly rebuilt on a scheduled job. Second, run EXPLAIN to understand where the bottlenecks are in your database queries. Third, be sure that you do not have very long queries and queries with many joins. If you have more than just a few joins and that query is executed frequently, you should revisit that design. Fourth, denormalize data as necessary and have the data act as a kind of side car to the "System of Record" tables. Finally, move things up into a distributed cache.

6. Use a Content Delivery Network (CDN) like Akamai or AWS CloudFront to deliver your media. The fastest responding system is the one that's never actually hit. That's true for web servers as well as databases.

Again, we're not trying to capture all the things you can do for performance tuning. That's a whole (very long) book. Of course you need to design your system properly, use the right level and type of hardware, and so on. If you don't do those things, adding CSS minification certainly won't save you. These are just a few simple, obvious, easy, low-hanging-fruit type things to do. If you do just these and little else on top of an otherwise solid design, they'll get you a great head start.

Separating API from Implementation

Often, teams know that they should separate the API from the implementation. In rushing to meet an aggressive deadline, they might simply create an interface and then implement it in a class in the same package. This also becomes a habit because, if you're using .NET or Java, those languages provide the interfaces in the same package as the implementations. For example, List (the interface) and ArrayList (the implementation of List) are both in java.util. Of course, we are free to create our own implementation of List in our own package, so it makes perfect sense here. But this acts as a silent teacher that can prevent us from seeing a practical extensibility and portability advantage we could gain by more cleanly separating them.

When you design your system, put the interfaces for a subsystem together in a package, and then make that its own buildable JAR or binary. Then, create a second, separate project with that binary as a dependency and put your implementation there. What you're doing is not assuming that your first implementation is the One True Light and The Way. Rather, you are assuming that this is one possible implementation of many. If you do this at the beginning of your project, it takes literally five minutes. And it opens the door to incredible extensibility for customers and other teams. Your service code remains mostly empty, with little real "business logic," which is in the implementation. Your code becomes an empty container, the possibility for that business logic to be executed.

The model here is the set of interfaces that support Java Database Connectivity (JDBC). These ship with Java but do no work. The database vendors such as Oracle, Microsoft, and open source projects then create their own database drivers that know how to communicate with their specific databases. But they allow you as a developer to switch between database vendors without changing the interface. So you must have the class implementation binary on your classpath, and that binary should be a separate artifact. I'm suggesting to do the same thing up one level further, too, with your engine implementations.

Following this model will prove to be an incredible time saver later when a customer wants to do it their own way, when another team wants to reuse the system shell for their own purposes, when you need to port to another platform or provider, or when you need to make a significant version upgrade. It will allow for wonderful extensibility, helping turn your regular application into a true platform that supports multiple implementations.

If you are writing in an interpreted language such as Python, you can still do this. Python has duck typing (you can pass a walrus for a duck as long as it's a quacking walrus) and as of Python 3 you can use Abstract Base Classes using the `@abc.abstractmethod` annotation and put these definitions in separate folders and packages from the implementations. Then, customers or other teams can provide their implementations that adhere to the same interface.

Languages

You might have more customers in Europe than North America, and APAC might be your fastest growing region. You might have a strong customer base in South America. You might be entirely run in London with no plans to expand beyond Brighton, but consider the multitude of languages, cultures, and diverse people in the world. English is only one language among many hundreds. When we default our application to English, and then later our Chief Strategy Officer wants to enter the Cuban market, we have to create a multimillion-dollar project that could have been free. Here are a few simple design rules of thumb for applications and services:

- Externalize all strings from your code so that internationalization and localization is made easier. You might exempt logged strings from this because it becomes overbearing and hopefully no one but you is reading your logs. These strings can be externalized in resource bundles, in the database, or in text files.

- For multiple languages, you can use an external service such as *translations.com*. That can get expensive depending on how much you use it. You can do a poor-person's version of this using the terrific *translate.google.com* service to start to get an idea of your key/value translations and test it to make sure that it's working properly. At the most rudimentary level, you're looking for a few basic things:

— When you specify another language, does it appear?

— Are you using UTF-8 in your application code, database, and accept headers, so that non-Latin characters display properly, such as when you need to represent the German "Straßenbahn" or the French "ça va"?

— Are you able to fully represent double-byte character sets, such as Mandarin, Japanese, and Korean?

— Are you able to represent right-to-left languages such as Hebrew and Arabic?

• Are you handling currency conversion properly? You can easily get a download once per day from Bloomberg or xe.com for current currency conversion rates. You must also handle the display of the currency properly (using dots and commas properly for the different locales, and so forth).

Use the Google Translate service to get a few strings of each of the kinds listed above, and test your user interface labels with each of the different locales.

Every service should have three clear, named owners: when you list the services in your service catalog, associate the business owner (the VP of product management for that area), the engineering leader, and the associated architect expert. Maintaining such a map of your service catalog will be valuable.

Don't go overboard if you truly have zero customers from anywhere else in the world other than your neighborhood, and zero plans to ever get any. But doing just these few things now will set you up for a very well-designed system that will serve you well in an increasingly global commercial world.

Radical Immutability

As we create software in our development environment we must be sure that everything compiles and runs, and so we have references to what works and is allowed in development. These variables comprise database connection strings, caching locations, service endpoints, passwords, filesystem references, dependencies, and so forth. At worst, we write all of these references directly into the code and then make it someone else's problem, such as a release engineering or release management team.

They might then have tools that rebuild your software after rewriting these strings, which can be a manual or automated process. If you have seen such processes fail catastrophically as I have, you step back and consider how this could have happened. The real question is, given all the many variables and considerable differences in environments about which we maintain a pretense of sameness, why doesn't this happen more often?

We comfort ourselves that we have externalized our encrypted passwords and endpoint URIs and use an automated tool to rewrite these files as we deploy on through to certification, user acceptance testing, and production. We assume or hope that the binary artifact moving through these environments, which is getting rebuilt each time, is somehow the same. It is not.

This process is rife with opportunity for failure. This is a wonderful place for entropy to set it. There are small, barely noticeable changes that can offset the environment just enough to, when taken altogether, create a very different runtime than what we tested. Thus is the origin of the phrase "it works on my machine."

I wouldn't bother making this point except that in my 20-plus years in this business I have heard numerous developers say those words with apparent lack of any irony, as if that closes the case. Thus, the equation goes: it works on my machine == it works == no problem || someone else's problem.

We want to avoid this confrontation, avoid problems in certification and User Acceptance Testing (UAT) and production, and have more assurance that our artifact will behave predictably. When you test and certify something, and then redo it, your test and certification are both invalidated, obviously. Yet we often behave as if this were perfectly normal, or acceptable, or perhaps we're aware that it's nonoptimal but shrug in conclusion, "Well, what's a developer to do?"

Seek as much immutability in your design as you can. You minimize what you have to change if you design the change in. Instead of kicking the can down the road to this broken process, design your system as if it were a series of references to many varied and wild outside things.

The binary artifact you build must be as close as possible to what is tested, certified, and deployed to production. The way to do that is to never rebuild it: what you build in development is the same binary that is deployed in production. The only way to achieve that is to externalize every reference. Your software becomes smaller, does less, and becomes rather more like a schedule of references to external references. This means that your software is not the thing that does all the work; it is rather like a bill of lading. It's a receipt list of packages. It does little, and looks more like a list of references to things it otherwise has little awareness of. Invert your software by extending the idea of dependency injection into more aggressive, radical territory.

One approach is to match your development environment as closely as possible to your production environment. Using containers such as Docker or a virtual box such as Vagrant helps with this.

An important element in this process is to use a universal package manager. Treat your own code as if it were not the center of the universe with some ancillary dependencies, but rather one element, flat alongside the dependencies. The role of your code is to pull them all together. Here are some of the commercial and open source tools from which you might benefit:

- Apache Archiva (*https://archiva.apache.org/*) (this has not been updated in a while, but it's venerable, works, and is free)
- Sonatype Nexus (*https://www.sonatype.com/nexus-repository-sonatype*)
- JFrog (*https://jfrog.com/artifactory/*)

Of course, this also means that you must use the same process to deploy the software across all environments. You must not have different deployment pipelines, and just as your deployment pipeline is software, too, you want to be sure to externalize strings and related references there, such that deploying to the QA environment versus the staging environment is a simple matter of changing a target name.

Another benefit of this radical configurability is that you get improved portability. It's easier to move from one cloud provider to another, for example.

If you have problems with them at runtime, they are easily visible, and easily updated without a rebuild and redeploy process.

Specifications

Martin Fowler and Eric Evans invented a wonderful way to implement the frequently needed use case of searching for objects from a catalog that match certain criteria. For example, in an ecommerce application, you likely need to allow users to state their filtering or search criteria, and your code needs a fast and loosely coupled way to respond to the query. You might also need to validate a candidate list of objects to ensure that they are suitable for the task at hand. This is where the Specification pattern comes in. It is based on the real-world idea of shipping cargo and the separation of concerns of objects that get picked from the contractors doing the picking.

Original Specification Paper

You can read the original Specification pattern paper published in ACM here (*https://www.martinfowler.com/apsupp/spec.pdf*). The pattern is based (again, as so many good things are) on the crucial Gang of Four Strategy pattern. A more dynamic and sophisticated, but slower, version relies on a combination of Strategy and Interpreter (*https://en.wikipedia.org/wiki/Interpreter_pattern*). This paper goes into far more detail, variations, and applications than we do here.

Upon consideration, you can see that there are many applications for this pattern, beyond the ecommerce product filter/criteria search. These might include a set of candidate routes that an airline might propose to get travelers connecting flights from one city to another, or the right set of containers for certain kinds of products based on their size, whether or not they are perishable, or fragile, and so forth. Though it's a bit abstract, I like to think of the Specification pattern as kind of related to the more mathematical Knapsack problem (*http://bit.ly/2lYfJ7p*).

To realize the pattern, you create a specification that is able to determine whether a candidate object (such as a product in a catalog) matches some criteria. The specification features a method `isSatisfiedBy(someObject) : Boolean`, which returns `true` if all criteria are met by `someObject`. The important move in the Specification pattern is that you are treating the specification as a separate object from the candidate domain objects that use it. You create the search criteria independently and let the domain object inform you as to whether it satisfies them.

As usual, we want to start our design from the outside in. We want to write the dream client that we wish we could have, and then fill in the code that makes that client possible.

Consider a proposed use case from the travel domain. A guest wants to search for a hotel room based on criteria she specifies. She wants a hotel room that costs less than $800 with a size of at least 22 square feet that has an ocean view. We want a readable, maintainable, flexible, business-oriented client for our room finder service that might look like Example 7-1.

Example 7-1. Criteria client search

```
Criteria criteria = new RoomSearchCriteriaBuilder()
.withPrice().being(lessThan).value(800).and()
.withSquareMeters().being(largerThan).value(22).and()
.withView().being(View.OCEAN).build();

List<HotelRoom> allRooms = ProductRepository.getRooms();
List<HotelRoom> matchingRooms = new ArrayList<HotelRoom>();
for (HotelRoom room : allRooms) if room.satisfies(criteria);
matchingRooms.add(room);
```

This code builds a criteria based on the supplied user parameters and then searches the hotel for rooms that match those three criteria. Matches are then added to a results list to be passed back up to the user.

So we need a few classes to satisfy this dream client. As demonstrated in Example 7-2, first, we'll make a `Product` interface and a `HotelRoom` implementation (this is just close/pseudocode to give you the implementation idea, it's not meant to be perfect).

Example 7-2. Product basics

```
class Product {
    double price;
    public boolean satisfies(SearchCriteria criteria){
        return criteria.isSatisifiedBy(this);
    }
}

class HotelRoom extends Product {
    int squareFeet;
    View view;
}

enum View { GARDEN, CITY, OCEAN }
```

We also then must define our `Criteria` classes, as shown in Example 7-3.

Example 7-3. Search criteria listings

```
public interface SearchCriteria {
    boolean isSatisfiedBy(Product product);
}

public class Criteria implements SearchCriteria {
    private List<SearchCriteria> criteria;
    public Criteria(List<SearchCriterion> criteria) {
        this.criteria = criteria;
    }

    public boolean isSatisfiedBy(Product product)() {
        Iterator<Criteria> it = criteria.iterator();
        while(it.hasNext()) {
            if(!it.next().isSatisfiedBy(product))
            return false;
        }
        return true:
    }
}

public class PriceCriterion implements SearchCriteria {
    public PriceCriterion(Operator operator, double target){
        //
    }
    public boolean isSatisfiedBy (Product product){
        //do price check
    }
}
```

Now we need to fill out the builders and connectors that are similar to what would be part of any Fluent API following the Builder pattern, as illustrated in Example 7-4.

Example 7-4. Builders

```
public class SearchCriteriaBuilder {
    List<SearchCriteron> criteria = new ArrayList<>();
    private PriceCriteriaBuilder priceCriteriaBuilder;
    public PriceCriteriaBuilder withPrice() {
        if(priceCriteriaBuilder == null)
            priceCriteriaBuilder = new PriceCriteriaBuilder();
        return priceCriteriaBuilder;
}

public PriceCriteriaBuilder and() {
    return this;
}

public SearchCritera build() {
    return new Criteria(criteria);
}

public PriceCriteriaBuilder {
    Operator operator;
    double desiredPrice;
    public enum Operator { lessThan, equal, largerThan }
}

public PriceCriteriaBuilder being(Operator operator) {
    this.operator = operator;
    return this;
}
public PriceCriteriaBuilder value(double desiredPrice) {
    this.desiredPrice = desiredPrice;
    PriceCriteriaBuilder.this.criteria.add(
        new PriceCriterion(operator, desiredPrice));
    return PriceCriteriaBuilder.this;
    }
}
```

Then, you can add the code for other criteria in the same manner.

The result is a very flexible system that allows you to develop and add to the design in a tidy and compatible manner. Things are loosely coupled and follow patterns that help your code communicate and stay maintainable.

A Comment on Test Automation

In a modern system, we really must radically automate testing.

There are times when we will need to do manual testing, but we should not rely on this as the primary practice of our testing department. We should have engineers who

---

are not secondary to the application engineers, but who work right alongside them writing automated tests.

Just as a programmer would put writing unit tests first in Test-Driven Development (TDD), the test engineer should sit with the business analyst as the stories are written and provide input into the Acceptance Criteria to ensure that it is testable. Acceptance Criteria should be specific, measurable, and verifiable.

The tests are not ancillary to the code base as the marginalized term of that binary pair; they are written in code, are committed to the code repository, enjoy an automated pipeline, are versioned, and might not only be written before the code, as in TDD, but might also inform the stories themselves that are built.

As we have discussed, your test suite topology should include the following:

- Unit tests written by developers
- Canary/smoke tests
- Integration tests
- Regression tests
- Load tests
- Security penetration tests

That's a big job. And they all need to be separated, automated, and treated as first-class citizens.

A Comment on Comments

Encourage your development teams (require them, in fact) to write comments about their code. Make them meaningful and helpful, not perfunctory or merely restating the obvious.

Anything that is checked in to the code repository—including YAML, CFTs, Python, Java, JS, CSS, RunwayDB scripts, pipeline scripts, machine learning code—anything someone will need to read and understand and use, all should have meaningful comments.

Have the developers secretly aim, however, to make comments unnecessary because their code is so well named with such high cohesion and behaves in such a clear and obvious way that anything they would write into the comments would be redundant. After they write the comments, encourage them to read over it and see whether, instead of making a comment, they can make some tweaks to the code to try to actually put comments into the working code itself to make it better.

Here are a few good examples taken from the Java APIs themselves, as some instructive examples of comments, but the ideas apply to any language:

Enum (http://bit.ly/2kjR78C)
This is quite short but directive about a specific point of interest, and points the reader to considerable deeply detailed information in the JLS.

UUID (http://bit.ly/2m2eVyd)
This too is short and to the point, but clear on boundaries that would make a difference to the programmer, and points the user to an additional related class and an RFC for further usage implications.

TimeUnit (http://bit.ly/2knF2PN)
This tells you exactly how things are defined within the class, gives examples for proper usage, and states what is and is not guaranteed.

PhantomReference (http://bit.ly/2mnim2T)
Same. This is fantastic. The sweet spot.

List<E> (http://bit.ly/2kTinep) and Set<E> (http://bit.ly/2miJArf)
These both are quite good. For both, it is for an interface, which is different. It gives an overview of what the interface provides so that you don't need to read the code to find out; it does not speak beyond what it can for an interface that has different implementations (that's the purpose after all). It has documentation for the type parameter (<E>). It talks about why Lists/Sets should exist at all, what is special about them in distinction with the other items in Collections, and how to use it.

String (http://bit.ly/2m190ti)
Clear guidance and examples on usage, implications, and equivalencies.

Formatter (http://bit.ly/2lXuYgS)
This is an interesting case that I call out for a specific reason. The JavaDoc alone must have taken a full week to write; it's pages long. If you have to take a week to write the JavaDoc to explain usage like this, you have probably designed a class poorly, in a non-object-oriented way. In this case, however, it makes perfect sense because Formatter is specifically intended to replicate the 1970s C printf function, so the code looks like that on purpose. Thus, it has to take a week to write the JavaDoc. This is a rare case to illustrate longer doesn't always mean better, but in this case it is appropriate. Hopefully, your developers won't write books like this comment and don't write classes that would require them doing so.

These are all great lessons for how to write proper comments. Most of these would not take forever to write and are helpful for maintainability, clarity, and efficiency for future developers.

Summary

In this chapter, we covered significant ground. We examined how to discover the services in your domain, the structure of services, how and when to add eventing, and how to use machine learning to go beyond pluggability into radical extensibility.

In Chapter 8, we examine the data aspect more specifically.

The Data Aspect

We don't eat lollipops, do we mommy? They're not true.
   —Alison Brown, *Fear, Truth, Writing*

The API and the data model represent the most obvious ways in which your concept is practically realized in the software.

In this chapter, we examine some of the tenets for us as semantic designers to keep in mind when creating data services. Following these ideas, we can create very resilient, scalable, available, manageable, portable, and extensible systems.

We don't skip the crucial step that is the one real difference between successful software and failures: first we decide what ideas will populate our world and what they mean.

Business Glossary

Define your terms.

This is the single most effective thing you can do to help your software and your business.

Identify key terms within your business. Make a spreadsheet. Put it on the wiki. What is "Inventory" as opposed to "Availability"?

Be very clear on the distinctions. Leave no ambiguity. Make them mutually exclusive. Don't allow fudging.

Sometimes this is called a "Data Dictionary." That's fine, too. Either way. For us, this is not a difference that makes a difference. Call the document what you like, but be ruthlessly exacting with respect to defining its constituent elements.

After you define them, use them consistently with their definition when it's time to make a data model or API.

Strategies for Semantic Data Modeling

Throughout this book, we have been sometimes practical and sometimes abstract. That is on purpose because I want to spur your imagination and thinking. It is also because the semantic design method, by definition, is not a prescriptive method. It is holistic. It is a mindset, a shift in mental models, supported by accompanying processes, practices, and templates. Examples are sometimes useful.

Here are some tenets, or oblique strategies, questions to ask yourself to make sure that your data model is rich, robust, and correct. The book has given us the context, the description of the semantic mindset. Refer back to Chapter 3 on sets.

Here are the kinds of things that, having that semantic mindset, we ask when making our data model.

You are representing the *world*. Your job is to make a clear depiction of the actual facts about *the actual world*. That mostly means thinking about fine distinctions and understanding relations and attributes.

Your first job is to ask: what is *true*? What is the actual case about each thing, their constituent things, and how they relate?

Then ask, what is *important* about all of those things? What is *significant*, which (literally) means *what here is capable of making signs*, of participating in the language?

Then ask, to whom? This gains you a vector of perspective.

The main lesson that all of these roll up to is this one: *be clear on where you are drawing the boundary in your semantic field*.

Here's an example. Your restaurant might serve different kinds of wine and beer and soft drinks. The wine and beer are regulated differently, and sold both individually (by the bottle) and by a pour (from kegs or in glasses of wine). So tracking is easy in one case and difficult in the other. You might care very much from an inventory perspective about tracking the specific bottles of each kind of wine sold and print them on the check so that the customer knows that the 2012 Cakebread Napa Cab was $25 per glass and the Merlot was $18. But you aren't interested in tracking whether you sold a Coke or a Diet Coke, because it's self-serve and you order it by the syrup box, not the bottle: you have less of a match between how you order it and how you sell it. Your customers get free refills. So you think you can call that a "Fountain Drink" and roll up all of the brands of soda together under that name.

That moment right there, where you posit the name "Fountain Drink" into your world so you can dim the horizon and get on with life instead of tracking each individually has lost details that still exist in the actual world. Your representation in this moment degrades to being a little bit less true. This idea is not that important to the customers and is not that important to the inventory keeper. But computers understand only True or False. Thus, you have made a fuzziness on purpose so that you can ship software. "Coke" versus "Diet Coke" are now beyond the boundary: they no longer have identities and are outside the inventory field. The real world in its infinite conjuncts carries on merrily with Coke and Diet Coke, however. I can't tell you whether it's right or wrong to say Fountain Drink here. I'm just saying to be clear and purposive, that this is where you created the semantic boundary. Because this is the place where the representation stops matching the real world and our semantics become incorrectly dimmed or inconsistent, and therefore this is where software starts to go wrong. We must do it. We need to ship. Just be aware, is all we're saying; live on this line.

With that context, here are some questions and simple guidelines:

- Next turn to your business glossary. That will be an easy anchor. You want to be consistent with it. "Availability" in your glossary should reflect what it means in your data model or there is a different word.

- If you're struggling to understand a word, break it into two words. Does that work better?

- What is the *perspective* of this database table? That is, who is the use-case driver? Who makes data enter this table and why? Perhaps you're looking at an Order table and a Vendor table, and you have them both pointing to a set of OrderReferences.

- Can you delete this table or column completely from the semantic field, the vocabulary? What do you lose if you do that? Do you gain anything?

- Try to make everything NOT NULL. Any column in the data model that wants to be NULL might be in the wrong table. Anything that wants to be allowed to have null values must claw and fight its way to earn that status for a very clear reason. If you have a column in your order table for "PointsPaid," because you reason that customers can pay with cash or with points, but they're different, so you need a column for each, and the one they didn't pay with will always be null, this is lazy. Allowing null columns should be very rare. Consider any column with a null constraint a red flag. Can you decompose further?

- Be suspicious of anything called "Type." "Type" doesn't mean anything. It's a programmer overlay. Modelers who say "type" a lot also use enums a lot. Wrongly. If a valid value in your "WhateverType" column is "Other," you don't have a type. Break it out into a referenced list. There is no such thing as "other."

- Avoid false sectioning. A false section is much related to the Type problem. This is an antipattern when you take something that's on a spectrum and break it into multiple categories: "Child, Adult." These are two sections of the idea of "age." But you could have Toddler, Senior Citizen. What is a "child," anyway? Is that a person age five to twelve? Three to seventeen? What if one vendor defines it the first way and another vendor the second way? Did you provide for them to do that in your data model, or presume one universal idea of these sections that are false overlays? Childhood didn't even exist until it was invented 250 years ago. What about Infant? What about Minor? "Minor" doesn't mean the same thing across different states in the US, or across the world. When you section a spectrum, it's always an overlay. Overlays are almost always false. That's where your semantics will fail, and consequently that's where the maintenance programmers will need to build a lot of time-consuming, expensive workarounds that will chip away at the integrity of your model. It's where entropy alights.

- Consider who will input this data? Why? Who will use this data after it's there? Why do they care and when do they no longer care? Can you state that as a universal truth across all time, space, and dimensions? Be culturally sensitive to make it right the first time. That usually means making your previously binary distinction into a list and separating it into a referenced table. It's free and takes 30 seconds to do now, and it takes a million dollars and six months to do in three years.

- Always test, interrogate, and challenge common words. If you have a column for CurrencyType what precisely does that include: Bitcoin? Is Bitcoin flat with USD and Yen in your semantic space? What if loyalty members can pay with points? Are the valid values of that column "Bitcoin, USD, Yen (and so forth), and Points"? What if you have multiple customers each with their own loyalty program? Decompose and refine away any assumptions.

- "Customer" and "User" or "Guest" are not the same. If I buy two ice cream cones, and give one to Alison, the vendor sees one customer with one order with one name on the credit card, and two ordered items. There are two guests. Don't conflate things unless you're doing it on purpose because you know that's your boundary. Because at a restaurant you might have one order (the "check"), and the table might want to split the bill either 50/50 or by which customer ordered what items: one table, two customers, two checks.

- Narrow to the lowest possible scope you can for a single data item until it feels like you're considering the most obviously useless detail. Then, start to edge back up in your scope until you get to where it feels still tight but also useful. This helps to ensure significance. Do the same again, but on the trajectory of who it's important to, who the use-case driver is.

- Don't make vague distinctions. "ShortDescription" and "LongDescription" don't exist in the world. Assign a stronger type based on the context in which they're used to better match the real world. The real world doesn't have short and long descriptions.

- Be careful when you write "PrimaryChannel" and "SecondaryChannel." What's the difference? From whose perspective? This is a hierarchy and it's a common software guy overlay. There is no such thing in the real world as primary and secondary channels. They are channels. What about the "TertiaryChannel"? This is a cousin of the "ShortDescription" and "LongDescription" problem.

- There are only three numbers in the universe: zero, one, and many.

- Does "Price" really belong on the Product table? It seems like with only the input of the Product table we don't have enough information: we need Vendor, too, because the same hose at Alice's Hardware might cost $30, whereas at Bob's Hardware, it's $25. That's because even though colloquially we speak that way, it is a false representation of the world that a Product has a Price. An InventoryItem has a price—that's the moment in time the product meets the vendor. So it's truer and therefore less error prone. Also, a Product doesn't typically have one price, but the "rack rate" or "base price" and then a military price, or educator discounts apply, and so on. The point is that things are almost always more complicated. Examine the complexity so that you can make the truest statement that makes sense for what you're doing. Usually things come in lists.

- You make a split brain when you make something referenced at two levels. Consider who is the use-case driver and how they enter the data model and then make the reference only at the lowest level from that actor if you can. Sometimes, there are multiple valid perspectives on the same table, and you need to accommodate them. Then that's not making a split brain, and it's fine.

Ask yourself these questions while making your data model.

Polyglot Persistence

Consider the relational database, invented more or less by Dr. E.F. Codd in 1970. In a relational database, you define entities as the nouns represented in your tables: Customer, Product, ProductGroup, and so forth. It seems to me that "relational" has always been a bit of a misnomer given that the relations are not even defined as first-class citizens in the model and are only apparent in the join routes in the SQL code. Even the so-called "join table" that provides a many-to-many definition (such as StudentsToClasses) is not defined any differently in the model than any other table. Which is to say that the relations are often thought of secondarily, and as a result, we can have a pristine data model with perfect entities and queries that require 10 or 15 joins or considerable processing logic to get the work done. Such queries can be quite slow.

The relational model has become the *de facto* standard in our industry, and many teams jump directly to thinking in a relational model without first considering whether it is the optimal model for their design. In the past decade, however, the

NoSQL movement has seen dozens of very different kinds of persistence models, each with their own set of advantages and use cases for which they are well suited.

My hope here is that you survey the landscape of available persistent stores, look at what they're good at, and thoughtfully pick the ones that make the most sense for your use cases.

Notice that I did not say to pick the *one*, or the one most appropriate for your *application*. Instead, we recognize that the data is really the rocket fuel of any modern application. Data is the backbone of machine learning and artificial intelligence (AI). Data is the point of any application.

Applications, for all the drama surrounding them, are really simply window dressing on the data. We don't use a single language for our applications and services: we regularly and unquestioningly use HTML, CSS, JavaScript, Java, Python, JSON, and myriad frameworks supporting all of those in our application code. No one hardcodes HTML into a Java servlet for their display, or, worse, uses a Java applet for the display layer because that's the One Language you've chosen for your application. It's absurd. Yet we often still maintain an idea that there is the One True Data Store to Rule Them All. Why the application should enjoy all these tools that are very well suited to the specific job they perform, and the data, which represents the real purpose of any application, should be crammed into one store suitable to do one job well is beyond me.

We have columnar databases such as Vertica, time-series and row-oriented databases such as Cassandra, document stores such as MongoDB and Couchbase, key/value stores such as Dynamo, object databases such as Postgres, graph databases such as Neo4J, hybrid "NewSQL" databases such as Google Spanner, and more. They're all good at different things, and selecting the ones that make the right sense for your use cases will help your system scale in the best and most cost-effective manner.

You might have an Oracle database for your set of tables hosting your services. But then you need a place to store the denormalized BLOBs representing your orders each time they are confirmed or updated, or need an Audit table so you know when things were changed. Those can be separate, in something that is optimized for writes and rarely read. Cassandra is perfect for that. Use the best tool for the job that you can afford and that your team knows or that you can hire for.

Persistence Scorecard

As you consider the appropriate persistence implementations, you might create a scorecard or grid of your own that illustrates the advantages and disadvantages of different implementations. Table 8-1 presents one to get you started down the path of thinking about having a scorecard like this.

Table 8-1. Persistence scorecard

Tool	Hosting	Storage type	Replication	Modeling	Transaction support	Scaling model	Master/ slave
Mongo Atlas	Cloud-only	Document	Good	Easy	Document level	Horiz.	Yes
Cassandra	Cloud/on-prem.	Wide row	Best	Worst	Row level	Horiz.	Peer to peer
Neo4J	Self-managed	Graph	Good	Best	Good	Horiz.	Yes

Of course you can be more scientific in your approach, run tests in a lab and do a real bake-off, score things more numerically, and use more criteria. The idea here is just for you to consider *polyglot persistence*, and to have some way to judge in a rubric which are right for your different services, depending on your actual needs.

With polyglot persistence, you will gain improved scalability, performance, and suitability, and be encouraged to follow the "database per service" dictum. You will also encounter additional challenges with manageability (dealing with multiple vendors) and maintainability (having development teams need to learn more than one system and model). Architecture is always about trade-offs, so just be sure that you're picking what's right for your business.

Multimodeling

Extend the idea of polyglot persistence into the realm of your modeling. Here, we're not referring so much to the daily work of doing modeling in a tool such as Embarcadero or something similar. If you get hung up on your tool, however, and assume that the tool you have for modeling is your allowed universe of possibilities for modeling, that's a category mistake that will cost you. For this reason, I generally avoid data modeling tools and instead use, on purpose, the wrong tool for the job. I use a whiteboard, paper and pencil, spreadsheets, plain text files, and drawing programs. I like these tools for data modeling because they force me to never mistake the tool for the concept I am trying to express.

As a data modeler, you are creating the concept of the data and their relations, not filling in forms in a predefined tool that might restrict and severely modify how freely and imaginatively you think about your data.

You do not want to consider your data as a static light, which having one database, especially a relational one, strongly urges us to do. We want to design for evolution, for change, for fluidity as best we can. To do so, we want to consider what the data will become and how it will evolve and be augmented and changed over time. Consider the time vector of your data. I don't mean timestamps of when that row was written. I mean the stages of life through which it will evolve.

Your application might feature 20 services, and each service has its own database, and perhaps there are three different databases you use for the different primary benefits a group of services would realize: a wide row, a graph, and a document store. You will need a different data model per service, and the models will need to be created very differently in accordance with each of those database types.

Because we cherish first the concept of our data, consider it as a whole, including the typically marginalized aspects of it, and are not led around by a tool, we have the following models to make:

- A distinct data model per database implementation, per service to run the application.

- A model for each service's data according to a temporal trajectory within the runtime: how it will enter the world of the software, how and when it will be cleaned, stored, moved to long-term storage and purged. What is the source of batch data, and what are the sources and destinations and uses of it?

- A security data model per service: where are the Personally Identifiable Information (PII), Payment Card Industry (PCI), and Service Organization Control 2 (SOC 2)–controlled systems? How will the data be encrypted? How will it be surfaced in APIs, for reporting, auditing, compliance checks, or machine learning consumption?

- A model for logs-as-data. Developers must be mentored to not think of logs as the disposable runoff or leftovers from an application that they are grudgingly asked to provide. Instead, consider the life cycle of logs. How do they tell a story if read in trace or debug or info mode? How will they be rotated, shipped, aggregated, stored, and removed? What regulatory restrictions surround values in them?

- A model for each service's data according to temporal trajectory as a roadmap. We make roadmaps for our products all the time, stating that we'll release this set of features on this rough timeline. We can make roadmaps for our data as well, stating what data we can add at what stages of the service evolution and what new sources we can get for it.

- A model per machine learning use case, per service, to map the machine learning use case to the data you will need to support your feature engineering.

- A model for the cache. We often don't model the cache itself because we think it is a mere reflection in memory of what we've already modeled. In a wonderful deconstructive move, the old application Coherence (created by the very smart Cameron Purdy and eventually sold to Oracle) inverted the database, moving the "primary" store into memory, with the persistent on-disk layer as the secondary. This can also include how will you create indexes, materialized views, and denormalization strategies.

- A model for events. What events are published, what Claim Checks are needed by what services to fulfill event subscriber needs, and where will they retrieve that data? Complex Event Processing systems invert the database, too: they essentially store the queries and let the data flow on top of it, and when a match is noticed between the criteria in the query and the data, a function is executed.

- A model for streams. We will examine this separately below because it might be newer to you.

The modeling job can't stop with dutifully enumerating the nouns in your application, making join tables between ones that seem to matter to each other, and policing developers on column name conventions.

Data Models for Streams

Data streams allow you to perform real-time analysis on a continuously flowing series of events, without having to store the data first. The data may flow from a variety of sources.

There are several common use cases for streaming data, including the following:

Finance
Stock tickers provide a continuous stream of changing financial data. Trackers can update and rebalance portfolios in real time and make robotic trades.

Media streaming services and video games
Here the content of music or movies or audio books comprise the data stream. Metadata regarding usage of the content, such as when it is paused, rewound, the resolution viewed, the receiving devices, and so forth can be examined to improve your services.

Web ecommerce clickstreams
On an ecommerce website, applications can capture each click, and even each mouse hover, as an event and stream them for processing in order to understand user behavior.

Social media
You can capture tweets and other posts from social media outlets in real time and filter on hashtags or use natural language processing (NLP) in order to gain real-time understanding of customer sentiment or current news updates and take action.

Power grids
The grid can stream usage by location to improve planning and generate alerts if a threshold is exceeded.

Internet of Things (IoT)

In the hotel domain, for example, a property might capture stream data from a variety of on-premises sources, including thermostats, mobile key usage, minibars, and other guest activities and make management adjustments.

This is data; it's often not stored at all or is likely not stored in the same way as typical data in applications. It requires a different kind of thinking from the traditional model, which is all about understood entities and on-disk persistent storage.

There are several wonderful tools available to get you started with stream processing.

Apache Kafka (https://kafka.apache.org/)

Kafka, created originally at LinkedIn, is a distributed publish/subscribe messaging system that integrates applications and data streams.

Apache Storm (http://storm.apache.org/)

Storm is a distributed, real-time computation framework written in Clojure. Its model is a directed acyclic graph (DAG) in which the edges of the graph are the stream data, which is moved from one node to another for processing. In Storm, the data sources are proxied by spouts and the nodes that perform the processing are called *bolts*. Taken together, the graph acts as a data transformation pipeline. Storm excels at distributed machine learning and real-time analytics.

Apache Spark Streaming (http://spark.apache.org/)

Spark Streaming reuses Spark's Resilient Distributed Dataset (RDD) component to perform real-time analytics over small batches of data. Because of this minibatching, the Spark Streaming library can be susceptible to latency bursts. Spark Streaming has built-in support to consume data from Kafka, Twitter, TCP/IP, Kinesis, and other sources.

Apache Flink (https://flink.apache.org/)

Written in Java and Scala, Flink is a high-throughput, low-latency streaming data-flow engine with support for parallel processing, bulk/batch processing such as Extract, Transform, and Load (ETL), and real-time event processing. Flink supports exactly-once semantics and fault tolerance. It does not provide its own storage system, but instead features data sources and sinks for Cassandra, Hadoop Distributed File System (HDFS), Kinesis, Kafka, and others.

All of these systems have a basic variation on a theme: they are data pipelines that accept unbounded streams of data and have a particular way of representing that data to nodes that provide an opportunity to do some processing, filtering, enrichment, and transformation. They must start with a *source* where the data comes from and end with a *sink*, where the transformed or processed data ends up.

In your streaming model, consider the following:

- The data source and destination (sink).
- The interval by which the data is updated or at which you want a snapshot.
- Your near-term and long-term storage needs and restrictions.
- Your durability requirements.
- Your scalability requirements: what is the math on the data volume and the processing time/response immediacy requirements? Consider processing in parallel and batches for their server footprint, cost, and management implications. Does your chosen library support scale-out?
- Your fault tolerance in the storage layer as well as in your processing layer.
- Many of these have a SQL-like language that allows the developer to express matches. Consider your guidelines for developers regarding its usage.

These tools are rather young, and so are rapidly changing. They are also complex to use well and keep manageable. But don't assume that streaming data is at all what you're used to from thinking of data as a passive element at rest in a persistent store that gets operated on by application code. By designing your stream architecture in its own light, given its own special and separate concerns, you can do amazing things.

Feature Engineering for Machine Learning

Machine learning is becoming a more typical aspect of any modern application. Understanding how you as a data designer can assist the data scientists and machine learning engineers with a basic skill in *feature engineering* is important. It will prompt you to see machine learning more as a capability to be used throughout your application as opposed an exotic separate project that you tack on to the existing application design.

When you get data to be used in machine learning, you'll need to clean it. You'll need to fix structural errors, impute values to missing data elements, and otherwise prepare it for processing. In data science and machine learning endeavors, feature engineering is probably where most time is spent. This is where your domain expertise and understanding of how customers use your data as a data architect can be of terrific service.

In machine learning, a feature is a numeric representation of real-world data. The purpose of feature engineering is to develop the data you have to the point where it's most useful to your machine learning model, given the use case. It's a matter of determining what is most relevant and differentiating to the model for it to make accurate predictions. You take the raw data, clean it up, engineer the features, create the model, and gain the insights and predictions it outputs.

In this way, feature engineering is a *creative* process. You are imaginatively figuring out what features are needed in your machine learning model and developing them from existing values that you have in your raw data. In this sense, it is much more like application developing. You must approach feature engineering with equal measures of imagination, creativity, and analysis. Here, you as a data architect/data designer/feature engineer are inventing something rather than figuring out where to put something.

One of the primary theses of this book is that you are a *designer of concepts*, that architecture is about the generation and illumination of the concept of the system, and that the best approach for making better software is the mindset shift afforded by a *deconstructive* analysis. That is certainly the case for feature engineering.

Done well, feature engineering goes far beyond the typical concerns of the data architect who is tuning queries for performance given intimate knowledge of a particular database platform. With feature engineering, yes, it's a matter of analysis, but, done well, you quickly can get into the varied realms of marketing, semantics, philosophy, politics, ethics, and bias.

The basic overview of the steps in feature engineering are as follows:

1. From the scrubbed raw data, determine which terms matter the most. Isolate these and highlight them with an aim toward focusing the machine learning algorithms on these.

2. Use your domain expertise to combine the data into more usable inputs. These are called *interaction features* because they combine multiple data points into a new one. At this stage, you're examining the data to see whether two features can be combined to discover one that might be more useful. For example, in a real estate model you might assume that the number of schools is important to predicting housing market prices in an area. But combining this point with the quality rating of each school to create a new idea of school richness (number and quality) is smart feature engineering. You're making the distinction, a value judgment, a determination in the world of the concept that quantity of schools doesn't matter to the question at hand if they aren't very good. These interactions will result in mathematical products, sums, or differences.

3. Use your domain expertise to combine values that are sparse. That is, if you don't have enough data points across a variety of categories in your dataset, determine how the sparse values can possibly be combined into one category that abstracts them up so that you have enough data points you can count as the same for the purposes of your model.

4. Remove unused values such as IDs or other columns that add to the size and noise of your dataset.

5. Use your business knowledge to frame all of this feature engineering work by always relating it back to the underlying, fundamental question of what specific task this particular machine learning model is intended to execute. What question does it exist to answer? All feature engineering must clearly map back to the question of the model. Are you hoping to predict stock prices to determine where to invest? Or predict which product offers will delight your customers the most? Traffic and purchasing patterns due to external related events?

Feature Engineering for Machine Learning

For an in-depth and hands-on examination of this field (with plenty of code), see the excellent book *Feature Engineering for Machine Learning* (*https://oreil.ly/L8Sr2*) by Amanda Casari and Alice Zheng (O'Reilly).

The field of feature engineering merits entire books on its own, and requires a strong understanding of the mathematics required to feed machine learning models. Our aim here is to provide our particular perspective on it as something to add to your toolbox with a caution to start with the concept and the language and then do the math later. Do not let feature engineering be mathematics-driven. The math is just a mechanism for representing one format concept, no different than JSON as an exchange format.

Classpath Deployment and Network Proxies

Data accessor services should provide a network-reachable API endpoint that your engines can connect to. In this way, they present as services like any other, exchanging data via JSON or ProtoBuf (*http://bit.ly/2krrlzu*).

But they should also present a native API such that you can compile the data accessor services into a binary artifact and either add them to the classpath of the engines that use them or directly bundle them into the engines' deployment artifacts. Providing the option makes a little extra work, but will likely prove necessary if you need the flexibility of network access as well as the faster performance you get from avoiding a network hop and translation.

You can implement this using a Facade pattern. Your default option is to simply provide the native interface for direct access as a library via the classpath. Then, provide a facade interface that wraps the data accessor service with a service endpoint to exchange JSON or ProtoBuf, or what have you.

The Proxy pattern (*https://en.wikipedia.org/wiki/Proxy_pattern*) provides a simple way to change the behavior of an object without changing the original object. To do this, implement the original data accessor and deploy it with an alternative proxy that exposes the same functions but adds the necessary translations for the HTTP endpoint to receive requests and post responses via JSON messages.

Peer-to-Peer Persistent Stores

The master/slave paradigm for scaling databases is popular because it has obvious benefits: you can usually see good performance and response times while also replicating data to prevent significant downtime. You can perform reporting and analytics off of the slave databases.

Beyond the unfortunate name, master/slave databases suffer from the obvious problem of the single point of failure. This is common when you have such a clear and obvious binary opposition with a privileged term. In deconstruction design, we question underlying structures to see how we can overturn and subvert power relations like this to arrive at what will hopefully be an improved design.

The obvious solution is a *peer-to-peer database*, such as Apache Cassandra. In Cassandra, every node is identical to every other in its function within the topology. There are no privileged nodes. Because the data is distributed and replicated across multiple nodes, it is incredibly fault tolerant. It is also tuneably consistent, so that depending on how you define your quorum, you can set the consistency level to be strong or weak, depending on your use case needs.

Follow-Up with Cassandra the Definitive Guide

To read more on Cassandra and get into the details of how to set it up, model it, and operate it, see the book *Cassandra: The Definitive Guide* (O'Reilly), which I wrote (the second edition was by me and Jeff Carpenter).

Because we want to use the appropriate database given the use case the service supports, use the following checklist to determine whether Cassandra might be suitable for your service. Instead of choosing a database because it's what you already have or it seems like the exciting new technology, ask yourself if you have these needs:

- High availability.
- Linear horizontal scaling.
- Global distribution (you can define clusters regionally).
- Ultra-fast writes are much more important to your use case than reads.
- You can do most or all of your reading only by primary key.

- You have little need for any joins: data tables match the queries very closely.
- Time-series and log journaling.
- Data with a defined lifetime; after a time-to-live (TTL) threshold is reached, the data is automatically deleted, which is a great feature as long as you're clear on its behavior.

Because of these features, Cassandra is a great choice for workloads such as these:

- IoT updates and event logging
- Transaction logging
- Status tracking such as package location, delivery status
- Health status tracking
- Stock update tracking
- Time-series data

Keep in mind that Cassandra is probably the wrong choice if you have the following needs in the service you expect it to support:

- Tables will have multiple access paths, causing you to employ considerable secondary indexes. This will slow your performance.
- ACID support. Atomic, Consistent, Isolated, Durable transactions have been, from the beginning, a nongoal for Cassandra.
- Locks. These are not supported in Cassandra.
- Intense reading. Cassandra is far more performant on writes than on reads. If your data can likely have a very strong cache read hit ratio, you probably will be better off with another implementation.

When we find a technology exciting, it is tempting to tell ourselves a story about how we can use it for use cases that don't quite seem to fit and to make up for shortcomings ourselves. We might suppose that we will write our own locks and transactions on top of Cassandra, for instance. This rarely works out. Pick the appropriate tool for the business use case.

When you have a write-intensive application, and need massive horizontal scaling, global distribution, and unbeatable fault tolerance, Cassandra is an excellent choice. Using a database with a flat peer-to-peer design as opposed to a hierarchical master/ slave design is in keeping with our overall deconstructive design paradigm.

Graph Databases

A graph database has three major conceptual components: *nodes*, *edges*, and *properties*. Nodes are the entities in the model (such as user or product), and edges represent the named relations between the nodes. The relations can be one way or bidirectional, and multiple relations can be defined between nodes. Properties are attributes that can be assigned to both the nodes and the relations. Nodes are typically called *vertices* and the relations are typically called *edges*.

The underlying storage model holds these all as first-order components in the implementation. Queries in a graph database can be very fast, because the relations are stored as first-order objects along with the nodes. This means that data in the store is linked together directly according to the relations and can therefore often be retrieved with a single operation.

Graph databases also allow you to readily visualize the data model because it closely and intuitively mirrors the actual world in its representation. They support and even promote the idea of modeling heavily interrelated data. Moreover, they are perfectly suited for semantic querying.

For all these reasons, graph databases are an outstanding example of the deconstructive design paradigm.

A key concept of the system is the graph (or edge or relationship), which directly relates data items in the store to a collection of nodes of data and edges representing the relationships between the nodes.

Popular graph databases include OrientDB and Neo4J, which we take a look at shortly.

When would you want to consider using a graph database? If you have any of the following use cases, it is worth checking out:

- Social media graphs (understanding relationships between users and making recommendations)
- Ecommerce (understanding relationships between disparate products and other datasets, and making richer recommendations)
- Fraud and security detection by identifying patterns in real time
- Personalized news stories
- Data governance and master data management

Check the Licensing

Be sure to check the licensing on your graph database selection. For example, Neo4J is a popular choice, but has a General Public License (GPL) license and is "freemium registerware." OrientDB, on the other hand, has a more friendly Apache license. Both have commercial support from parent companies.

Graph databases are a terrific choice as the underlying support for your service if its job is to answer questions or perform operations such as these:

- What is the list in ranked order of products recommended for purchase with this product?
- Who are all the managers between this employee and the CEO?
- What are the names of the musicals that won a Tony award and are produced by this person and are composed by that person?
- Who are friends of my friends?
- What is the distribution of companies that people who work on this project have also worked in?
- What are the most popular recommended activities for people staying this hotel?

From a certain point of view, the entire universe can be viewed as a (very long) list of things that each have a list of relations to other things, and both the things and relations have a list of properties. If you view the universe this way, you can see that a graph database is capable of most closely representing the world and creating the least impedance mismatch in so doing. It is therefore well suited to many data modeling tasks of any even modest level of complexity and richness.

OrientDB and Gremlin

OrientDB is perhaps the database with the greatest intellectual kinship to deconstructive design. As a multimodel database, it's incredibly open in terms of allowing you to pick the storage model that best supports a variety of workloads. It supports not only graphs, but also key/value pairs, objects, and document storage.

In addition to the multimodel, OrientDB offers the following features:

- Horizontal scaling
- Fault tolerance
- Clustering
- Sharding
- Full ACID transaction support

- Relational database management system (RDBMS) import
- Works with SQL as opposed to a proprietary language

And it's free and open source. It also comes with a standard Java Database Connectivity (JDBC) driver and other options for integrations.

OrientDB also supports Apache TinkerPop Gremlin (*https://tinkerpop.apache.org/ gremlin.html*), which is a powerful and flexible graph traversal language. Gremlin is composed of three interacting components: the graph, the traversal, and a set of traversers.

From the Gremlin site:

> Gremlin is a functional, data-flow language that enables users to succinctly express complex traversals on (or queries of) their application's property graph. Every Gremlin traversal is composed of a sequence of (potentially nested) steps. A step performs an atomic operation on the data stream. Every step is either a *map*-step (transforming the objects in the stream), a *filter*-step (removing objects from the stream), or a *sideEffect*-step (computing statistics about the stream). The Gremlin step library extends on these 3 fundamental operations to provide users a rich collection of steps that they can compose in order to ask any conceivable question they may have of their data for Gremlin is Turing Complete (*http://arxiv.org/abs/1508.03843*).

Gremlin supports imperative and declarative querying, host language agnosticism, user-defined domain-specific languages, an extensible compiler/optimizer, single- and multimachine execution models, and hybrid depth- and breadth-first evaluation.

Check out the wonderful Tinkerpop Gremlin Getting Started Tutorial (*http://tinker pop.apache.org/docs/3.4.0/tutorials/getting-started/*) to see how it works.

Because of the power of Gremlin, picking a graph database with this support is a good idea.

Data Pipelines

Historically, developers would get an idea of the platform on which their work would eventually be deployed to, and they would make some close approximation of that in their local environments. They would work on the code and then on rare occasions at major milestones (or, commonly, only once) transfer their work to a production environment. This was considered perfectly reasonable because why would you deploy something to production that was not fully ready?

In recent years, the idea of the Continuous Integration/Continuous Delivery (CI/CD) pipeline has gained popularity. A CI/CD pipeline is a set of end-to-end automations that use tools to compile, run, test, and deploy code. Because it is automated, all of these steps can be executed by the single command.

Some of the advantages of a pipeline include:

- Problems with the code are detected early and the team gets feedback on what happened so that it can quickly address it.

- It prevents compounding errors in a code base, keeping your project more predictable. General quality is promoted.

- Automation makes your program more testable and reduces single points of knowledge in your organization.

For a deconstruction designer, you want to design your pipeline early, up front, so that you are deploying a simple "Hello World" type application. In this sense, your application code base acts as a mock object for the testing of your pipeline.

You want to design the pipeline first because then you can increase predictability and efficiency in your project. Give your developers a single command to invoke, a single "button to push" to build, test, and deploy their software. If it is easy to invoke the deployment, they will do it a lot. The more they do it, the more you learn about your environment and application, and the more surety and stability you will have throughout your project.

Of course, your pipeline is software, too. As you execute it, you are making sure that your pipeline works properly and covers all the use cases you need to. If you have put the basic structure in place early in your project, you can add specialty items to it easily. These might include security scans with a tool such as Veracode, UI tests, regression tests, health checks following deployments, and more.

You might have a few pipelines:

- One for creating and tearing down the infrastructure, using the Infrastructure as Code (IaC) pattern. This works if you are using a cloud provider with APIs that allows you to do this in a "software-defined datacenter" manner.

- One for deploying the standard application and services code that you create as your product.

- One for the database creation and updating automation. You can do this with a tool like FlywayDB (*https://flywaydb.org/*), which is a scripting database migration tool with APIs. It's open source with an Apache license and supports about 20 different databases.

- One for the machine learning services and offline aspects of your application.

All of these will be jobs that you create to be executed in independent steps using an automation tool such as Jenkins (*https://jenkins.io/*).

Pipelines can be initiated automatically every time code is committed to the repository. A listener hook in Jenkins makes this easy be simply pointing to your repository.

After the job is kicked off, the pipeline should create a new instance so that only one build is tested at a time. If the job fails, developers can be notified immediately.

Here is the outline of a flow for you to use in building your own pipeline for your application code:

1. *Commit*: this stage is kicked off on an approved pull request or code commit. It should execute unit tests. You might also want to include executing "A/B" tests at this stage. Here you are checking that the basic functionality works as advertised.

2. *Integrate*: For an application of any size, you won't want to re-create the environment every time. Instead, use this stage to promote the changed or new code into the environment with the rest of the existing passed code. This is an integration environment. Here, you run a battery of regression tests to ensure that the new functionality doesn't break existing functionality. Here, you should also run a battery of security tests and scanning (with a tool such as Veracode) and penetration tests, too. To do that, you'll need to expose your build to the internet.

3. *Production*: If you are ready to release this new code to production, you will execute this phase of the pipeline. Here you run smoke tests to ensure that your build actually connects to all of the proper environments with the production settings. Smoke tests are essentially just quick verification tests. You can execute them by pinging a health check function on your services.

Health Check Function

Chris Richardson has a clear and practical writeup of how to implement the Health Check function (*http://bit.ly/2lVAMYo*) on a service using Spring.

Note that not all software can or should be continually deployed. If you are making large-scale operational software for companies to run their businesses, that would not be desirable or responsible, so choose production schedules as is appropriate for your business. The aim with pipelines is that the technical teams are not the bottleneck, that you *could* theoretically release 10 times per day if the business wanted to; that doesn't mean you must or should.

Code Coverage

Your code review process should include a test coverage tool, such as the old Java Cobertura (*http://cobertura.github.io/cobertura/*), though this project is not actively maintained any longer. Most developers have moved on to use SonarQube (*https://www.sonarqube.org/*), which also has a Community Edition if you don't have the cash for the full version. These tools are a great way to check how well your unit tests are checking the cyclomatic complexity in your code. This is essentially a measure of how many ways there are in and out of a method. Your code might throw a checked exception or a runtime exception such as NullPointer, or it might pass or fail some condition in the business logic. Do not test only the Happy Path: write tests that truly cover the cyclomatic complexity and monitor your teams' test coverage. SonarQube is not only interested in test coverage and cyclomatic complexity, but the richer idea of "continuous inspection" to call out warnings when it sees potential issues with your code. Employ this tool and watch your resilience score go way up.

You should aim for creating a single artifact that you build once, and that then moves through all the production pipeline stages intact. If you rebuild software at each stage, or tamper with its settings or replace things, your tests are all essentially invalidated.

Machine Learning Data Pipelines

As deconstructive designers, we don't make frozen pictures of software we advertise; we will build and assume that the system will actually work or look that way. The system is a representation of a concept. Neither do we make frozen software that is locked, fixed, and predetermined. Not because we are on a religious quest, but because it fits the world better and therefore is more successful software. We design deconstructed systems to be a more organic and generative system. We find ways to make a generative architecture, an active design where the system helps create itself. The obvious mechanism for this is machine learning.

To help the system you're designing have the biggest impact, expect to design machine learning capabilities *throughout* the system. At least take the entire system into account so that you can prioritize how you apply machine learning from a holistic point of view. Although it is not likely appropriate, desirable, or cost effective to make every aspect of your product machine learning enabled, it is certainly important to inspect your system and its set of use cases, top to bottom, and consider how it might take advantage of machine learning at each of these.

For example, in a shopping system it might be obvious to see that you want to use machine learning as part of a product recommender. But not all of the great uses for machine learning will be customer facing. There are internal opportunities to proactively predict when you might have the next outage.

For any of these use cases, it will quickly become important to have a machine learning pipeline in place to allow automation to keep the data and resulting machine learning predictions fresh and tuned. A data collection workflow to help gather and prepare the data for your machine learning algorithms will be necessary and save you a lot of headaches trying to manage it later.

The data collection pipeline has the following responsibilities:

- Decentralize data intake. Agent adapters can pull data in from their original sources.
- Parallelize data intake for different data sources and data types to execute quickly. Each of the data intakes can stream with a throttle mechanism or can be awakened on timers or triggered by events.
- Normalize and munge the data to prepare it for use in data science use cases including ingestion, data cleanup, imputing missing values, and so forth.

Designing data pipelines will make it easier for you to add new data sources later and make your machine learning richer and more robust. Figure 8-1 shows an example process and set of responsibilities for a machine learning data pipeline that you can use.

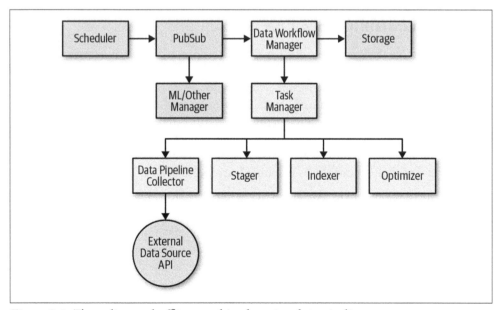

Figure 8-1. The online and offline machine learning data pipeline

Here is the basic flow for a data pipeline similar to how we use them as designed together with a great architect, Holt Hopkins:

1. At code time, create a separate project and package for your data pipeline. Create a set of interfaces that you deploy as an API separately from the implementation classes associated with any particular data pipeline. Say, for example, that in the travel domain you have flights and trains and you want to use schedule, change, or cancellation data as an object of machine learning in order to optimize your application in some way. You would make separate implementation artifacts (WAR or JAR in Java) that adhered to the data intake interfaces: one for the flights and one for the trains.

   a. These interfaces include a Scheduler, a Workflow Manager, a Task Manager, and a Data Processor Engine.

2. At runtime, a Scheduler interface implementation determines when to initiate a job. This will typically be for one of three reasons: an event was published that the scheduler consumes, a certain hour of the clock was struck, or it's continuously running or running at intervals capturing a stream of data (such as from the Twitter streaming API). If the scheduler is notified through a publisher/subscriber (pub/sub) mechanism that something has happened and it decides it should open a pipeline, the scheduler invokes the proper implementation of the Workflow Manager through its interface.

3. The Workflow Manager, like typical manager services as we have discussed, represents the orchestration layer and does no other actual work but to track the state machine of progress across the use case through to completion and to ensure that asynchronous notification messages are published so that Task Managers can do their work.

4. Each Task Manager receives the message appropriate for its task. There are tasks for Collecting, Staging, Indexing, and Context Optimizing. Each of them can represent a long-running process.

   a. A Collector acts as a Data Processing Engine service, which is an implementation that knows how to connect to its data source (typically through a network API) and retrieve and save the raw data for local storage (say, in Amazon S3). Data should be stored in its raw form, as from the source. That way, if anything goes wrong in the processing, you can revert to this step without retrieving it again (which might not be possible in the case of streams).

   b. The Stager puts data into a common format, cleans it up, normalizes it, and generally prepares it for consumption. The Stager performs conversions from tab-separated to comma-separated values (CSV), renames columns for file consistency, imputes missing values, and normalizes numeric values on appropriate scale. The Stager is specific to its API client. For example, a single Task Manager might be invoked to refresh the "social media" data and that could kick off two Collectors and two Stagers (one for Facebook and one for Twitter).

c. The Indexer has no awareness of the source of the data. It is aware of the use case in which the data will be used, and how. It knows how the data will be filtered and queried. Multiple Indexers can be at work for a given use case. For example, one could index according to date, another could index according to user, and another according to content category. The Indexers will break large files into small ones that are optimized for read retrieval, rewrite files with the proper order, update a database, and store metadata in case range queries are needed.

d. The Optimizer performs the last offline step. This is necessary only for intensive, high-traffic systems. It can precompile and add to caching in order to optimize shopping performance. In this way, it acts analogously to Facebook's HipHop precompiler, or a Maven "effective POM." It can denormalize data for speedy retrieval, prepare any anticipated runtime rules, and add it to a distributed cache if necessary.

5. At each step, the Task Manager should update the Workflow Manager from time to time regarding what percentage complete its job is or otherwise update on the status of the job. The Workflow Manager receives the job status update and records it in a database for exposure to tooling.

6. When the jobs are complete, the Manager service notifies a topic. The machine learning Manager can then understand that the data was updated and execute any processes it wants to, such as pulling the data into its store. The raw data can be deleted if desired to save space, cost, or comply with data privacy rules.

These steps are all performed "offline" and are not in the standard use case runtime path.

Now with your machine learning algorithm running as a service, the fresh circulation of properly prepared data acts like the fresh circulation of water through a fountain.

Metadata and Service Metrics

Define the metrics that your services will use. This must be treated as data because it must be defined, collected, massaged, and put into a usable form. The metrics must be engineered by you as a data architect/data designer. Table 8-2 shows examples of service metrics that you might consider employing in your own organization.

Table 8-2. Sample service metrics

Metric name	Description
Request Count (Total)	Total number of requests, per service operation, by millisecond, second, minute, etc.
Response Time (Average)	Average response time, per service operation, by millisecond, second, minute, etc.
Failure Rate Count (Total)	Total number of failed service requests, by millisecond, second, minute, etc.
Success Rate (%)	Percentage of successful service requests over the total number of service requests

Metric name	Description
Failure Rate (%)	Percentage of failed service requests over the total number of service requests
Service Availability (%)	Percentage of availability, per service operation, by hours, days, etc.
Fault Count (Total)	Number of times a technical fault has been registered, per service operation
Transaction Response Time (End-to-End)	Average end-to-end response time, per service operation, by millisecond, second, minute, etc.
MTTR (Mean Time to Recovery)	Average duration in minutes from a service incident to its complete recovery

These are by no means the only metrics, just some that I've used effectively in the past. The point here is to give you a jump start toward tracking the behavior of your services so that you can understand how well they are working and how to improve them. This is a matter for you to design to ensure they are meaningful; do not merely leave this up to the operations team.

Auditing

You will need to add auditing to your system so that you can trace who changed what and when.

For auditing purposes, tables that supply configuration options, user access, PII data, and certainly PCI data should maintain columns such as the following items to support auditability:

- When created
- Who created
- When last updated
- Who last updated

For a robust security measure that can really help you out in the event of a breach or unauthorized use, also maintain columns for who and when last viewed. You can implement this as part of the eventing framework discussed earlier.

ADA Compliance

Your software user interface design in its various forms (including desktop, tablet, and mobile) must comply throughout with the Americans with Disabilities Act (ADA). Any consumer-facing web application must meet Web Content Accessibility Guidelines 2.0 (WCAG) (*https://www.w3.org/TR/WCAG20/*) to ensure that the application is perceivable, operable, understandable, and sufficiently robust for users with disabilities.

Companies that do not comply with this federal regulation are subject to fines of $25,000 per day for every instance of a violation, which becomes a million dollars in fines to your company for every three sprints it takes to correct.

Therefore, it's an excellent idea to test your software on a regular, frequent basis (prior to every release) using the following tools:

- JAWS (required) with the IE browser
- NVDA and Zoom Text Only (required) with the Firefox browser

Your software could also be tested on a less frequent but still regular basis (quarterly) using the following tools:

- IE-Edge with the IE browser
- GoogleVox with the Google Chrome browser
- Totally: an accessibility visualization toolkit
- MAGic: a screen magnification tool
- Voiceover and TalkBack for Apple and Android tablet and mobile devices

Keeping your software ADA compliant is not only a way to make better software, it's the law. Your public-facing consumer software will be particularly susceptible to this, but although that's where designers tend to focus their activity, your internal applications are subject to it as well.

Summary

In this chapter, we looked at new ways of thinking about and implementing rich data designs to support the new needs of modern applications.

CHAPTER 9

The Infrastructure Aspect

In this chapter, we take a look at the kinds of services to create at the infrastructure layer. We explore a variety of infrastructure-related concepts that are important within the universe of deconstructed design, including Infrastructure as Code (IaC), Pipelines for Machine Learning, Chaos, and many more tools and methods.

Considerations for Architects

Sometimes, architects are viewed as only a part of the application development or product development team. They limit their specifications to only the software and services layer. Just as we saw that the effective architect's purview also includes the business view, this individual also must contemplate the infrastructure, seeing all the aspects of business, application/services, data, and infrastructure working together.

As you consider how to design your infrastructure, the following are critical issues to address:

- Definition of approach to infrastructure creation in support of your project, including containerization and IaC
- Toolsets in support of these
- Release engineering and management
- Process definition for Continuous Delivery, Continuous Deployment, and Continuous Integration
- Process definition for change control
- Budgeting and financial management of the infrastructure
- Capacity planning
- Patching

- Disaster recovery
- Monitoring
- Logging and auditing
- Roles and responsibilities definitions for DBAs, DevOps, architects, and application owners and/or system owners

These are all important considerations in the purview of the effective enterprise architect. They should be captured and addressed in your Design Definition Document. Although these aspects of your infrastructure are critical, they will be specific to your business and project needs.

If you are working in a cloud environment, many of these will change from your on-premises approach. For example, the saying goes that in the cloud, you treat your infrastructure as cattle, not pets. This refers to the cloud best practice of never actually patching servers. You instead take them offline and entirely replace them with a complete upgraded server using your automation tools.

Disaster recovery is another area that tends to change dramatically from on-premises to cloud. Historically, you needed to have two different datacenters, and grudgingly negotiate vendor contracts that have a separate disaster recovery datacenter. The application here tends to not have the same capacity, the same setup, and the same version of the application and data. There is usually some lag because there is less urgency to keeping these perfectly synchronized because disasters don't happen every day. There is also significant cost associated with something you hope to never actually use. If you design your services properly, to statelessly run on top of automatically replicating peer-to-peer data services, you can have a very resilient application running across multiple datacenters, even across multiple continents in an active–active configuration. This puts your services close to your customers and maximizes both your resilience and the cost/benefit.

Architects assist in the budgeting and financial planning aspect by using tools such as cloud provider cost calculators to estimate the infrastructure and the monthly rental costs. Make sure when you do this to specify different needs for development, testing, integration, User Acceptance Testing (UAT)/staging, and production as necessary. Defining your infrastructure across several environments like this can become expensive. This is one reason why automation through IaC is crucial: it allows you not only to scale up, but to scale back down. You can shut down entire environments when they aren't needed, to save costs. If all you need to do is push a single button to kick off the automatic creation of your entire infrastructure and deployment, you'll be more likely to manage this closely and carefully.

Capacity planning will also require significant changes in how you operate in the cloud. Instead of trying to guess up front, months in advance before you have any real traffic patterns or load to plan for, you can take advantage of autoscaling groups.

These allow you to define rules such that when a trigger circumstance is met (for instance, when a server reaches 80% CPU and stays there for some time), you can have the cloud automatically provision another server and add it to the cluster behind the load balancer. Likewise, for cost management reasons, you'll want to define rules that remove a server in the event that usage becomes very low.

This all means that your infrastructure is more closely related to your business than ever, and potentially more closely coupled to your applications than ever. We have been used to two separate horizontal layers in the false dichotomy of infrastructure versus application. But we deconstruct that false binary opposition, and with the cloud and IaC, see the entirety of our servers, networking, and application all defined as versioned plain text and code in a single image, automated, and all working together in near real time.

Make sure that however your relationship with the enterprise operations/run team is structured within your organization that you have clearly defined the aforementioned items. The one place no one likes surprises is in the infrastructure. Your goals should be clarity, predictability, transparency, and cost-aware resilience.

DevOps

Another story that we comfort ourselves with in software is patently false: if we use this tool, this framework, this practice, we will "save time" by eliminating effort. The person who invented the ship also invented the shipwreck, which reminds us that every solution creates new problems; we are often not solving problems so much as trading them for others we (hopefully) would rather have. If we focus on the idea that we are "solving problems" and "saving time," we will miss much of the picture. Similarly, we must let go the idea that we are eliminating effort. Effort, like problems, is typically just moved, not eliminated. This presents one of the major difficulties in DevOps today.

DevOps attempts to conflate the two jobs of development and operations. It is encouraging that DevOps is a deconstruction of the traditional binary opposition between development and operations. But the responsibilities of the two jobs do not go away.

The stated aims of DevOps are, as you might expect, improved productivity, speed, scale, reliability, collaboration, and the other usual suspects that have been the aim of most initiatives in our industry in the past half century.

There are a variety of DevOps models, and we as an industry have been discussing and debating the practice, what it is, and how to go about it for more than a decade. For our purposes, let's do a quick overview to make sure we have defined the term and highlighted some of the key principles that might make the most material difference to architects/designers:

- In DevOps, the application developers and the operational folks are not siloed in a Plan/Build/Run–type model in which the builders throw completed code over the wall to the runners. Instead, they work together on the same team for a more integrated lifespan of the project, and share practices and duties. Development, infrastructure, and security are viewed as part of the holistic set of concerns everyone shares.

- DevOps focuses on IaC as a practice, which requires that traditional infrastructure folks work more as developers, but with an infrastructure and operations mindset. They need to be not just more aware of developer practices such as Agile methods, code repositories, testing, software design, commenting, and so forth, but they need to be very skilled in these practices.

- It represents a philosophical shift in mindset wherein both roles are focused on developer productivity, resilience and reliability, automation, and security. Instead of serializing the customer needs on through to product management and then development and then infrastructure, the DevOps engineer is less abstracted from the customer by working side by side with the application makers.

Although the way different organizations have tried to realize DevOps can vary, there are a few practices that seem consistent and important across applications:

- Small, frequent updates as opposed to large, infrequent major pushes. This requires a CI pipeline, and a continuous (or at least frequent) delivery pipeline. Such pipelines allow you to be more responsive to your customers and improve reliability because changes are isolated to small batches instead of large and less predictable updates.

- Service-oriented development. Aligning a single function with a single service that is independently deployable, scalable, and versionable, and in turn aligning that service with an Agile team on your org chart can also help productivity, accountability, speed to market, and reliability.

- Other important practices include IaC, configuration management, and integrating monitoring and logging with the application development practices as we will discuss throughout this chapter.

These are the principles and ideas that will be most relevant to you as you consider your infrastructure angle further in light of your organization's position and needs.

Infrastructure as Code

IaC allows you to describe declaratively in plain text the infrastructure that you want to create. Software systems read those declarations and spin up the infrastructure to match it. Instead of negotiating contracts, enlisting the procurement department, and spending capital dollars far in advance to provision your datacenter in a nonrepeatable and hard-to-visualize process, IaC allows you to define your entire datacenter with plain text using a configuration syntax. This gives you a blueprint of your datacenter. There are tremendous advantages here:

- You can readily understand the comprehensive picture of your datacenter and all of the components that underpin your applications and services.

- You can also repeat that datacenter to deploy across multiple cloud regions by simply changing the region or zone names.

- Additionally, infrastructure definitions can be shared and reused by other teams to give them a jump start on their projects.

- Because they are plain text files, they can and should be stored in your code repository, which means your IaC definitions can be versioned. You can roll back entire datacenters to a Last Known Good state if something gets out of whack.

- Your infrastructure environment becomes more testable. You can (and should) write a battery of tests for checking the health and compliance of your infrastructure.

- You can define Governance as Code, checking that resources are properly provisioned, tagged, and compliant with guidance.

For these reasons, IaC is an important element of deconstructive software system design. Anything in your business applications sphere that can be code should be code, so that it can be presented with an API and invoked through automated processes.

Following are some of the popular tools for implementing IaC:

- Provision local and remote systems with a tool like Vagrant (*https://www.vagrantup.com*). Vagrant is a free and open source tool created by Hashi-Corp that allows you to create a portable complete environment inside a single file called a "box." You can then share this file, which defines your complete environment across teams so that everyone has the same repeatable, working OS with all the same versions of all the same tools. This goes a long way toward combating the "It Works on My Machine" syndrome. You define your Vagrant virtual machine boxes using Ruby. You can also search for existing boxes to give you a jump start.

- A popular Platform as a Service (PaaS) tool is Heroku (*https://www.heroku.com*), which assists you by provisioning and orchestrating containers (which it calls "dynos"), managing and monitoring their life cycle, and providing proper network configuration, HTTP routing, log aggregation, and more. Because it's a full PaaS tool, the platform regularly performs audits and maintains PCI, HIPAA,

ISO, and SOC compliance, taking a variety of necessary but often cumbersome tasks off your plate. With Heroku, you can add extensions for Kafka, Redis, Postgres, and more. Heroku supports Ruby, Java, Node.js, Scala, Clojure, Python, PHP, and Go.

- Define, manage, and test automated systems with Chef or Puppet. These tools allow you to perform configuration management. Puppet requires that you declare dependencies between resources, which Puppet then satisfies. Chef, on the other hand, satisfies all resources in the order in which they appear in the file.

- Automation of creation production infrastructures can be done with Jenkins, Ansible, and Terraform (*https://www.terraform.io/*). These help you to deploy on environments including Amazon Web Services (AWS), Google Cloud Platform (GCP), OpenStack, and Digital Ocean. Terraform, also by HashiCorp, lets you define and provision datacenter infrastructure using a high-level, proprietary configuration language called HashiCorp Configuration Language (HCL); you can also use JSON. With Terraform, you can configure your corporate GitHub account, dynamically create servers across multiple IaaS providers, register their names at another DNS provider, enable their monitoring from a third-party monitoring company, and specify to send the application logs to an aggregrator service.

Depending on your environment and needs, any of these in combination can be helpful to you. You can use these in conjunction with Docker and Kubernetes to create a more portable infrastructure foundation.

If you are using the AWS cloud, you would likely use AWS CloudFormation as the templating system, and something like Ansible or Jenkins to help you execute the scripts. AWS CloudFormation is essentially YAML. You can use it to describe the Amazon EC2 servers, the autoscaling groups, the security groups, databases, network routing and DNS, edge services, and basically everything you can create in AWS.

The primary mental shift that you will need to negotiate with your enterprise operations teams is this: historically, the operations and infrastructure folks want nothing to change. Change of any kind is often viewed as nothing but an opportunity for failure and uncertainty that keeps people up and night away from their families and rest. IaC asks you to embrace change, and provides a set of practices and accompanying tools that support this mental shift. Changes in an IaC world are viewed as an opportunity for improvement, rather than an obstacle or hardship.

The second challenge you'll see organizationally is that people sometimes do not want to give up what they know or are reluctant to learn new ways of doing things. They can feel threatened or think that their jobs will go away or change and they'll lose power and control. Don't underestimate the force of this kind of resistance, and include the enterprise operations teams who might be running traditional datacenters, or (worse) bring a traditional datacenter operations mindset to the cloud.

Metrics First

In our rush to make deadlines, and in the absence of any demand to produce metrics numbers for a product that hasn't been launched yet, we often begin designing and coding without consideration of metrics.

If you don't create a few key metrics up front, you'll not only miss out on showing how successful you've been, you'll also have nothing to start reporting from when deadlines grow near and when budgets are almost used up and management begins asking questions.

Define the metrics for success of your overall project up front. Then, before actually recording any values, check with executives to see that these metrics, if you did the work to track against them and give them real values, would in fact tell them the story that they need to hear to determine whether you're being successful in the ways that matter to them. This is a crucial point of difference for us as deconstructive designers. It's like Test-Driven Development (TDD) in which you create the test from a client point of view, it fails because there's no code to fulfill it, and then you fill in the code to make the test pass. You want to do this on an organizational/project level, and defining the metrics up front is like defining your own set of tests for the project.

If you define them at the end, you will be doing a "Texas Two Step": right at the point when you're all exhausted from the big push of delivering your project, you'll have a second small project on your hands to figure out what the right metrics are, hope that you have things in place to procure them, add those tools and processes in when you inevitably don't have them all, and then go through weeks, if not months, of remediating your product for performance or security, right at the worst time.

With respect to the broad infrastructure, you should consider the following success metrics:

- Are there health checks on every service? To get a jump start on adding health checks to your services, you can check out the Netflix runtime health check library (*https://github.com/Netflix/runtime-health*).
- Do you have a battery of automated tests for the infrastructure itself to show that all the correct services are present and properly networked and connected?
- Do you have regularly running Veracode scans to produce an Open Web Application Security Project (OWASP) secure coding practices report? This is especially useful throughout the project so that you are keeping the security tidy and manageable throughout. You don't want to get to the end and discover that you have a long list of security bugs to work through before going live.

- Do you have a mechanism in place to measure mean time between failures (MTBF) through your monitoring tool?

- Do you have a mechanism in place for recording mean time to recovery (MTTR)? This is the more important metric going forward, but often not really measurable until you have an incident in production. You should, however, decide up front and agree on how you will measure this. Usually the Ops team will have a virtual room or Pager Duty type tool and process defined for capturing the duration of incidents.

At the application level, you want to set up certain metrics that will tell you how well your application is performing. Although these are not strictly infrastructure-related, their collection and measurement will probably need to be defined in collaboration with your Ops team. Here are some of the key infrastructure-oriented performance metrics to define, collect, and reflect:

Latency per service

This gives you a concrete measure of how long it takes to perform a task, whether that time is consumed in travel, processing, or response time. Focusing sharply on the latency in your mission-critical services will be an important key to success. Being able to consistently measure, say, your shopping response times, will help you find bottlenecks in performance and fine-tune your infrastructure or your code to improve them. It will also help with forecasting financial needs and scalability ceilings. Don't forget offline batch jobs: create service-level agreements (SLAs) around them and measure how frequently they complete on time.

Traffic

This is the measure of load and demand on your system so that you are clear on how much work each component is doing. Collecting traffic data will indicate whether you need to provision more supporting infrastructure, or if you can redesign a component to do more work in parallel, or whether asynchronous processing can be employed. As you measure your traffic, you should look to view it in patterns and trends. If they swing significantly, this might indicate where you can add or fine-tune autoscaling groups to scale up and down accordingly.

Availability

This is important and notoriously difficult to consistently measure. People seem to argue about it all the time. So it's good to be clear on what you mean when you say "available." For this reason, it's common to see advice suggesting that you measure primary functions during business hours, all functions during business hours, and both of these in a 24x7 measure. You can consider the nature of your application or product, and the impact that availability failures can have at different times. If you have a financial reporting application, that can go offline for hours on the weekend with little or no user impact. Does your measure account for planned or only unplanned downtime? Define it in whatever way makes sense for your business and your product, but make sure you're consistent.

Incidents
> Number of production incidents measured by severity (priority one, priority two, and so forth). I don't see a lot of value in defining more than a few priority levels because they tend to just incite arguments and defensiveness and cause people to lose sight of customer focus.

There are other metrics that your organization might prefer. The point here is to be sure to define measurable metrics, start figuring out early on how to track them and report on them, and be sure that they are metrics that drive the behavior that you want to see.

Compliance Map

Depending on the size of your organization and the role of your department, you might also consider having a *compliance map*. This would essentially be a list of applications in your purview and how well they comply with your next generation toolset. Create a spreadsheet with the list of applications and several columns to capture specific aspects of the application current state versus your target or future state toolset. Next, you can assign a score with a color code of red/yellow/green to indicate how far away each application is. Then, you can assign a business priority to each application. This would generate for you a score in a 2x2 type quadrant: applications with high strategic business value that are far out of compliance might be prioritized first.

You can then use this as a data view to discuss with your executives and product management to create a prioritized roadmap for application remediation.

Automated Pipelines Also First

Often, we go through projects and we add automation close to the end, when we're almost done. We wait until we have a significant part of the work done and need to turn our attention to deploying to certification, staging, or production environments. This creates a second, hidden project.

Instead, we want to start with automation, even when you have nothing. We create the simplest "Hello World" project, and then immediately begin automating the build, testing suite, and deployment across the IaC. That's how you get the most bang for the buck because you can use your own automation throughout the development of the project. This adds efficiency and predictability overall. Moreover, when you do it in this order, you are less likely to start with application-specific needs (because the application is just a kind of empty shell at this point), and your automation pipelines can enjoy more reuse across the organization.

The Production Multiverse and Feature Toggling

We in software tell ourselves many comforting stories. One is that we have a reliable staging environment that is very much like production and that if we test our code here, we should be good in production. The problem with this story is that it's almost never true.

You must decouple unit tests from integration tests as well as performance tests and penetration tests. Think of these as separate matters that can be kicked off, or not, as your current situation demands. Penetration tests by definition occur in production. But the rest occur before you get to the production environment.

Try this thought experiment: imagine that you had no staging environment at all, and imagine then what you would need to do differently to perform responsible deployments. It is impossible to test completely.

One problem with our typical way of thinking is that we have an idea of a perfect piece of software in a perfect environment (whether that is staging or production) and these ideas are all monolithic. Even if your application is decomposed into microservices, the *idea* here is monolithic, unified, perfect, complete.

If you abandon the idea that there is a perfect application, a perfect environment, you can start to create compensatory actions as a native and integral part of your design. And these compensatory actions will not only make up for the fact that you are not relying so much on the false foundation of staging, but will create new benefits.

If we see our application as rhizomatic (as being made of decentralized root systems), that is a more honest and accurate view of the world that will benefit our software. Although that sounds abstract, consider this: your source code management system exists as a series of roots. They can be merged back to the trunk, and different people can be working simultaneously on different areas of the code. In a large development project, there is no single, unified field of the code base. The code base is a set of multiplicities. One key reason our software is less resilient and higher quality than it could be is not, I wager, that we didn't spend a million dollars on a staging environment that looks "exactly" like production. That is a fantasy that we must abandon. When your uptime availability is measured in ten-thousandths of a percent, a "pretty close to production" environment is not even in the ballpark. No, I think the reason is instead that we are happy with the idea of a multiplicity of code bases in development, and force ourselves into an inaccurate translation that there must now be a single, unified, monolithic idea of "The Production Code" right around staging time.

The idea that staging will save us does not serve us well enough. We cannot replicate the complete production environment precisely. You won't have all of the exact same licenses, which can be prohibitively expensive. We certainly don't have the same network setup, firewall rules, and routing tables. Is everything authorized to third-party

APIs the same way, with the same throttling and service level? No. Are all the file paths identical and security groups identical and URLs identical? The data is not the same, the keys are not the same. Clinging to this idea hurts us.

If instead, we carried that multiplicity of development branches forward into production, what would that mean? What benefit would it give us? What would we need to do? What if we gave up on the idea of staging, and moved that matter into production? We would need to build those paths, that extensibility, that configurability, into our code base and subvert the idea of production in order to make it more resilient.

In what I hope by now is a more intuitive first thought in our deconstructive design, we look for the binary opposition, see which term is privileged, and overturn the hierarchy in order to determine how they are interrelated and interdependent and how they can inform each other to create a new space for an improvement. In this case, we would not privilege production over nonproduction by treating it as pristine, wholly distinct. Yes, *of course*, we must have it properly secured. Nothing here is saying to play fast and loose with what surely must be a hardened, resilient, secure production environment or to encourage sloppiness or entropy.

The point rather is to suggest that the code base itself, as deployed in production, might have many credible paths through it that can be turned on and off for different users, different countries, different percentages. I have heard it said that there are hundreds of "versions" of Expedia.com all running simultaneously in production. Consider production less as a single monolith and more as a choose your own adventure book, or a set of train tracks at a major rail station: the tracks can be switched to route trains (user requests) through to various points.

A good way of achieving this is through *feature toggles* or *feature flags*.

Implementing Feature Toggles

There are two primary use cases for feature toggles. One is that you have a new version of an algorithm that you want to try out on a subset of users. You might not be sure how it will perform or whether it will convert shoppers at a higher rate. So you want to introduce it slowly to a subset of your site visitors rather than rolling it out in speculation *en masse* and hoping it works; if it doesn't, you are faced with rolling it all back and figuring out what to do. Feature toggles deconstruct this binary opposition of "all or nothing" and "totally on or totally off." They allow you to see the world on a gradient and implement new features or algorithms accordingly.

The second primary use case for feature toggles is rather similar: you want to have two versions running at once in an A/B or multivariate testing scenario and gather data to learn which performs or converts better. This is common in ecommerce, where we're likely to have a few different merchandising messages, colors, photo placements, and so forth. You might have different button labels with variations on the same message, such as "Buy Now" or "Add to Cart" or "Book it!" and you want to show these to different users of the same kind in order to measure which is more successful. If the "Buy Now" button shows a conversation rate 10% higher, you might want to settle on that wording and eventually let the other label candidates go at the conclusion of your test.

Let's consider how we might implement feature toggles. In the most rudimentary way, you could comment out the old lines of code in favor of running the new code and then redeploy and switch back if it didn't work out. This is not, however, what we're talking about. Beyond the fact that commenting out code is a terrible practice, it does not achieve our aim of separating the idea of deployment from the idea of what is "released."

A slightly more advanced way to do it would be to make the flags dynamic so that you can have both options of the functions/algorithms/whatever you're toggling available, and then flip a Boolean in a configuration or runtime parameter to state which to run:

```
if (flagEnabled) { return exciting new thing }
else { return standard thing }
```

You can get more fancy with this, such that you have a function to determine which path this runtime request is in. You can even build a UI to make it easy to see all the flags you have and turn them on or off. The inadequacy here is that a Boolean just means on or off; you must pick between one of two states. But worse, your code will become littered with conditional logic all over the place, and the state machine you're creating will become far more complex to picture with the more flags you put in place. In this situation, the chances of having at least some users wind up in a bad state becomes much higher.

A more sophisticated way of doing this is to use a Strategy pattern. This is my preferred method. If the development teams know that when designing every microservice they must ensure that the service contains no actual business logic, but rather that all business logic is "injected" via Strategy pattern, you will be able to keep your code very clean, intuitive, readable, and manageable while still providing the ability to feature toggle. You can have one strategy with the exciting new algorithm and one strategy remaining for the old one. Then, you can create a toggle router component that sets the Toggle Context. This has a plain-text configuration to associate various strategy implementations with runtime attributes. For example, you might want to send 5% of requests as selected by the load balancer to the strategy A path, and the rest to strategy B. Or you might select a path based on country of request origin, geolocation, logged in users, loyalty members, random cookie settings, an HTTP header setting, or whatever suits your needs. Using the Strategy pattern should be standard in your microservice design, and for feature toggling, it allows you to avoid any conditionals littering your code.

Strategy Pattern

We've discussed the venerable Gang of Four Strategy pattern ear-lier, but it's always a great time to be reminded of this simple, pow-erful design technique. See the explanation, diagram, and examples at DoFactory (*http://bit.ly/2m3136T*). The examples are in C#, and I like to refer people to it because the explanation is very clear and it's easy to translate.

You can find a good article on thinking about and designing feature toggles at Martin Fowler's website (*http://bit.ly/2m316zB*). It is very long, so you are making a commit-ment, but if this idea is important to you, it's a good read.

Finally, if you really love this idea of feature toggling and find yourself wanting to go all-out with it, you might also be interested in feature flags as a service, which you can check out at Launch Darkly (*https://launchdarkly.com/*).

Putting the idea of feature toggling first, and assuming that you will have multiple production environments running at once is an excellent way to learn what your users truly prefer, how they use your application, and what works best for your business.

Multi-Armed Bandits: Machine Learning and Infinite Toggles

An outstanding extension of this idea is the Netflix user interface. Instead of deciding which toggle path to chose, the more modern and advanced way of doing feature tog-gling is to do so much toggling on so many aspects that you end up with many thou-sands of simultaneous versions of your application, such that the entire idea of toggling sort of goes away and is sublated into the realm of machine learning. This level of personalization represents a key facet of deconstructed design.

They use machine learning to select not only the selection of movies to recommend to you, but even the image thumbnails for movies, based on your preferences. I highly recommend reading up on how the company does this on its engineering blog (*http://bit.ly/2kH70GC*). Using a multi-armed bandit machine learning algorithm, Netflix selects the best image for you personally, based on items you have previously enjoyed. For example, if you have watched and liked several Matt Damon movies, the image Netflix selects for you when recommending *Good Will Hunting* would include a picture of him. If you've never watched another Matt Damon movie, but enjoy lots of comedies, it might instead select an image from that movie featuring Robin Williams.

The name "multi-armed bandit" (MAB) is derived from the image of slot machines, colloquially called "one-armed bandits" because slot machines "steal" your money. You pull the arm to place a bet. If you find a machine that you think is "hot," or that is paying off well, you might tend to stick with it and continue pulling the arm of the

---

same machine. However, in the row of slot machines before you, others might pay off better. You'll never get the optimal payout unless you fashion a combination of continuing with machines that you know work and occasionally trying other machines that might work better. These two axes on which a MAB operates are known as "exploit" and "explore": you continue to execute what you know works (exploit) in an optimal balance with exploring other options that could work better. The machine learning algorithm converges when, after many executions, it learns this optimal balance. This is how a basic recommender engine works, suggesting that the people who bought the sleeping bag also bought the flashlight, and then occasionally recommending something that might have less chance of hitting but which would represent a higher revenue point and profit margin, like recommending a tent, too. What your MAB should be optimizing here is not the number of conversions but the total revenue or total profit.

Your data scientists should be able to pull together a good multi-armed bandit in short order. If you don't have a strong data science team or want to test it yourself quickly, Jason Liu has put his multi-armed bandit library for Java (*https://github.com/ jxnl/bandits-java*) on GitHub. That's an easy way to get started.

As you can see, it's difficult at this point to say that there is one "Netflix website." It hardly makes sense to refer to "*The* Netflix website" as if there is one and it's always all the same. The same is obviously true for Google, as well, in which you see personalized results based on patterns, but even results that no one but you sees.

In your design work, ask yourself how you can unravel the idea of the single monolithic unified application in ways that make sense for your users and workload. What would make things quicker and easier for them? Have you designed a single monolithic workflow as the One Grand Narrative to rule them all? Or have you considered that you have both novices and power users, and thought about how you can distinguish between the two and in real time modify the workflow steps or the additional controls you reveal to them? This is a silent, seamless, wonderful way to make the easy things easy and the hard things possible.

How can you introduce paths for the production multiverse?

Infrastructure Design and Documentation Checklist

In your lookbook or Design Document, you will want to be clear and directive with teams regarding the infrastructure decisions you have made. The following should all be things that you outline and take a clear, declarative stance on in your architecture:

- Statement of what infrastructure provider you are using. Will this be on-premises, in cloud (if so, which one), or a hybrid?

- Operating system. This should include whether you want to use a cloud vendor's version of software. Often it has the advantage of getting regularly patched and updated as a service, alleviating that responsibility from your teams.

- If you are in a public cloud, you must explicitly state which region you will deploy to. Base your decision on where your customers are, latency between that cloud region and any home runs the systems there will need to make back to your datacenters, and the tools available in each. Not all regions have the same capabilities even within the same cloud vendor, so be sure to check.

- How many datacenters ("Availability Zones" in AWS) will you deploy to within that region?

- Will you be using an edge cache? Through which vendor?

- Are there particular infrastructure requirements for your application's design? For example, you might choose to forego web servers altogether, and instead deploy your static assets such as JavaScript, CSS, and images to a storage service such as Amazon S3 and have them served from your edge cache.

- Define how you will handle Security Groups and Access Control Lists (ACLs). Which services will be in which security groups and how will you balance the complexity challenge of maintainability when they each are accessible only via their own load balancer? What connections will you require between datacenters? Will you use a Direct Connect? Do you require use of a bastion or jump server to control access to environments?

- Define how you will handle key management.

- How do you anticipate scaling? What will be next one or two regions you expect to deploy to?

- How will you handle disaster recovery (DR)? Or you might choose not to have DR, but rather what I refer to as "built-in DR," where you run active–active in three or more datacenters and merge your DR investment with your active runtime investment. This, of course, must be designed into the application.

- To support your related infrastructure practices such as IaC, you should specify the design of your pipelines. Also specify some of the seemingly small matters that can end up making a big difference, such as disallowing anyone from using the cloud provider's UI console to make changes. Instead, mandate that any and all infrastructure changes occur only through the IaC automated process.

- To help control costs, you should specify how you will do resource tagging. If you're an AWS user, be sure to read its tagging guide (*https://amzn.to/2ksO5z8*).

- Of course, you must specify the typical matters such as load balancers, DNS names and relevant IP lists, firewalls, routing, reverse proxies, and the infrastructure communications setup including what type of servers, from what vendor, with what power and capacity, and how requests will route through them. What protocols will you allow and disallow?

- What monitoring must be in place? What alerts and triggers do you have?
- How will you perform autoscaling? What are the thresholds defined for those rules?
- Will you employ service or server virtualization? Gateways? How will you throttle traffic from the internet? Do you need to have tiers of API service (in which case, you must be able to identify traffic properly)?
- List the environments you expect to have. Is this Production, Testing, and Development only? Or will you also have Integration, Demo, Staging, UAT, Certification, and Load Test, or do these overlap in some way? Be very clear on this because it becomes the specification for the IaC people to build, and it has significant implications for cost and manageability. Be sure you're clear on who will use them, when, how, and for what purpose. Put this in a chart. It seems obvious, but it will require at least two meetings to sort out, and then another one later to tighten the belt when either it's not being followed according to the specification or when finance comes to find you.

Make sure that you do the calculations and projections for costing as you make these choices. If you end up with an incredibly resilient architecture that costs a million dollars a month to run, you might be asked to revise your plan. Make sure you are working with finance and product closely as you make these decisions. They are, after all, business decisions.

Chaos

As deconstructionist designers, we recall that an important part of our work in the production of concepts is to identify the values, the arguments, the principles, and the apparent superstructure in order to discover their opposites: we find the binary oppositions that adhere in the set of concepts we are working with. When we find a pair of binary oppositions, we can identify which term in the pair is privileged, and which is marginalized, secondary, or ancillary. Through analysis, we will discover how the privileged term actually relies on that marginalized term, how they are intertwined. Such analysis allows us to subvert that privileging, which is desirable because it will help us discover a more innovative, better design. It will be better because it will be a more accurate and less myopic view of the world, so our concept will be cleaner, richer, and reflect a truer state of affairs. This will improve our design, which is nothing but a transcription in code of our concept.

A very common binary opposition in our world is that of development versus production. Development is hopefully not the Wild West, but we expect it to be a bit messy and not at all presentable to guests. We expect it to be very dynamic, and that we must break stuff in development almost by definition because we are in the process of making the thing in the first place.

Production, on the other hand, should be frozen, the opposite of dynamic, pristine and perfect, which must never be touched and must be tread silently by, stepping delicately and not even looking at it or speaking above a whisper. Production is clearly the privileged term in this binary opposition.

Chaos Engineering is a term coined by Netflix around the year 2010. This is a wonderful, innovative practice that makes perfect sense for us as deconstructive designers: it has engineers invert the sacrosanct idea that production should never go down. Instead of thinking of production as the place you hope never breaks, and which you do everything to prevent breaking, you break production on purpose in order to make your application more resilient. It's beautiful. And if you actually do it, very effective.

The tool that Netflix made for this and eventually open sourced is called Chaos Monkey. You can think of Chaos Monkey as Failure as a Service. It does a few basic things to create problems for your application services. As you see how your application responds by creating these common problems and then observing how it responds, you can then design and plan changes to your application to improve its behavior under these adverse conditions. In this way, you're creating a terrific feedback loop. Perhaps by way of analogy, it's a little bit like vaccinations: you infect your application with a little bit of real world trouble in order to build up terrific defenses against it ruining things when it occurs in the wild.

It tends to work across a few lines:

Resource
> Starve your service of resources it needs to operate properly. These can include CPU, memory, or disk. In the real world, common problems like these are caused by runaway threads, stalled processes, and log files filling up due to improper configuration and (on Linux) too many open file descriptors.

State
> Change the state of your service's underlying environment. This can mean shutting down the operating system of one of the servers in a cluster, rebooting a machine, or changing the network time. It might mean removing a dependency.

Network
> Create simulated network stability problems. You can kill a specific process or flood the network.

Request
> Randomly create problems for specific requests.

Its popularity and usefulness within Netflix caused the company to spawn an entire "Simian Army," including Chaos Gorilla, which destroys an entire datacenter, and Chaos Kong, which destroys an entire region. Other monkeys are more "helpful," such as Janitor Monkey (*http://bit.ly/2M4GoLB*), which scans for leftovers and unused resources and cleans up, and Conformity Monkey (*http://bit.ly/2lW0yvF*), which runs at regular intervals and checks that all your resources conform with predefined rules, such as being tagged properly, creating a simple form of Governance as Code.

A great place to begin is to read the Principles of Chaos (*http://principlesofchaos.org/*). Then, you can download Chaos Monkey (*https://github.com/Netflix/chaosmonkey*) to run locally and read the documentation for how to install and use it there.

You can also try Chaos as a Service using Gremlin (*https://www.gremlin.com*) instead of trying to set it up and run it yourself.

Stakeholder Diversity and Inside/Out

We often talk about the customer as the person outside our company who is buying our product. In this binary opposition of inside/outside in which the external stakeholder is privileged, we might actually be doing them a disservice in not considering the many multiple customers we have.

If you do a thought experiment and imagine that your internal colleagues are your customers, too, that everyone's back end is someone else's front end, that the development environment is the production environment to a developer, you might change a few practices that can help your external paying customer.

Who really are all the users of the system? At different stages, there are many of them.

Developers are the first user of the system. There are a few things you can do to set the table for them that will pay off richly in happier developers who aren't dealing with the same low-level and uninteresting headaches every day:

- Invest in automation. This includes deployment, testing, and provisioning. There is a step that needs to be inserted in the software development life cycle before coding starts to make sure that the table is set for them. In a sense, you're building production first, but with the developer as the customer.

- Do everything you can as an architect and a leader of influence to take process bureaucracies away from them. The more time they spend filling out tickets just to get access to the environment that they work in every day, the more grumpy and distracted from the important work they will be.

- The developer is a user of the system after it's deployed into the hands of paying customers. Ensuring that they have commented thoughtfully and made the code readable and properly named and properly segmented will help to make their work more efficient when they are going back to fix bugs and make maintenance updates.

The Network Operations Center team and the Bunch of Poor People on the Phone at 3 A.M. on a Crit Sit Call are also users of your system. Make sure to put the following in place to take care of this customer:

- There must be proper monitoring for them to gain transparency and clarity.
- Log messages properly and actually design the logging subsystem and naming conventions thoughtfully. Consider how messages will be written in order to be quickly looked up, indexed by a system like Splunk, and consider how they will be aggregated.
- Can you build components as managed components (think of something like Managed Beans in Java as part of Java Management Extensions or JMX (*http://bit.ly/2kGZFH6*))? Wrap or decorate your services as managed components for vendor-agnostic viewing, monitoring, and even updating at runtime. The Apache Cassandra database does this, and it essentially turns the software system inside out, making all the runtime components available in this way. It's a fantastic feature of the system and allows vendors to build monitoring and manipulation control panels on top of it very easily and plug in existing ones.

Make Managed Components

Even if you're not using Java, that doesn't matter. The point is to use this idea of the managed component in whatever language. See how Apache Cassandra does it in the source code on GitHub with the CommitLog (*http://bit.ly/2ltMtW3*) and CommitLogMBean (*http://bit.ly/2krd6uu*). You don't need to worry about how Cassandra works or what a commit log is; this is just an accessible example.

Testers and auditors are also users of the system. Consider their needs along these lines. The obvious point is that if you think only of the "user" who is sitting in front of the UI clicking, your long-term product will suffer. Everything you do in the design to support this more diverse customer set will pay off.

Summary

In this chapter, we reviewed a variety of modern practices and methodologies that you can employ to make your infrastructure more scalable, resilient, predictable, and manageable.

There can be entire books written on the subject of infrastructure architecture that go into more detail about specific fine points of the areas we have touched on here. We have focused primarily on considerations for infrastructure with respect to building software products or applications, because there is no point in infrastructure in its own right; it exists solely for the purpose of providing a platform for some kind of application.

In Chapter 10, we turn our attention to broader development methods, operations, and change-management processes.

PART III

Operations, Process, and Management

In Part III, we explore your role as semantic designer within an organizational context. You are the technology Creative Director. After you have interpreted and translated the theory into practice using the templates and guides provided, you need to get your project and systems up and running. It also must be managed appropriately after you've accomplished that. Here, we explore some best practices for governing and managing your work operationally. It's filled with templates and practical guides to help you get your job done.

Finally, we close with a manifesto to capture in summary the main tenets of semantic software design.

CHAPTER 10

The Creative Director

Depending on the organization's size, industry, line of business, and culture, and the general role of IT or product development, architects can have a difficult time knowing what their role is or should be in order to be effective. I often see CTOs at smaller companies acting essentially like the lead programmer. Sometimes this is necessary, or is just the "Way It Is" at a given company.

Moreover, this book problematizes that even further with the suggestion that "architect" is not exactly the role that's needed at all, but that rather our work is in semantics and semiotics.

This chapter aims to help you define the scope of your role and perhaps expand it. Ultimately, you might well become the chief semanticist, principal semantician, chief designer, creative director, chief philosopher, or something similar to better reflect the practices here. Because everything is a potential subject of design, bringing your design mentality and toolset to a broader purview in the organization can help it be more effective, clear, and efficient.

The Semantic Designer's Role

I often observe that role clarity is a challenge in many organizations. It is difficult to rally around your job, invest in continuous learning, research best practices, and generally go all out to be the best if you're not sure what it is you're supposed to be doing or what success even looks like. Lack of role clarity accounts for considerable disengagement in organizations. People become overly concerned about boundaries that get crossed or gaps that are left due to nothing but lack of communication of the expectations. We regularly define service contracts in our systems design and programming work, and then forget entirely that we must do the same thing with our roles if we are to be effective and efficient.

So although I don't presume to have the precise definition of your role given your industry, organization, and culture, I do encourage you to take a shot at defining it.

First, you might consider the skills, or job-description type attributes, for an architect or designer on your team. What must this person know, what proclivities and talents must he or she have? Of course you can go on the internet and find a variety of job descriptions for an architect. That's not our present point. Rather, we're trying to state what you might do differently as a Chief Designer, Chief Philosopher, CTO, Chief Architect, Chief Concepter, or whatever title you're able to get away with in your organization. The following attributes would be representative of this role:

- Strong understanding of our industry and business: primary economic drivers and factors, competitive landscape, customer needs, threats and opportunities.

- Strategic thinker with a strong understanding of strategy consulting tools (for an excellent guide on this, see my companion book to this volume, *Technology Strategy Patterns*).

- Philosophical, analytical thinker with good command of logic, set theory, rhetoric, post-structuralism, and ethics.

- Ability to form and communicate concepts as foundational software designs to support business outcomes. Command of semantics and semiotics is imperative.

- Design-oriented, creative, aesthetic thinker with a background in one or more fields of the arts including music, theater, dance, or painting. An understanding of the concerns, methods, and needs of marketing and advertising.

- Data-oriented thinker who builds arguments based on data and communicates them in meaningful models. Capable of assisting in machine learning efforts.

- Strong teaching/mentoring ability. Communicates broad concepts and memorable stories to create context across teams, focusing on "where" and "why" as much as "how." Regularly and enthusiastically mentors and coaches team members in concepts and best practices

- Good breadth across all technical domains (business, data, application, technology) and a strong depth in at least one of these.

- Strong written and verbal skills. Ability to write long documents detailing comprehensive solutions as well as brief documents that make a clear point with high impact. Command of the language appropriate for highly analytical, discriminating concept creation. Compelling and inspiring public speaker who excels at listening to and communicating with customers.

- Effective formal presentation skills: your great ideas don't matter if you cannot communicate them in an clear and inspiring way to others.

- Ability to lead directly and by influence. Often few people, if anyone, will report to the chief architect or chief systems designer. Even the CTO can have a small organization, but even if it's the whole development team, they must be able to lead by influence with other business partners.

- Skilled at planning and project management.

- Skilled at conflict resolution, customer negotiation, and business development.

Notice that a primary difference between our list of desired attributes and what you'll find in a typical job description include a heightened focus on skills and background in *strategy, philosophy, aesthetics/the arts, teaching/mentoring, and data.*

When you see the world as a list of lists of things with relations, all of which have attributes, you can see the data in everything. Notice that it does not say "data-driven." We want to be informed by data, and use it to assist in judgments and assessments, but it's far from the only thing. This is the direction in which we need to develop our talents in order to be more effective in our organizations.

The responsibilities for us might include the following:

- Documents current and future state designs across applications, technology systems, business processes, organization, and culture. Proposes evolutionary plans for the transformation and assists in program planning and change management. This includes authoring Design Definition Documents (see Chapter 5).

- Solution consulting: responds to customer RFPs. Identifies possible solutions to a customer need and determines the optimal product combinations, configurations, third-party technology partnerships, and important gaps, and documents the strategic approach. Develops a strong customer fact base including business strategy, technology strategy, technical/infrastructure capabilities and requirements, FAQs, and organizational capabilities and constraints.

- Use data-driven methods to determine design decisions.

- Able to quickly create clear and communicative models for large-scale and local problems and solutions.

- Guides technical/development teams through images, lookbooks, wikis, patterns, and formal guidelines. Establishes a vision and strategic technical direction and communicates common goals and means to achieve them.

- Keeps abreast of trends in the economy, politics, technology, media, and the industry at hand and is able to create meaningful conclusions and advise senior leadership with recommendations to senior leadership about strategic business and technology direction.

- Create formal methods and innovative models for viewing concepts throughout the organization, whether they are people, process, or technology related.

- Understands and negotiates trade-offs between people in technical disputes.

Some additional responsibilities depending on the seniority level might include the following:

- Identifies technical risks and makes recommendations for remediation.
- Determines, documents, aligns, and communicates design decisions.
- Formally expresses system design in a document, lookbook, architecture definition, architecture approach document, or other concept-capturing artifact.
- Illustrates formally how the system's design (whether a software system, process, or organizational change) will support the "-ilities" of Extensibility, Scalability, Availability, Portability, Manageability, Monitorability, Security, Performance. Include perspectives for Business, Application/Services, Data, Infrastructure.
- Drive integrity and capability readiness across the entire business portfolio.
- Review designs, code, environments, and tests.
- Establish processes, project and program management rubrics and milestones, and design executive steering committee meetings to ensure the design definition is actually realized in the solution as implemented.

Defining and publishing and communicating the role is a really good idea: it helps others know what your job is so that they don't imagine or assume it's something else and then continually wonder why you're not doing it. It helps people know when to engage you and for what purpose, and when to leave you alone to think and get stuff done.

Creative Directors Across Industries

Peter Drucker, father of business consulting, famously stated decades ago: the purpose of any business is to create a customer. A business does that with only two functions: marketing and innovation.

Everything that isn't marketing or innovation is a necessary support function, like Legal and HR.

The question we must ask ourselves is this: how do I create value in my organization?

Designers and makers of software create value through innovation. Innovation, by definition, is making something novel, something new. It's not repeating the same thing, as if on a factory line, such as with hardware.

Everything in a business that is not innovation or marketing is a cost. Architects must be value creators, and not clerks.

Apple and Microsoft and Amazon have jobs with the title "architect" in them. In general, Facebook and Google do not employ architects. We are at an inflection point in our industry's journey toward maturity, and in the discovery of new ways of working that best achieve our aims given changes in technology and the evolution of our practices.

Architects must create value for customers. All too often, they do not. If you have a spectacularly knowledgeable and collaborative developer who works very fast, they will do the "application architecture" work naturally themselves. Same for the role of project manager: you wouldn't need one if people did what they said they would do on time. But they don't.

Someone on the project must collaborate across fields to achieve the real aims of the business, which is less about telling engineers what to do, and more about collaborating to create a vision and unifying concept to meet the diverse needs of marketing, product, infrastructure, compliance, and strategy. To do so, you must perform a double, and apparently contradictory, action: you must innovate and you must make your innovations repeatable. You are making a system of systems, prescribing not the system itself, but the context in which the software system can spring to life with all these competing concerns met. You must at once define a practice that is measurable and can meet the budget and the timeline, and yet which supports the kind of innovation and invention that is the hallmark of value creation, which means that you can't merely always do what you did before.

Consider for a moment the production of film and television, music, advertising, media, and fashion houses. These industries have existed for far longer than the field of software, and none of them employ anyone with "architect" in their title. This moniker is not necessary, and perhaps has outgrown its usefulness for us.

But is there not a need for someone to see across multiple projects and ensure that they are aligned with the broader vision, to stand at the busy crossroads of finance, HR, management, compliance, technology, and material production across a variety of more defined internal disciplines and ensure that they all come together in a work of art?

There is, and this role in each of those industries is called the *creative director*. Let's survey them briefly; we can learn something.

In Fashion

The creative director at a fashion house is the most senior creative role, and frequently the most critical role in the company. Houses rise and fall most because of their creative directors. At Prada, the creative director is Miuccia Prada who is also co-CEO. She took over her grandfather's company after being told that a woman could not run the business. When she took the reins, Prada was a $450,000 company;

today it is worth several billion dollars. Tom Ford was creative director at Gucci and Yves Saint Laurent before opening his own house (he is also an Academy Award–nominated film director, writer, and producer).

The job of the creative director is not to design the clothes themselves. Their job is to *create concepts*. These concepts will apply to the collection or the label as a whole. Their work consists of the following:

- Understanding what the market needs, and what customers want that they might not even know they want
- Determining what designs should be made within the constraints and the possibilities
- Expressing an overarching concept that allows many different local designs to support the innovation necessary to stay relevant, but also the consistency necessary to produce and distribute the realizations of the designs

In this sense, they are a meta-modeler. They make a design wherein designs can be made.

In Film

In film, the creative director might be the director or the production designer. They must do all of the following:

- Manage teams.
- Lead by influence.
- Bargain.
- Stick to a budget.
- Understand how the music, the characters, the dialog, and the edits and pacing all work together to tell the story to reveal to viewers what they need to know when so that they both understand what's happening and have enough mystery to figure out to keep watching.
- Design the props and settings and scenery and lights altogether to make a unifying concept.
- Express the unifying concept to the local designers responsible for each of those areas, such that they can in turn produce their own designs for their respective areas.
- Figure out with the team how to invent something familiar enough to be appealing to audiences and yet new enough to get them to buy a ticket.

The creative director is who gives a movie or a show its look and feel, its mood, its unification with the script, the actors, and the goals and constraints of the studio.

It is perhaps easy for the more scientifically minded of us to dismiss or deride artists as people who are disorganized or who do not understand the rigors of applied knowledge in business. Although software projects being late by months or a factor of two or three are the norm, when was the last time you heard of a play not opening on the advertised evening? Films do go over budget on occasion, but the director is responsible for assembling the creative team but also ensuring proper execution at every stage of preproduction, filming, and postproduction. In a sense, the making of a movie is similar to a software project. You have the script (the requirements), you storyboard in simple and cost-effective sketches before filming to allow everyone to envision how it will come together, and you manage all the people and places and things with a budget of a million dollars up to $200 million and more.

How Raiders of the Lost Ark Got Made

This tale is told in the 2017 HBO documentary *Spielberg*. An iconic movie of the 1980s was *Raiders of the Lost Ark*. George Lucas originally had brought the script idea to Spielberg, who was enthusiastic to direct the movie. But the script was rejected by every major studio in Hollywood. Eventually Paramount signed on, but the studio would not allow Spielberg to be associated with it, because although his prior movies such as *Jaws* and *Close Encounters of the Third Kind* were very well received, their productions had gone over budget by two and three times what the studio had signed up for. Lucas fought for his friend Spielberg to direct, arguing that he was the best person for the job. The studio finally agreed on one unwavering and practical condition: Spielberg would never be allowed to go a dime over their allowed budget of $20 million. He could hardly imagine making an epic movie of this scope on such a relatively modest budget. But he made the promise as well as many trade-offs and adjustments along the way in order to keep it. The movie was completed with Spielberg's newfound need to be disciplined and keep to his budget, which he did through a variety of practical measures: often films do 30 or 40 takes of a shot, but they could only afford three or four takes, so Spielberg storyboarded every scene of the movie, drawing them out with pencil and paper like cartoon strips before doing any shooting. When one of the actors became sick, someone on the crew would jump in and do the part to keep things on schedule (the movie was actually completed sooner than schedule).

The movie became wildly successful. The movie was entered into the Library of Congress for its historical and cultural significance, received eight Academy Award nominations (including Best Picture) and remains nearly 40 years later one of the highest-grossing films of all time.

The lesson for us is that $20 million is not that different than the budget of many software projects, and that creatives, like software folks, need to use their experience and ability to adjust to make something wonderful within the confines of a very real business setting. Storyboarding your concept helps you do that.

An important similarity here is that what the director must be good at is understanding the creative process of himself and the entire team, as well as practical matters of making an artistic product that must "work" within a business context.

In Video Games

The creative director is critical in the making of video games. This person, like Vitruvius' architect of old, must be skilled in many disciplines including art, graphics, illustration and fine art, math, physics, computer science, management collaboration and leadership, and outstanding ability in reading and writing. Their precise skills depend in part on who the person is, and what their own background and proclivities entail.

In Advertising

The creative director in advertising guides the entire creative department in selection of visuals, music, and themes for an engagement. They lead directly and by influence. They will often work with key clients as a project manager and lay out the entire chronological order of how a campaign and all its constituent elements across many media outlets will be arranged. They are charged with working for maximum impact, cost management, and efficiency, and must meet deadlines.

They might also perform copy writing and art direction and have a degree in journalism, psychology, media communications, film making or language arts, or, more rarely, business.

In advertising, creative directors are not uncommonly promoted to chief creative officer, and chairman of a firm.

In Theater

In the theater, this role is called the artistic director. This is the person with overarching control over the artistic vision of the organization, as well as choices of the plays to be produced and directorial choices. Their job in practical terms is to plan the season of what will be produced. They frequently speak to the press and represent the theater and often will engage in fundraising and meeting with prominent donors. They are frequently former directors and often apply support in the form of counseling and recruiting.

In ballet, they hire choreographers, and ensure proper training of the dancers. They are almost without exception former dancers.

In Technology

If you thought your job in technology was to be the creative director, what would you do differently?

You would not police the developers. You would create a context in which they can design well themselves.

You would not be overinvolved in metaphors about skyscrapers—things made of concrete and steel and intended to last many decades of being battered by physical elements. You would see that software has a shorter shelf life, and that you are not the designer of a building, but the designer of designs: you would make a factory not of software, but a factory for designers of software.

You would not create mere taxonomies and classifications, and become devoted to making hair-splitting distinctions between the role of the solution architect versus the software architect and the application architect. Each company is too different for these to have any traction or much applicability outside their own walls, and the employees within the walls too transient for anyone to care. Rather, you would be in the business of creating value for customers, like the plucky and resilient creatives: by any means necessary.

You would see, and embrace the fact, with joy, that software is a creative process and that there is no shame in that. You would look beyond the factories of the asphalt jungle and cannery row for inspiration, and turn to architectonics of music, games, and film.

If we were to learn from our esteemed leaders in the artistic community of filmmakers, dancers, video game creators, theatrical artists, fashion designers, and advertisers, we would have turned the dial a bit in our focus.

In such a configuration, the ~~architect~~ creative director in technology would be a role that is responsible for understanding and finding ways of applying these things in practical ways to create value for customers:

- How will people work together? What is the set of expectations across disciplines? What organizations are necessary, what roles and functions are needed? What training? How can we help recruit the best talent to reach our aims? What sense of collective culture and individual craftsmanship will obtain the best results?

- What processes will be employed? Processes are a system and can be designed with the same level of rigor and imagination that we use to design software systems. A set of repeatable practices are necessary; how can they be optimized for efficiency, impact, and delight?

- What tools will the people employ to best realize these practices with the least friction and waste? What attributes should any system have to ensure that functional and nonfunctional requirements can be readily met?

- What must systems adhere to in compliance and regulation? What balance of budget and timeline and quality should they demonstrate?

- How does your corporate and departmental strategy inform the way systems will be made? What internal projects, such as the moving of a datacenter or a pending merger/acquisition, inform system design across teams?

- How can you help your organization grow, scale, differentiate, and compete across these areas?

- How will you manage projects and design the implementation of projects for maximum efficiency?

- How will you collaborate with internal stakeholders in marketing, communications, product management, development, infrastructure, procurement, finance, HR, management, strategy, and executive leadership to create a unified vision and the organization that can realize it in a coherent, compelling way?

- How can you represent your organization in the press, in interviews, in speaking engagements, and in public writing to advance your organization's position as a thought leader? How can you attract and retain key customers and assist in marketing efforts?

This emergent role is a collaborator, a presenter, a leader across disciplines, who is able to assemble across disciplines and to synthesize across industries, including fields in philosophy, set theory, logic, history, cultural difference, religion, linguistics, math, physics, marketing, management, music, art, advertising, theater, systems engineering, writing, rhetoric, customer service, retailing, psychology, strategy, and computer science and its attendant history. This is not an entry-level role. You must first understand making, and have been a maker for a long time, of different kinds of systems, in different fields, with different organizations and among different cultures.

The creative director is in the business of making meta-models: the model of how models are made in your organization, taking all these disciplines into account to create that meta-model, the space in which other disciplines such as software developers can do their best work. This is the creative director. You are not creating the thing; you are creating the space in which everyone else can create their things.

Don't see yourself as making the architecture and design for one building, one piece of software. Rather, move up the value chain, and make the design of how designs are made. Lift your visor to take as your domain not only a software system, and not only a collection of software systems, but the design of people, process, and technology at your organization. This is what is needed now. But we do not need this old architect metaphor anymore. Creativity by definition can never become a commodity.

What's In a Name?

It is well understood that the architect's role is not particularly well understood. Despite this, we presume to attempt to be "effective" at our pursuit of the work. In so doing, I have suggested modifications and updating of the way we approach our work, and the scope and activities of the work we do to help our organizations.

In this book, we have taken issue with even the moniker "architect" as being an inappropriate metaphor for the work we do, the tools we have at our disposal, and the material we have as our subject. But just fighting with a name and replacing it with a different one would serve little important purpose.

Perhaps, given all the existing conferences and HR job descriptions, we must remain satisfied with calling ourselves "enterprise architects"? But there may be hope (to paraphrase Churchill) to shape this title, and thereafter the title will shape our work. Recall that "Scrum Master," a wildly outlandish title that comes from the game of rugby, didn't exist 20 years ago, and soon came to be considered *de rigeur* in any software organization.

But there is a job to do. Considering the multivariate functions we perform and the new ways this book suggests to help us be more effective and, well...perhaps another title is more appropriate now. Maybe chief semanticist.

Other names come to mind. The title *creative director* makes a certain wonderful sense. Of course people might think you're at a marketing agency or fashion house with that title. But then has there not been considerable clarification at cocktail parties as to whether you're an architect of buildings or of software; have you not even made the distinction to say "real architect" when referring to those who make buildings? I want to say "concepter," but it sounds a bit high-falutin'.

Or maybe *executive producer*. Consider for a moment the work of the theatrical *producer*, which has no obvious analog in business. This maps better to how we see the role. The Broadway producer has the following responsibilities:

- Assembling a compelling creative team
- Helping ensure that the right talent is available and managing the balance between star power and cost (note that in the theater, "talent" refers to the people onstage, whereas "creatives" refers specifically to the director, writer, and composer)
- Making the case to win the money from a variety of backers
- Finding the right space for the production
- Managing talent throughout the process

- Setting expectations for a wide variety of stakeholders, dealing with very concrete matters such as number of seats, marketing, and the contractural arragements for the size of the font for the star's name in relation to the title
- Setting parameters and providing creative input as the show is being developed
- Helping negotiate and manage contracts and meet competing requirements
- Pulling together the many disparate elements to create a financial and critical success
- Doing anything necessary to ensure that the show will go on

Perhaps *executive producer* is at least as good a metaphor for helping us think anew, think differently about our work so that we can be more effective. They are there to help conceive the show when it's just an inkling, and they see it all the way through writing, workshopping, rehearsals, and staging. They are the "quarterback" of the theatrical production. In successful projects, this is what this role is about: creating the concept, communicating it to others, ensuring that the implementation matches the concept, and ensuring its successful rollout. Then, someone else can take over.

As we further consider our better role, consider the following:

Perhaps we can do better by forgetting about the conceptual legacy of architecture. Or not forget it entirely, but take up what matters from the discipline, not get too caught up in the name, and step into our future.

Perhaps it is not so much a problem. Perhaps some titles no longer serve us. Do they hamper more radical thinking? There weren't always architects in technology. It is not *necessary*. No one knew they were supposed to have Scrum Masters until a little more than a decade ago. Things evolve as they must. It's time for something new.

Consider yourself, your own situation. How would your world change if you were the chief semanticist, the creative director, chief philosopher, or the executive producer of your organization? How dramatically would that change what we do, how we focus, how we advance our field? The signs, the language is real, and not only real, but *signs in a semantic field are our only material* and beget our systems and make us think and create differently.

The future of computing will not be programming. It will not involve human programmers writing code in syntax for static compilers.

The future of computing will be visual.

We have the nagging need to show up at our work tomorrow and do something we hope could be called valuable, perhaps even important, innovative, or beautiful. We hope to act beyond the haunting chains of our inherited language and thereby our inherited identity, to learn the lessons of our failures, to make something creative, something meaningful, something that's useful and capable of creating wonder and perhaps even joy. Something new. Something *better*.

Are you ready?

What will it be?

CHAPTER 11

Management, Governance, Operations

After you have done all this wonderful work as we've discussed throughout this book, you must continue to manage it through to success and operationalize it. If you don't, your work runs tremendous risk of collecting dust somewhere in the shadowy recesses of the wiki where no person ever visits.

So, this chapter offers a set of practical tools and templates to help you govern and manage your portfolio. It's not intended as a definitive guide exactly, though you can use it that way. These tools and practices can help you improve the management, governance, and operations of the product development organization.

Strategy and Tooling

You must ensure that your concept aligns with the business vision. The best way to help connect those dots is to read this book's companion volume, *Technology Strategy Patterns*. All too frequently I see architects and even CTOs who consider themselves as a kind of lead programmer. They are incredibly interested in the bleeding edge tool of the day. You can identify these people because they proudly and vocally will argue at lunch or over beers from a fervent viewpoint on the comparative merits of some particular JavaScript framework versus another.

We're not interested in arguing over JavaScript frameworks. They don't matter.

Raise your visor, think strategically, focus on getting the concept right, and you will have the best chance to define and create something maintainable, extensible, evolutionary, maybe even interesting, innovative, and groundbreaking.

Work at the level of the idea, the concept, and be ruthlessly pragmatic and detailed in your analysis. Argue the concept, the view of the world you are representing. This is where all the difference is made in a successful project versus an unsuccessful one, a costly and late one versus an efficient and on-time one.

Let the programmers pick their tools. They'll be eager to become concept designers as soon as they realize how little difference is made between Ember and Angular.

There are only a few reasons that you want to weigh in on the tool selection:

- You have done homework the developers haven't and have good reason to believe that one tool is more generally popular and therefore might be easier to hire for and will have better chances of living a longer life.

- You're clear (without irrational bias) that a particular tool fits the concept well—for example, a graph database.

- You're clear that a particular tool offers more portability and extensibility over another candidate tool.

- The tool represents a major new shift in direction or a wholly new kind of technology for your organization. If your organization has never done blockchain and has decided to go down that path, you need to do the homework yourself, read as much as you can, install what you can, and work with them a bit and create a comparative rubric with data to illustrate the thought behind your recommendation.

These things do matter, and should be squarely within your purview. Otherwise, tool arguments are nothing but minor border skirmishes, posing, and religious battles.

ThoughtWorks Radar

You can also use the neat ThoughtWorks Technology Radar (*https://www.thoughtworks.com/radar*) to assist in your research.

The fact that one language has duck typing and another doesn't is interesting and quite important to a lot of people, typically those who might be designing languages or compilers and the like. To be clear, that is a fascinating and wonderful discussion to have, and any intellectual pursuit will only help you and your colleagues. I am only saying to not invoke minor technical differences in one framework or language and think you're doing effective architecture. That's all an important conversation, just not for us, not for these purposes.

One thing I do recommend is to study tools and processes from outside your industry. For example, if you work on business application software, look outside your domain and examine the software used by DJs, screenwriters, or composers for example. Consider the software tools you use every day that are outside your domain, whether these are ecommerce sites, social media sites, audio books, your car interface, and more. What can you learn from them and apply back to your domain? What can you learn from a MasterClass (*https://www.masterclass.com/*) in chess, poker, cooking, or directing? You and your users will be richly rewarded.

Oblique Strategies

A common human trait is confirmation bias. We tend to quickly interpret new evidence, whatever it might be, as confirming the status quo or supporting our existing views. This is an efficient and important trait in navigating the world. We can't look at every stop signal and wonder afresh what red might mean in this context, just because we've entered a new intersection. But such habits leak out into our thinking and shut it down. This is harmful for us as designers. It curtails, hampers, and dilutes our thinking until our conclusions are so pat and obvious that we are not prepared to make something new or exciting. It's painful and awkward to challenge our own thinking. But that act of challenging might in fact be the only thing that can even be called "thinking." Because we are creatures of habit, we must find ways to challenge ourselves in order to innovate.

One fun easy way I have found to help with this a little bit is called *Oblique Strategies* (*https://en.wikipedia.org/wiki/Oblique_Strategies*). These are a deck of cards, invented in the 1970s by musician Brian Eno and Peter Schmidt. Each card contains a short maxim, suggestion, or remark that can be used to break a deadlock or dilemma you might be having.

The strategies include directives such as these:

- Do something boring.
- Make a sudden, unpredictable, destructive action; incorporate.
- Emphasize differences.
- Work at a different speed.
- Only one element of each kind.
- Would anybody want it?

Picking one of these and using it as a heuristic or a lens through which to view the current aspect of your project can be very illuminating and get you out of a creative jam.

 Fun Fact

In 1996, the illustrious computing pioneer Peter Norton persuaded Brian Eno to allow him to produce a deck of the cards for distribution to his friends and colleagues.

Here's one way to use them. Each morning, visit the free Oblique Strategies website (*http://stoney.sb.org/eno/oblique.html*). Or, if you really like it, you can buy a deck of cards with the strategies on them. Pull a new card and read the strategy, and consider it like a little mentoring guide for your work that day. You can pick one and then state it to the team in your daily standup, or mail them to the team. I've used this practice and although it's by nature impossible to measure the specific impact this has had on the designs, the teams seemed to enjoy it, and I'm sure it caused a few actions or decisions to be reconsidered.

Use Oblique Strategies to challenge your own conventional or default view. You're activating the synapses of critical thinking and imagination, and that will only help your concepting.

Lateral Thinking and Working with Concepts

You can also take the simple approach we discussed in the Oblique Strategies pattern and extend and deepen it using a technique called *lateral thinking*. Lateral thinking as an approach to creative thinking and creative problem solving was invented by Edward de Bono in the late 1960s. Dr. de Bono's PhD was in philosophy and he authored more than 70 books.

Lateral thinking is concerned with using an indirect, creative approach to problem solving. To do so, you use certain specific techniques to incorporate nonobvious methods of reasoning that help you arrive at conclusions that you might not otherwise get to using linear traditional logic. It's about how you can search for alternatives without using standard patterns. Traditional logic is concerned with determination of truth value of a given proposition. Lateral thinking, on the other hand, is more concerned with the slippage, reversals, or movement of terms in statements and ideas. As such, it is an important tool for us as semantic designers.

de Bono defines four types of *thinking* tools to solve problems in an unconventional or indirect manner:

- Idea-generating tools, intended to break thinking patterns that are traditional, routine, or simply represent the status quo
- Focus tools, intended to broaden the horizon as you search for new ideas
- Harvest tools, intended to ensure more value is received from idea generating output
- Treatment tools, intended to prompt consideration of real-world constraints, resources, and support

Dr. de Bono compares traditional vertical thinking with lateral thinking, which we present in Table 11-1.

Table 11-1. Traditional vertical versus lateral thinking

Vertical thinking	Lateral thinking
Selective	Generative
Moves only if there is a direction to move in	Moves in order to generate a direction
Analytical	Provocative
Sequential	Makes jumps
Must be correct at every step	Not required to be correct at every step
Use the negative to block certain pathways	There are no negatives
Concentrate to exclude what is irrelevant	Welcome chance intrusions
Assigns fixed categories, classifications, labels	Labels are not fixed
Follows the most likely Happy Paths	Explores the least likely
Finite process	Probabilistic process

You can see how well lateral thinking fits into a deconstructive designer's mindset and work in concepting. The more you design your software in this way, the better it will be.

This is a field of considerable study as well as controversy. But we should illuminate a few of the major tools here that you can incorporate into your concept work:

Challenge idea tool

We often ask the question "why?" to solve a current problem, and this begets Fish Bone Diagrams and root-cause analysis exercises. However, it's interesting to ask "why?" about something that is not an apparent problem, but a typical state of affairs. To ask why in a nonthreatening way about a current state of affairs or the way something is done can help us innovate and remove headaches and inefficiencies. You can apply it to processes, organizational culture, toolsets, and anything really. For example, in the United States, many states use Daylight Savings Time and roll their clocks forward and back one hour each year. We just do it, and that's the way it is. By asking "why?" and realizing that the original purpose was to support our agricultural society, which is no longer agricultural, we might stop doing that. Similarly, we might ask why certain conventions are in place for the treatment or expectations of children. It is perhaps shocking to learn that childhood has not always existed, and had to be invented. It is a social construction and not at all "necessary" or even a candidate for the realm of something "true." In fact the idea of "childhood" has only been with us about 250 years.

Reversal method

A swimmer swimming a lap in a pool will, as soon as they reach the opposite side, kick hard against the wall upon turning around, to move quickly in the opposite direction. Whenever a direction is indicated, an equal and opposite direction is also indicated. If you start in New York and move toward Paris, you're moving away from Los Angeles. If a person is supposed to obey the government, reverse the relationship and ask what the world would look like if the government had to obey a person or people. Embrace this opposite idea and consider the ramifications in order to put together a new idea. You purposefully and provocatively turn the status quo inside out, upside down, or around to see the world anew.

Provocation

A provocation is a statement that we know is wrong or impossible but is used to create new ideas. This helps you deliberately leave the mainstream in your thinking. Negate what you take for granted about a topic. That negation is your provocation. In *Serious Creativity*, de Bono gives an example of considering how to handle river pollution. He creates the provocation "the factory is downstream of itself"; this leads to the idea of forcing a factory to take its water input from a point downstream of its output, an idea which later became law in some countries. Other kinds of provocation include wishful thinking ("wouldn't it be nice if..."), exaggeration (if there is a quantity in your statement, wildly exaggerate it bigger or smaller), reversal (make an opposite statement), escape, and distortion.

Consider the *movement* in your idea. How can you use a provocation to advance a new idea?

Extract a principle

From this circumstance, provocation, suggestion, or implementation detail, can you define the broader principle that would lead to it? To what seemingly unrelated point can you apply this principle? First try to extract a principle. Then, discard the provocation and work with the concept with the new principle at work.

Random inputs

To escape the mainstream, randomize input that has nothing to do with the topic under discussion into your process and work with it. You start with the focus on your topic at hand. Introduce a random, irrelevant word and then list associations with that word. For each association, use it as a metaphor or descriptor for an idea that might then be related to your original topic and help illuminate an innovative solution or perspective.

Focus on the difference

Highlight and explore the points of difference between the provocation and your idea.

Moment to moment

Imagine or simulate what would happen, what would have to be true, to implement the provocation as is.

Positive aspects

Are there any direct benefits or positive outcomes of the provocation itself? Examine each benefit and see if it could be achieved by practical means.

Special circumstances

Explore for a moment if there are some special circumstances where your provocation might have some immediate use.

Related to the idea of lateral thinking is another book by de Bono's called *Six Thinking Hats*. Published in 1985, this book and its techniques were focused on business managers. In the 2000s, it found popularity in the UK government to help spur innovation.

The six hats outlines an exercise that you can do with your team:

White Hat

Concerned with data, definitions, facts, figures; neutral and objective

Red Hat

Intuition, feeling, emotion

Black Hat

Logical, careful and cautious, the "devil's advocate"

Yellow Hat

Sunny and positive, finds reasons something will work

Green Hat

Growth, creativity, new alternatives, provocations

Blue Hat

Cool, the color of the sky, the meta-hat, organizing, looking at the process

The idea is that these six forces impinge on our thinking and can scramble it. If we instead do a bit of role playing and actively represent the different positions embodied by each hat, we can be clearer in our thinking.

We can't cover everything about the six hats and lateral thinking presented in de Bono's work, but I do encourage you to check out his books *Lateral Thinking* and *Six Thinking Hats* to learn more about these techniques if you're interested. I hope you are interested, because lateral thinking represents an excellent way to work with concepts in a challenging, creative manner that will result in your best designs and products.

Conceptual Tests

It would be nice if all of the data which sociologists require could be enumerated because then we could run them through IBM machines and draw charts as the economists do. However, not everything that can be counted counts, and not everything that counts can be counted.

—William Bruce Cameron, *Informal Sociology*

The cost of finding bugs goes up exponentially for every later stage in which it's found. The sooner you find bugs, the quicker and cheaper it is to fix them. There's actually a lot of math done around this, in a famous National Institute of Standards and Technology (NIST) paper that reveals how these costs multiply, as shown in Table 11-2.

Table 11-2. Cost multiples at each stage of finding bugs

Requirements gathering & analysis/architectural design	Coding/unit test	Integration & component/system test	Early customer feedback/ beta test programs	Post-product release
1X	5X	10X	15X	30X

In the paper, which is actually more than 300 pages long, the authors demonstrate considerable and complex math and justifications to substantiate these numbers.

NIST Report on Software Testing

The NIST paper is an oldie but a goodie. Check out the NIST report (*http://bit.ly/2kTnQSC*) on the costs of software testing.

As round and neat as the numbers look, the cost increases are real.

The Concept Is the Thing

Table 11-2 reinforces the central thesis of this book: many problems in software and software projects are caused because we as designers have not understood that our primary job is to create a sound and accurate representation of the world, which is our concept, and that our software will be better all around if we make that our object.

The earliest you can find a bug in the software is before there is any software, in the analysis and design phase. The time you spend on the design will literally pay off later in a reduced number of bugs and reduced cost of fixing each bug. The time you spend making sure your concept is well designed and properly advanced will do wonders for creating high-quality code.

Your job as a ~~architect~~ designer who creates and communicates concepts concerns the following:

- Test whether your concept is *internally consistent*. Your design *is* your concept. Your concept is an argument (*https://www.iep.utm.edu/argument/*) for a certain representation of the world. You are making claims about how the world itself is, how it works, its causations, relations, attributes, meanings, implications, and boundaries. Some of it is a reflection of the existing world, and some of it might be a wholly invented world. But just as in science fiction or fantasy, even invented worlds are only components of what exists in the actual world. And they must have internally consistent rules. Even in a space fantasy such as *Star Wars*, nothing exists or happens that does not have some relation to the actual real world. And The Force might be invented, but its implementations must be consistent with the rules established when it was set up and presented to the audience.

- Test whether your concept is *valid (https://www.iep.utm.edu/val-snd/)*. Your concept is an argument which, like all arguments, consists of a collection of statements. The argument is valid if every comprising internal statement is valid. A statement is valid if it takes a form such that if its premises are true, it is impossible to have a false conclusion.

- Test whether your concept is *sound*. The argument your concept represents is sound if all its propositions are valid *and* all the premises are actually true.

- Perform the deconstruction on your concept.

- Test and challenge your concept using the techniques of lateral thinking, as we have seen.

- Ensure that its arrangements have lightness yet sturdiness, beauty yet fitness to purpose, integrity yet openness, harmony yet challenge, movement yet quietness.

- Test whether it is rhizomatic instead of arborescent: consider tagging, flatness, and contexts-in-relation, as opposed to rigid categories, hierarchies, and concrete entities-in-themselves.

To do these things, you can use the ideas and practical techniques discussed throughout this book. In the end, the test is about thinking through it yourself and talking with other smart people through these various lenses.

You must test your concept early, often, and vigorously. This need diminishes somewhat over time. Make sure that it is internally consistent, that all the components are named properly, and that you have made an accurate and true and rich representation of the actual world, and you will have made the biggest impact you can make on the quality of your software in the near and long term.

Code Reviews

I often see code reviews used to police programmers on compliance matters. Code reviews are important, but the code reviewer should not be forced to become the QA department or test compliance with convention guides.

Instead, your code reviews should be about encouraging and deepening your concept, broadening its understanding and application. Code reviews should support the development of the coder through sharing, mentoring, recommendations to best practices resources, and mapping to principles to reinforce them. They help you develop a better bench. You are reducing single points of knowledge across your organization if you can make them a positive and participative experience. You are helping to refactor the design.

The purpose of code reviews is not to put people in their place or to overindulge in nit-picking minutiae. They should elevate, not diminish, the programmer.

As the chief semanticist, designer, or concepter on the technical staff, you should be at least occasionally reviewing the implementation to ensure that your design is being realized properly.

First, be sure your concept is well tested as discussed in the previous section. After code starts hitting the repository, here are a few pointers or guidelines to help you determine the code review process that's right for you:

- Hopefully your team uses a version control system like Git and a tool like Bit-Bucket, which makes it very easy to for you to view commits and diffs on pull requests, make comments, and treat it as a bit of a conversation. The code can't be committed until approved by reviewers. This is typically a very good thing. Reviewers must respond quickly to pull requests.

- Encourage developers to notice, use, and take action on the refactorings and recommendations in their IDEs. For example, Eclipse, JetBrains' IntelliJ Idea, and Microsoft Visual Studio all have capabilities of reading source code and making recommendations. Your developers are doing it wrong if you're using code reviews to catch possible null pointer exceptions. Use tools for that job and elevate the nature of the code review.

- Use a continuous inspection tool such as SonarQube (*https://www.sonar qube.org/*) to improve code quality. It will detect bugs, vulnerabilities, and red flags in the code construction. Have developers run this before pull requests so that your code reviews can be more robust and interesting.

- Review a small batch at a time. If you're presented with 20 files to review, you will skim and hit only the obvious things. Maybe three classes or a few hundred lines of code is best.

- Make two checklists. There will be things that your developers' IDEs should just capture. You might be able to tune it to insert your rules to capture low-hanging fruit, using something like Appraise (*https://github.com/google/git-appraise-eclipse*). The second checklist should be things that your developers will commonly violate that the IDE can't capture as easily. I find these are things like uncommented or poorly commented code, exception handling, proper "discoverable" logging, avoidance of null pointer exceptions, improper use of enums, and so on. These are common things that act as a preliminary review for the developer, to save everyone the brain damage of repeating the same low-level observations at every review.

The manner in which you conduct code reviews should improve your culture. They should encourage transparency, interest in having the best idea win instead of your own idea, conversations about quality so that it stays top of mind, and a brave and open invitation to scrutiny in our work. Code reviews reduce your "truck factor," so even if you haven't gone as far as pair programming, you still will get more people with more familiarity with the broader code base.

Of course, if you're designing the next space shuttle, print out every line of code and review the minutiae in a locked room for weeks before allowing anyone to do anything. For all the rest of us, make it a fun, collaborative learning and team-building experience.

Demos

If a developer on a typical Scrum team finishes his first story in a sprint, he might then wait for a week or 10 days before getting to demo it. Why wait so long to demo code?

As an alternative, when code is done, invite the team to demo it later that day or the next. This aligns your development in an event-driven way, when your story is done. Don't wait until the end of the sprint if you use those (though Kanban is more consistent). I have used this in the past in a Kanban-like style, and the teams loved it. The sense of progress, competition, drive to complete work, and frequent little public celebrations all conspire to generate a palpable sense of energy, movement, and camaraderie. You can make a party of it. Send an email when a story is done and let everyone gather at the end of the day in a room used for this purpose, put it on a video for the distributed team members, and demo the story. It's fantastic!

The Operational Scorecard

As deconstructionist designers, we see the whole as well as the parts, and we understand that it's not only software that are our design candidates. You probably have, or should have, monthly operational meetings. These typically are boring reviews of dead history that cause participants, who are generally forced to be there, to disengage. This in turn makes the meeting worse.

What you want to do instead is design this meeting. As we always do, we begin with one of our key questions: *who it is for and what do they want or need to know to make a decision or do something differently?*

You can elevate your organization by encouraging your executives and peers to design their meetings. Everything is a potential object of design. And when you take the holistic view, every constituent part becomes improved. As designers, architects, executives, leaders in the business, we will spend a nontrivial portion of the time reviewing performance against our key metrics across the business. That performance will include people, process, and technology and product views. The goal is to understand performance trends, discuss issues we need to address, and get quick updates on improvement efforts underway that will affect our performance. In your operational meeting, the expectation is that each functional leader will speak to his or her metrics, with questions, issues, suggestions, or concerns being discussed with the broader team.

The goal of the meeting should be:

- Give you and all participants a comprehensive view of the actual progress, the important elements that will give us confidence about how we're actually doing for our customers.

- Give you a seamless transition to subsequent reporting out to senior executives; the data should cover similar items to minimize repetitive busywork.

- Make a template that is repeatable and easy for your team to update each month.

I urge you to create an operational scorecard template that you can use in the operational meeting. Each meeting simply provides a forum for leaders in each area to present the current state of their organization through this lens.

Your scorecard might include the following as a sample from which you can create a template to share with the leaders to fill out each month in preparation for this meeting:

Roadblocks
Just like in a standup, what remains in your way that might need visibility or executive action?

Risks/mitigations
What problems do you anticipate becoming roadblocks next, and what are you doing to mitigate these?

Major misses

What did we recently mess up? Including this and covering it in a way that is nonjudgmental can help engender transparency and improved collaboration, and makes sure that any relationships that need to be smoothed over are repaired.

Major accomplishments

Who is due some recognition from the leadership team? What went right that we can replicate?

Contracts/budgets

Any deals that need legal or executive review? What seems stuck in procurement or finance or HR or otherwise needs pushing?

"10X" initiatives

What are you doing to "10x" your performance, to compete with the very best in the world at what you do? How are you driving your team to go above and beyond mere maintenance, the status quo? Instead of just doing our daily jobs, how is your team working to take a big step forward across People/Process/Technology to be the very best in the industry?

Critical skill gaps

For People, what technologies or soft skills do you see that your leaders need to focus on?

MBO/OKR/goal tracking

How is the team progressing against stated goals at the organizational level? Whether you use Management by Business Objective, Objectives and Key Results (OKRs), or any other framework, how close is your team to completing what the leadership team expects?

For each major product by area

State the availability/uptime since last reporting period. How many Sev-1 and Sev-2 production defects does the code base have? Measure mean time to recovery (MTTR) and show that on a graph: we will have failures, the point is to work toward improving how quickly things get noticed, identified, and resolved so that customers are back up.

Cloud spend

What is the Amazon Web Services (AWS) monthly spend (incorporate the reports from CloudHealth, for example, gained through your cloud provider)? What are the recorded security defects reported for each major product as reported by OWASP/Veracode scans? How aligned is the product with the overall enterprise architecture/design and strategy?

For each major initiative

How is your team progressing on an initiative that is not simply specific product creation or maintenance? These might include a modernization effort, cloud migration, database migration effort, datacenter move, disaster recovery (DR) overhaul, a process reengineering effort, and so forth. Report on these right alongside products so that they are measured and visible, too. These might need a different kind of summary with success metrics specifically tailored for each initiative given that they are not product based.

Then, to ensure that you're taking the comprehensive view and including People as well as Process and Technology, review these items as well:

- Current headcount FTE/contractors
- Current recruiting efforts (number of open positions, offers out, new hires/ conversions)
- Terminations/people on Performance Improvement Plans

In your monthly operational review meeting, instead of just having vice presidents attend, you might also consider including folks one level down (the senior directors or directors). This then helps you to build your executive bench. It acts as a kind of training ground for them so that they see what executive meetings are about, how they are run, what the expectations are, and what the conversations are like, and generally helps bring them into the fold for developing their careers. This alone can be a really good motivator. It has the benefit to you as a leader of helping create context, so that you can be more comfortable and confident pushing decisions down to them. With the understanding they've gained attending this meeting, they'll be better equipped to make decisions that are in alignment with your overall strategy.

The Service-Oriented Organization

In this section, we tackle the exciting subject of effective organization design. To do so, we look through two lenses: Conway's Law and software design principles.

We introduced Conway's Law earlier in the book. It's the idea that software designs are copies of the communication structures in an organization. This is often interpreted as a warning that if your organization has lots of committees and lack of clear roles in decision making, you won't have high cohesion in the software created by the teams in that organization. But we can look at it from the other direction and use this to our advantage as we design our organizational structure. Imagine and refine the set of services you think best define your future state platform. This will include some services as they are now, and some that might not exist yet but represent the direction in which your business is evolving.

To begin, be sure you have a diagram or sketch outlining the set of services your platform provides, grouped together by domain. Consider the following as you sketch this catalog:

- Find a level of abstraction that's right for *several groupings*. You don't want too few or too many groupings within your domain. Fewer than three or four is maybe not granular enough, and more than seven or eight is maybe getting too complicated and thus too difficult to track, manage, and govern. There is no "right" number, but this will rather depend on the size of your company or business unit and where you are in your life cycle.

- The catalog should be *balanced* so that one grouping is not responsible for 85% of the critical services in the catalog, whereas the others are left anemic with a few random stragglers.

- Consider the items that tend to *change at the same time*. Group services together that tend to change together. For instance, you probably don't typically need to change the Profile service when you need to make changes to the Shopping service. But you might need product-related services or distribution-related services to change with them. The point here is to not settle into what seems a "logical" grouping, but rather to consider the efficiency gains you will have if you can limit the number of people helping make a particular decision, attending the meetings, or weighing in on emails.

- Consider *process divisions*, such as supply chain, offer management, order management, and fulfillment. Viewing your service catalog groupings through this lens will give you another perspective to consider.

- Consider the specific *customer segments* you have. Who are the primary customers or users of your services and applications? This will allow you to line up your portfolio in lanes along with your different customers. Serving a B2B customer is different than B2C; serving an enterprise-sized customer is different than an SMB, and so forth.

- Consider the future *strategic direction* versus the current leaders and what sets of services and applications they own. There might be some left over arrangements from various leaders coming and going that don't make sense any more. The leaders will be the champions (or detractors) of the required change management to make your service-oriented organization successful. If the people involved do not all have something interesting and important to do while overseeing their domain, they won't be on board. This is an important element to keep in mind. Sometimes the organization will need a tweak here and there, and sometimes a major overhaul.

Essentially, you are starting with the aforementioned lenses to look at your organizational catalog, and you'll find the one that alights the best path. By viewing the potential groupings through these different perspectives, you will ultimately arrive at the most effective service catalog groupings to which you can make your future state organizational recommendation. Then, you can socialize this with leaders and work to make the organizational changes accordingly.

As you consider together your service catalog and how you organize it, and how you propose an organization to best support its efficient operation, we can see it as a system. As a system, we can look to the standard tenets of good object-oriented (OO) design to consider how these ideas, usually intended for the realm of software, can also help inspire the design of a great people organization. After all, it's a system, too. Here are the SOLID principles of OO design:

Single responsibility

Things should have one and only one reason to change. Teams should be organized around the services they offer and are accountable for. Minimize the number of people on the email, at the meeting, and on a call to move more nimbly.

Open-closed

Things should be open for extension, but closed for modification. Therefore, teams should be flexible enough to move where the business heats up. But the teams must be cross-functional enough to have all the expertise they need internally to complete their work. This requires some common technology across teams so that new members can get up to speed quickly. It also means that you don't modify the teams frequently, moving members around and expecting that developers are somehow the commodity equivalent of interchangeable blade servers. Get the right mix of seniority and expertise on cross-functional teams and then don't mess with their members very often; let them go through their inevitable Storming/Forming/Norming/Performing phases.

Liskov Substitution Principle

Objects of a derived class should always be substitutable for a parent class. What this means to us is that you need to build your bench so that others can step in for you. If you have a conflict, you want to be sure your team can speak for you with the same message, the same emphasis, and the same principles. This means that as a leader (whether it's with direct reports or dotted lines as you lead by influence), leaders must build their bench and spend time mentoring others and illustrating the vision, regularly preparing others to step into their place and lead the customer engagement or design meeting without them and still feel confident that it will be done properly.

Interface segregation

A client should never be forced to implement an interface that it doesn't use. When teams do not create their own interfaces and define the proper way to engage them and the set of inputs and outputs that they generate, it can be awful working with them. To be respectful of other teams, define clearly how they engage you, when they engage you, for what purpose, how long they'll wait, how they can get permissions or exceptions, and so forth. When teams do not do this, they need to be managed by the team that is depending on them; typically this means engaging with several different members and trying to coordinate them from the outside. It's just crazy-making. Ideally you would set this up like a version of your own Unix "man" pages within your architecture department first. Do this as practice with your own department, and learn how it feels to create the proper documents to set expectations and then to socialize them. Then branch out to make a recommendation for how others can do this using scalable business machines (which we discuss shortly).

Dependency Inversion Principle

Things must depend on abstractions, not on concretions. The high-level module must not depend on the low-level module. Therefore, hide your organization behind a clear strong interface and contract. Have defined inputs and outputs and do not require other teams to get into your internal business or manage/corral your organization to get their work done.

Now that you have considered your organization through all of the principles and lenses, there is a practical matter. You're ready to draw up your service-oriented organization in an image. Each organization might look like what is shown in Figure 11-1.

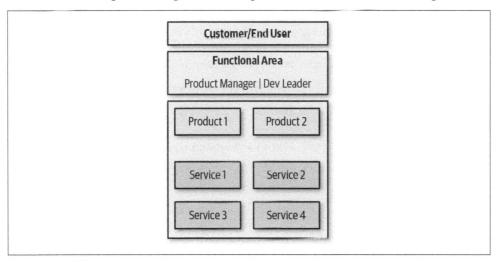

Figure 11-1. The structure of your service-oriented organization representation

Do this for each organization (each VP, probably). You start with the customer, enter the organization at the point of the product VP for that area, and fan into product development VP and assigned architect. These are the named buddies that will work together most closely. They control the portfolio of applications as well as the portfolio of services to govern within their subdomain.

Cross-Functional Teams

Within each of these subdomains, it can really work to your advantage to form your teams with dedicated, full-stack developers on cross-functional teams if you can swing it.

The talent on each team should include people with knowledge of the following:

- Business domain knowledge
- Systems design
- UI/UX
- API design and service creation
- Familiarity with and interest in the overall strategy
- Testing
- Automation
- Data
- Infrastructure, networking, your datacenters

As you populate teams, minimize any cross-team dependencies that threaten the accountability of the outcome. It's important to persist these teams, keeping them consistent. Don't frequently swap members from one team to another. They need to go through the "storming/forming/norming/performing" phases. Meddling managers often rob teams of their productivity by moving members around.

With such teams, I have found that you will get more natural leadership, accountability, sense of shared success, free collaboration, curiosity, shared understanding, and habitual reevaluation of quality.

Each cross-functional team works within a single domain. The architects and project managers coordinate across the teams when a complex multi-domain solution is required. This is shown in Figure 11-2.

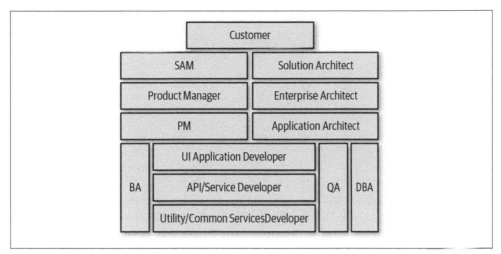

Figure 11-2. The cross-functional team composition

Within a single domain that corresponds to a named set of salable products, your cross-functional teams should have this composition, or some close approximation. If you do, you will get the most velocity and productivity, the most team accountability and happiness, the best overall throughput for product development, and the most efficient and clear management mechanics. You will get to take best advantage of things like all the pipelines you're building, reusable libraries, and services and practices like DevOps.

It's on purpose that I don't specifically call out "DevOps" developer or something like that here. Although you can (and should, at least for a while) have named developers doing the pipeline and automation work, they're still developers. Recall that in Agile there is only the role of "developer."

The Designed Scalable Business Machine

A *scalable business machine* (SBM) is a representation of the inputs that come into your organization, the outputs you produce, and the principles that underpin the internal processes by which you create those outputs for use by others. The purpose of an SBM is to define your work in a clear process to help set expectations for other organizations with which you work. In a sense, you are defining the interface, the API, for other departments to work with you. It's important for us to do this because we so often float between product management, strategy, and product development. Defining your own SBM will help you move from the potentially murky realm of adviser into a more clearly effective participatory role, and help make your entire organization more performant and responsive to customers.

The SBM consists of a few main parts:

- Principles
- Inputs
- Processes
- Outputs
- Tools

Principles are propositions that serve as foundational statements for a system of beliefs. Explicitly stating the principles that you want to see enacted in terms of people, process, and technology can help your entire organization be more effective, especially as you undertake large-scale modernization efforts. To create your own set of principles, refer to "Principles" on page 73 to get some ideas.

Inputs are the raw materials that come into your team. These are the conversations, ideas, documents, and external parameters you use to build your solutions. You don't define or control them yourself. You might get them directly from customers, the product management team, the strategy team, executives, or a central compliance group.

Processes are the defined activities that you undertake to convert the raw material of inputs into the new, useful outputs. These should be internal to your own team and can be treated like a "black box." They are the engine working behind your API.

Tools are any helping software programs or other concrete means that you use to produce your concepts and documents.

Outputs are the result of mixing the inputs with your own internal processes using your tools. The outputs should be of clear use to a clear set of customers. Consider who cannot make a good decision or take their next action without having some declaration or direction from you. Then think of how you can formalize that and turn it into a template your team can repeatedly use. Identify what deliverables and metrics matter to the customer. Define metrics incentives internally to drive toward great customer outcomes.

Figure 11-3 shows a sample template that you can use to define your own SBM.

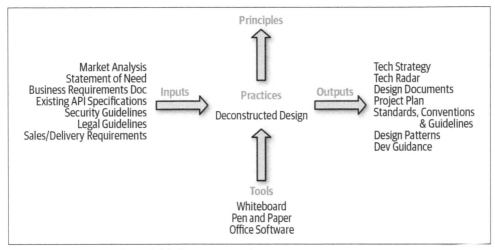

Figure 11-3. A sample scalable business machine

The principles are not listed on the template, but they could be. Here are some examples of principles that you might adopt and adapt:

- Primacy of principles.
- Solutions must first comply with laws, regulations, and standards.
- Nonfunctional requirements must be considered on equal footing alongside functional requirements.
- Data is an asset, shared, and accessible, and requires stewardship.
- Solutions must be service oriented, and designed in accordance with the service design framework.
- Development work must be aligned with the stated architectural strategy.
- Solutions must be globally deployable.
- Solutions must be cloud native or cloud ready.
- The organizational structure must be aligned with system governance.

The goal of creating an SBM is to maximize efficiency, maximize speed to market, scale the business better, delight customers, win back customer trust, increase employee engagement, and so forth. These are the typical goals of any business. Orient your SBM around these goals depending on your current needs.

This book's companion volume, *Technology Strategy Patterns*, elaborates on the idea of the SBM more thoroughly. I encourage you to do this for your own architecture-design department. You will likely have different principles, tools, and inputs, and that's a good thing. Introduce the SBM idea to your team and have a workshop to construct your own diagram. This will help you to create a contract-oriented interface with other organizations and set expectations properly.

If the effort proves effective for your own department, I encourage you to lead similar workshops for other departments in your organization. Of course, if you decide to do that, you must first get the understanding and approval of the senior leader in that area, and work with that person.

Managing Modernization as a Program

There are large initiatives that architects might be invited to participate in or assigned to run. The effective enterprise architect will not try to execute these from the bottom up, or as small, local, individual, unrelated projects. Instead, view them as a holistic program that requires management from a senior program manager, as shown in Table 11-3. You can apply a mindset here to "think globally, act locally."

Table 11-3. Managing modernization as a program

Program management plan	Description
Detailed work plan	All milestones, deliverables, tasks, and subtasks in a work breakdown structure. Start and finish dates, dependencies, critical paths, resources.
Staffing and resource plan	Organizational structure, communication, retention strategies. Roles and responsibilities.
Risk management	Conduct pre-mortems. Develop checklists to monitor, identify, analyze, and remediate risks.
Quality management plan	Establish a consistent method for automation and standards, service-level agreements, and quality level.
Configuration management	Describes the approach for identifying and controlling project configurability in source and deliverables.
Change management	Defines and develops sign-off on architectural changes, resource changes, and goal and scope changes. Records changes in a log, ensures proper approvals according to impact to stakeholders.
Issue management	Identifies prioritizes, assigns, monitors, remediates, closes issues in a RAID.
Time and schedule management	Approach, control, and change thresholds to manage project schedule.
Communications management	Policies, values, practices. Include a communication plan with all contact information and communication trigger events.

Writing the code is maybe 15% of a software project, and less if the project is a digital transformation effort. They are change management efforts. Because this is one of the top three reasons that projects fail, we address it in our method.

As an architect or systems designer, you are not likely to be expected to be in charge of these areas. But you can have a tremendous impact on the overall success of the program. Seeing your large-scale effort as requiring true program management and change management is essential to its overall success. If your PMO is mature, well-staffed, and powerful, architecture might be more on the production and participation end of such programmatic management. Either way, you can play a central role in helping to bring these proper activities, business guardrails, and processes to the fore. As a deconstructive designer, your comprehensive view of the semantic field that includes promulgating the need for these activities, and for properly representing your team's perspective in these areas, will help to make your programs a success.

Change Management

Change management is the active, programmatic management and leadership of an organization through some large change. Is your organization going through any of the following efforts?

- Large digital transformation programs
- Modernization programs
- Service portfolio management efforts
- Mission-critical systems overhaul
- Datacenter migrations
- The creation of a platform
- Mergers and acquisitions
- Organizational restructuring
- Large-scale business process reengineering

Any of these should be considered change-management efforts. They will result in the redefinition and reallocation of funds and other resources, changing processes, retraining, and more. They will create the need for considerable communication and nurturing of the staff and other stakeholders throughout the process. They will need programmatic oversight and architectural involvement.

Typically, an executive will be the sponsor for such efforts and appoint a leader to act as the named accountable party. As an architect, this might be you. Even if a different leader is accountable, architecture will likely be a responsible or recommending party for one or more of the activities in the overall change-management effort. The effective enterprise architect can serve as the locus of many interrelated activities across a variety of departments, helping guide the effort to success.

Figure 11-4 presents my change management framework, which you can use or adapt for your own needs.

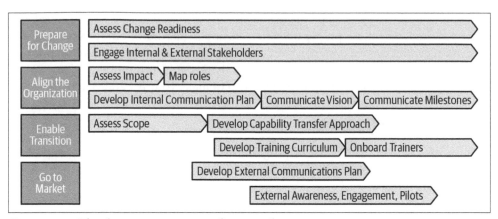

Figure 11-4. The change management framework

Depending on the nature of the change management program, you might have more or less need for each of these activities.

Don't Forget the Culture

Peter Drucker, the father of modern management methods, famously stated, "culture eats strategy for breakfast." Check out this article (*http://bit.ly/2kJxbMT*) for a good reminder on how to ensure that you are considering and actively supporting the cultural forces at work in any change-management program.

Analogous to these four phases of change management illustrated in Figure 11-4 are four phases of a project or development method. Whatever your software development methodology is, you will go through the following phases:

Define
Create the vision, goals, parameters, and definition of successful completion for the effort.

Design
Create a set of concepts from which you derive systems: new business processes, new data flows, new software, new infrastructure.

Develop
Do the work to realize the designed system.

Deliver
Complete the transfer of the work product to the customer.

If you follow more of a waterfall process, these phases can be very sharply delineated with phase gates. If you follow more of a Scrum or Kanban method, they might be more iterative or less formally defined. But you'll still touch on each of these concerns for at least some time. The point is to be consciously aware of them and define the expectations for your stakeholders. Moreover, it will help us to remember the many diverse stakeholders in a program and recognize their different needs and plan accordingly. Helping to set good expectations is one of the best ways for you to help your organization overall.

Figure 11-5 illustrates the activities and documents you generate in each of these phases. As an effective enterprise architect, you can help to guide the product management, program management, legal, HR, development, and other teams through these steps as necessary.

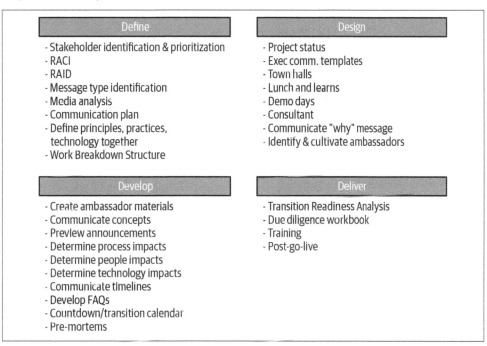

Figure 11-5. The change management activities in each phase

Change management is a huge field of study on its own. Your company might employ legions of Deloitte or Accenture consultants for millions of dollars to help define and lead these efforts. For the rest of us, the framework provided here should give you a good starting point, set of reminders, checklist suggestions, and other tools that you can adopt and adapt for your own needs.

Governance

To advance your service catalog with clarity, purpose, and alignment with the overall vision, create a governance committee. Its working members should include architects/designers and development leaders.

Goals

Like your design principles, clearly state the goals of your governance board. These might be sample goals for the governance committee:

- Reduce training time
- Improve consistency and best practices across the service catalog
- Improve technical documentation
- Limit risk for the team
- Save time in supporting consuming teams to get economies of scale; reduce pressure on one central team
- Reduce time for rolling deployments
- Reduce time for testing
- Reduce time and risk of rollback
- Help go to cloud
- Improved quality because of focus and hardening

Again, this is just a sample, and you should make your own. Keep in mind fixing broken things, avoiding problems, and taking advantage of opportunities.

Don't do much else until you and the executive sponsor can agree on the goals.

Metrics

After you have your goals, define the metrics. People often do this last. But it's like setting acceptance criteria for the governance board: if you know how success will be measured, you will make a better board more efficiently.

These are some examples your might consider tracking:

- Deployment time
- Availability
- Stability including number and duration of Sev-0, Sev-1
- What is the maturity model?

- Capture the number of internal and external clients consuming them to illustrate service reuse.
- Adoption percentage: total number of consumers out of the total number of clients expected.
- How much did we save/cost avoidance because we reused this?
- Number of services total
- How fast are we growing in TPS?
- What is the total cost to operate each service?
  - VM initial cost and cost to maintain * number of servers
  - How much disk space does the database consume?
  - Network
- Metrics that illustrate success for each service

Service Portfolio

One of the goals of governance is to improve the understanding of your portfolio so that you can manage your business better. Be sure that your governance regime is focused on more efficiency and better support for product teams, customers, and business outcomes.

The activities of the committee might include some of these:

- Evangelize the platform and service orientation
- Teach the organization services best practices
- Create a service cookbook for the organization to use
  - Define standards (say, for event headers)
  - Define patterns to reuse
- Create a service design review checklist
- Define your design review process
- Define your code review process

Help with some of these items is covered in this book.

Service Inventory and Metadata

Defining the semiotic signs and their interplay and relations is, in my view, critical because it's the structure of the semantic field of your software application. Naming things properly is one of the most important things you can do. But I'm not a big fan of the kind of architects that nerdily classify services for hours on end, debating whether this is a "business service" or not. These folks are bureaucrats but don't even know it. They aren't innovating, and they aren't creating value, as Peter Drucker said. Architecture cannot be a Drucker Support function. That's what it becomes when you classify all day.

However, there is some use value in terms of understanding what you have, why you have it, and where in its life cycle it is, as part of an active governance regime:

- Clearly define the life cycle stages of services.
- Maintain the service registry with each listing its name, purpose, life cycle stage, version, owner, deployed location, code location, and so forth.
- What is the protocol and data format of each?
- What events do they produce?
- What security (auth/auth) mechanism is required?
- What is the capacity (ceiling) for transactions per second of each?
- Document the set of known workflows and consumers of each service.
- What is the roadmap of features per service?

Answering these will help you to make good decisions, understand the impacts and complexity, set proper expectations with product management, and manage timelines well.

You have to, as always, ask yourself: if I do this work, produce this result, who is able to make a particular decision or go do the thing they couldn't do before? If the answer is "no one" or you don't know, stop doing that thing. There's no value.

These questions are probably difficult to answer. They would be hard to even find an answer to with some effort; you'd need to have load tested and stress tested every service to be able to answer that question. The point is that what gets measured and managed gets done. If you govern your services with this as a guide, you will be in far better shape than most organizations. Part of the idea is that it forces you to get better practices in place if you're going to be able to answer these questions.

Schedule a monthly meeting or whatever cadence makes sense for your stage for the governance committee to meet. Include not only architects, but software development directors, product managers, and project managers. Understand whether you will report out externally, such as to the sales team or leaders because there's something of value to them, or if you will use the meeting for your own internal management. Either way's fine; just decide consciously which one you're doing.

But at that meeting you'll need a document to review. Can you put all of this on a KPI Dashboard? Make something fancy in D3 that jumps. Or just use a spreadsheet.

In addition to the working members, expect that there are other stakeholders who will want to be kept apprised of the progress of the service portfolio. These might include executives, sales and account management, and parallel organizations such as labs or other business units, UX teams, and others. For them, have the governance program manager send an update on the catalog.

Service Design Checklist

Your governance should exist as a structured organizational body. This is a cross-functional committee of architect/designers, development leaders, and product leaders who can work at a high level with a view across the entire portfolio of services. This ensures that overall what your teams are developing is actually accruing toward the vision for your platform or general product strategy.

But you must also have a practical means of checking the work at the local level. As each individual service is developed, you want to make sure they are developed in accordance with the many nonfunctional requirements that operate alongside the functional requirements. For this purpose, it's helpful to have a checklist that ensures proper service design.

Automate Me!

If you can, automate the things on this list to the extent possible. It's far more efficient to have them actually checked by tools if you can. This will depend on your working environment, so I present them as a list here, hopefully to help serve as an automation requirements document for some of the items, as applicable.

Here is a sample list that you can adopt and modify for your own purposes.

Service Design

1. Describe the concept of this service. What are the abstractions you employ?

2. Where have you embraced the complexity of the abstractions and their relations in order to make it simpler for the end user? Where are the semantic boundaries, the points at which your service is no longer representing the semantics explicitly and the implicit ideas begin?

3. What is the general category of this service?

    a. Stateful business process (employee onboarding, return merchandise)

    b. Business entity (nouns such as employee, customer)

    c. Business functions (verbs for atomic actions in a process such as shopping or booking); these can also be Event Handlers

d. Utility (perform a non-domain-specific application-agnostic function such as notifications)

   e. Security service (handle identity, authorization, privacy)

4. If this is a new version of an existing service, have you tested directly for backward compatibility issues according to major/minor versioning guidelines?

5. Illustrate how you started with the client/customer goal. How simply is that fulfilled from their perspective?

6. How have you accounted for this service in terms of the platform-wide capability it represents? How is it reusable in other contexts? Trace the assumptions made in the semantics: what is the assumed client context?

7. Where are the tightest couplings with other services or systems? Are manager/orchestration services used to invoke other services such that dependencies are at the proper level?

8. In what other systems can this service potentially be reused? Beyond the current demand, what else might this service enable or support?

9. What patterns from your service design patterns catalog have been employed?

10. Have you followed relevant organizational implementation standards (coding conventions)?

11. How have you accounted for internationalization? How will your service support localization (e.g., return different data based on geographic location, formatting concerns for currency, language, and other items)?

12. What protocols and message formats does your service support? Why were those selected? What basic message exchange patterns are used for this service?

13. How is user configurability supported? Does the service make use of or allow for user preferences (e.g., number of results returned)?

14. How does the design support an event-driven approach?

15. What are the binary oppositional structures in the semantics (primary/secondary, main/ancillary)? How have those been flattened?

Service Operations

1. Does the service support purely stateless connections (unless it is a business process service)? Can the binary artifacts be easily horizontally scaled, such as in an autoscaling group?

2. Do service operation definitions support typical variations in the domain?

3. Have you avoided any messages, operations, or logic that are consumer specific?

4. Are all operations capable of being executed independently without necessarily relying on any previous invocation of another operation? Is HATEOAS (or at least the ideas behind it) achievable?

5. Are data operations (as applicable) idempotent?

6. Does the service offer a variety of operations for retrieving minimal, most common, and full datasets? How is data filtering and pagination supported to balance user needs and pressure on the network and database?

7. Does the service use only standard logging facilities and approved log rotation strategy?

Business Processes

1. What named business processes (order-to-cash, account management, etc.) use this service?

2. What business rules have been identified that can be extracted to a business rules management system or external rules engine?

3. Does the service reference any business rules that might feature thresholds or other items that could be configured by a business user? How is extensibility specifically accounted for?

4. What specific customer-oriented KPIs have been identified for the service?

Data

1. Describe how this service accesses data, what data it accesses, and where.

2. Are transactions required? How does the design handle transactions? Has compensation been considered as an alternative?

3. Describe how this service fully encapsulates its data. If it cannot at this point, what is the transition plan for doing so?

4. How does the service perform validation on incoming data? How does the service respond to invalid inbound data?

5. How does the service account for data quality?

6. Have you externalized all strings used in labels, buttons, notifications, and so forth?

7. Has the user interface been designed and tested in accordance with ADA (Americans with Disabilities Act) guidance?

Errors

1. Does the service use only standard message return codes and user-friendly descriptions?

2. What runtime exceptions are likely to be generated from the service? When consumers receive runtime exceptions, what opportunities for compensation or next steps do you offer?

3. Are exceptions logged specifically for surfacing in Splunk, AppDynamics, or other instrumentation agents?

Performance

1. What is the measured latency of service response in testing?

2. What SLAs have been defined for this service? What mechanisms are in place to prevent SLA violations? What mechanisms are in place to report SLA violations?

3. What steps in an orchestration can you design to be executed in parallel and joined later?

4. How does the design encourage asynchronous invocation through events or pub/sub?

5. Does your design allow for clients to select variations on an operation based on their context? For example, can you offer both doXandWait(m) : Response and a doXLater(m) : Void operation options?

6. Are the operations designed at various levels of appropriate granularity so that they are not prone to network chattiness and do not return data clients are not likely to need?

7. How does the design delineate between operations that must be performed quickly and operations that are long running?

8. What is your caching strategy behind the service implementation? Can known consumers easily cache data in front of the service? How will this be managed (eviction policy, invalidation, etc.)?

9. Do your services exchange binary data? How is that encoded and stored?

10. Has edge caching been employed?

Security

1. Does the service require authentication? Authorization? Single sign-on? Are these implemented according to the internal standard tool?

---

2. What other regulatory constraints (PCI, GDPR, Sarbanes-Oxley, SOC 2, etc.) might affect this service contract or deployment? How have those been directly accounted for in the design?

3. Are logs free from PCI or PII information? Do you have masking and scrubbing in place?

4. What are any additional security requirements for this service? How are they fulfilled?

5. How does your service specifically accommodate auditing?

6. Has Veracode or another security service scanned the code base to ensure a passing score against OWASP issues?

7. If this service is public facing, have you run penetration tests?

Quality Assurance

1. Is the unit test coverage at the set threshold according to a coverage tool such as Cobertura or SonarQube?

2. Are all unit tests independently executable?

3. Were test cases created for every user function? Did the tests use a variety of data inputs (valid, invalid, null, many different combinations of length and character)?

4. Were test cases created for all exception conditions and the "Unhappy Path"?

5. Are the unit tests in version control and versioned in clear correspondence with the service so that the environment can be entirely reproduced?

6. What functional tests were written if a consumer is available?

7. How was the service load tested? What metrics were recorded? Are they run regularly to inspect the trends?

8. Are integration tests run regularly?

9. If the service uses asynchronous pub/sub or fire-and-forget operations, were these tested by subscription?

Availability and Support

1. What are the availability requirements? How will these be met? What is the business impact (in revenue and other measures) if the service is down for 1 minute? 5 minutes? 30 minutes? 1 hour? 4 hours?

2. How will availability be measured (see the previous details)?

3. Have you employed a circuit breaker or Resilience4j kind of mechanism to prevent catastrophic or cascading failures?

4. How will the production support team receive messages or alerts regarding the current state or health of the service?

5. How will runtime issues with the service be addressed organizationally? Has an on-call schedule been established?

6. Is the service instrumented to natively surface metrics in an independent manner through tools such as JMX, DataDog, SNMP, and so forth? Have you measured and recorded the execution time of all key services? Have you done the same for unhandled exceptions, trace data for response codes?

7. Does the service require planned downtime for maintenance? How much time, and how often? What work do you expect to be done during this time? What design would allow you to avoid this?

8. How have you involved the infrastructure operations team in the creation and design of this service?

9. What is the plan for future maintenance of the service after it is successfully deployed?

Deployment

1. Have you made a simple deployment diagram so that upstream and downstream dependencies are understood?

2. Can you move the same binary artifact through multiple environments because you have externalized necessary variables?

3. Can you deploy with the "push of a single button" in an automated process, such as through Jenkins or similar tool?

4. What services if any in the existing catalog can be retired or sunsetted after this service is deployed?

Documentation

1. Have you captured the design in the Service Template?

2. Have you followed relevant guidelines for code-level documentation?

3. Have all test execution results been recorded and posted (such as through the wiki or a generated Maven website)

4. Have you completed necessary go-live documentation, technical readiness, operational review documents, attestation on compliance, and so forth?

Your list might (and likely should) vary. But the idea is to inspire you to have a checklist like this, and to create the appropriate one for your teams' needs. Require your developers to go through it before making pull requests. In a larger, more formal organization, you might have them prepare documentation attesting to how these concerns are specifically addressed in their services.

To help ensure this is happening, you can make it part of your governance process. A good way to catch things early on is to have the analysts add it to the Acceptance Criteria of your user stories. Then, in the sprint review or event-driven demos, developers can illustrate how they've accommodated this guidance.

Further Reading on Organizational Design

- Aronowitz, Steven, et al. "Getting organizational redesign right" (*https://mck.co/2lUnXxx*), *McKinsey Quarterly* (June 2015).
- Davis, Stanley M. and Paul R. Lawrence. "Problems of Matrix Organizations" (*http://bit.ly/2lYbPvh*), *Harvard Business Review* (May 1978).
- Henshall, Adam. "How 4 Top Startups are Reinventing Organizational Structure" (*http://bit.ly/2kQm4Sb*), Process Street.
- Morgan, Jacob. "The 5 Types Of Organizational Structures: Part 1, The Hierarchy" (*http://bit.ly/2kR6WnC*), Forbes.com.
- Neilson, Gary L., et al. "10 Principles of Organization Design" (*http://bit.ly/2lUBZzc*), *strategy + business* (Summer 2015).
- Peters, Tom. "Beyond the matrix organization" (*https://mck.co/2mpmXBP*), *McKinsey Quarterly* (September 1979).
- Sisney, Lex. "Rethinking Product Management: How to Get from Start-up to Scale-up" (*http://bit.ly/2lVAgcU*), Organizational Physics.
- Sisney, Lex. "Predictable Revenue: How to Structure the Customer Success Role" (*http://bit.ly/2kI2vLZ*), Organizational Physics.
- Stuckenbruck, Linn C. "The matrix organization" (*http://bit.ly/2moBeP2*), *Project Management Quarterly* (September 1979).
- Tollman, Peter, et al. "A New Approach to Organization Design" (*https://on.bcg.com/2krreny*), BCG.
- Whalley, Brian. "SaaS Company Structure: Learning From 13 More Companies" (*http://bit.ly/2mlxg9L*), InsightSquared.

CHAPTER 12

The Semantic Design Manifesto

Should I, after tea and cakes and ices / Have the strength to force the moment to its crisis?
—TS Eliot, "The Lovesong of J. Alfred Prufrock"

We have come to the end that is hopefully a beginning.

What here are we proclaiming? A definitive answer? No. A different path forward?
Yes.

Proclamations of that order seem to require a manifesto.

The Manifesto

Any manifesto will reject the supposed values, claims, methods, and models of the
past, proposing to replace them with new ones. An exciting age of expansion and
prosperity is heralded, but only for the true-believing radicals who can see the
promise of the proposed One True Light and Way. Astonishing advances have been
made in the reach and power of software in the past 50 years. So we do not wish to
trumpet quite such claims, which doubtless will ultimately prove facile and reduce to
a fascism of the mind.

But perhaps something has occurred in the history of software that could be called
the architecture of our concept of software itself. Within this field of signs, directives,
meanings, and metaphors, we shape our words, and thereafter our words shape us.

Our practices have countless times failed to achieve our aims. This is obvious in our
collective landscape, littered with growing project failures. Seven out of ten software
projects fail by not meeting budget, timeline, or feature requirements. More than
eight out of ten big data projects fail. One in six software projects fail so spectacularly
that they threaten the very existence of the company. Project failures abound, costing
three times, ten times, twenty times as much as proposed; they take longer, do less,

and if they don't destroy the company, they leave unhappy customers and unhappy makers. Projects churn, with large portions thrown away and redone. And the problem has grown worse over the past twenty years, not better.

Received architecture frameworks, Zachmann, TOGAF, DODAF have not saved us in this, having done more to relegate architects to the Ivory Tower of Irrelevance than to realize the promise of project success.

Agile in its merriment has not saved us in this. But its religion has had a (possibly purposeful) side effect of relegating architecture as something unnecessary, or as a facet of the hated enemy other-method, Waterfall.

We see a major contributing factor as a failure of comprehension of the complexities and contradictions in the world. The world is an infinite conjunct of propositions and their predicates. Software and systems design demands we bound a context, to represent our ideas in the system, translating them to instructions. When these concepts and our language falter, we wait, as one waits for Godot, forever, for the "requirements."

There are no requirements. There is only fecund imagination, and the subsequent work of reduction into rigorous concepts. Rigor here does not mean rigid: quite the opposite. Any further conceptual demarcation in the system's design and naming that fails to embrace context, complexity, contradiction, and change will act as the kernel of its eventual upset, across many possible vectors.

We identify this is a key contributor to our history of failure. And this is what we here address.

We can do better.

How?

With X.

We call this method, this conceptual model for design "semantic software design," "deconstructive design," an "Architecture X."

Why "Architecture X"? "X" is provisional, temporary. X refers to the horizontal axis, the flatness of the extending horizon on which rhizomes work, rather than falsely hierarchical Y-based systems; it is used to represent the in-between of time. "x" in the art and fashion worlds is used to signify a collaboration between two or more artists, as in "Jane x Jill"; in other fields, "x" is the unknown value, which we embrace in seeing that our software is a representation of a concept of the world—our work suffers when we disavow its complexities and paradoxes, as by extension software presents the world view of its designers. "x" in mathematics represents the independent variables—they are the inputs or causes; that is, potential reasons for variation, which can confound the system. "x" is one sign we use for the multiplying operator—x is generative and fecund, not reductive; x is a kiss. X marks the spot. X crosses boundaries of disciplines, and its cultural allure alights in cross-pollination.

Yet, and "so," X is not X. Because X represents, in one usage, the unknown, we might easily replace the term "Architecture X." We can be united in our ideals, but recognize a panoply of names, each foregrounding some different facets, each true and useful; we might here be doing "Generative Architecture" or "Oblique Architecture" following Brian Eno, "Active Architecture," "Dadaist"—provocative against the architecture of the day. Or the X is for "x-perimental." Or rather it is a "deconstructed" architecture following Derrida, a "thousand plateaus" following Deleuze. So we emerge from Architecture X into Semantic Software Design.

Because it is in fact no architecture at all, precisely not architecture. There are no architects in fashion houses, but rather designers. Is it so different? Music has composers. Is this more estranged from our work than making a concrete building in legally demarcated physical space? We are precisely semanticists, whose only tools are language and logic. We have no material but these, and imagination, creativity. Our work is in producing, challenging, and inhabiting the semantic field we demarcate to produce a properly structured concept of our software. This is the piece that's missing from our failures.

We assert: an image of thought called architecture has been formed historically, and even though we don't agree on job descriptions and practices, this effectively stops people from thinking. The X architect must *create*. We reject architecture as categorizing and classifying. No one with a P&L has any use for such endless classification of the animals. This is not Ivory Tower architecture: quite the contrary—Semantic Design, Deconstructive Design, X Architecture is street-fighting architecture, firmly rooted and working in the gritty, real world of customer demands, annual budget cycles, arbitrary strategies, mergers and acquisitions, our own independent flights into the unknown.

We recognize that that real world is richly complex, abounding with contradiction and deferral, and if we refuse or ignore or are blind to that, we will continue to make weak systems and fill them with accidental complexity later, making them very expensive and difficult to maintain. So we embrace the tools of deconstruction. Software is, to paraphrase Samuel Beckett, not about something—it *is* something. The code represents the design; the code is not the product. The code is a design factory, which emits into production only once invoked. So our work is further complicated in that the design is the primary object of our design. Recognizing this double action is critical. Recognizing that our true materials for construction are semantics is critical.

What you are creating is not architecture, not anything like a single building that won't be changed over decades and hundreds of years: very far from. You are designing the concept. You design the design in semantic space.

So Architecture X is not *architecture*. We use the term "architecture" here *under erasure*. As X Architects, X Designers, Concepters, we not only read but hear, and hear "*Ex*-Architects," and we do not in fact practice architecture at all. We practice semantics and design ("of signs"). We leave architecture as a metaphor, adopted decades ago at a conference in Germany in 1968, as one proposed option among many, to help find a language to talk about how to talk about how to talk in software. Perhaps it has served us to some extent: one needs to put a stake in the ground. But we assert, no longer. "Architecture" itself is not what we do, but there our job titles sit in fields in the totalitarian wisdom of HR databases. Yet it is a metaphor that, like all language, can't help but generate ancillary metaphors, like "blueprint" and "plumbing," which lead us further away from our efficacy.

X Architects/Semantic Designers see that our language prescribes a space, demarcates our words and as such our thoughts and expressions of our work. As such, we recognize across the spectra of writing and speech the sound quality that presents us: *ex*-architects. We abandon this metaphor while we recognize its pervasiveness, and deconstruct it from within, in search of a better model for our work.

Our work, hardly fully captured by the term "architect," is making software, designing software, designing whole systems, designing data models and infrastructure and datacenters and managing teams and projects, thinking, mentoring, researching, changing the structure of organizations, recommending, coding, reviewing, deciding what and how and when and why and writing, presenting; we are the philosophers of the organization, its fools, in the classical sense: we advise the king. We support mergers and acquisitions. We make broad strategies and tactical fixes. We debug, we curate. We arrange the semiotics of what names and labels and words mean what in relation to each other. We *design*. "De" = "of" + sign. Design = "of the sign." Comprehensively, not merely software, but across all these vectors. So *little* of the work of making software has anything to do with the coding.

And we design from nothing, no cloth, no marble—nothing but our concept. There is no ground we are given as in other fields. We *invite* our constraints like few others. Our design subject is *systems*, of all kinds—systems of thought, organizations, datacenters, and software. And the work we apply to them is design work. We have forgotten how to think and lost our words. We mustn't, because a key job is naming the things in the semantic space: the infinite Turing tape of propositions and their predicates.

But it is frivolous and impotent to merely replace one word with another and keep doing the same things. We care less for the worry over the word as the concern to shift our focus, to rethink what our work actually *is*, to improve the outcome. "Scrum Master" is a metaphor borrowed from the game of rugby—what in the world has that to do with software development? Yet fresh-out-of-college HR recruiters happily repeat it, echoing the phrase into the internet as if it were a thing. As indeed it is. So it does happen.

X Architecture, X Design, this notion of not-architecture but *concepting*, is a recognition of the world as an infinite conjunct of propositions, and that systems require demarcating a semantic field in a way that paradoxes take hold at the boundaries, and these hurt the unprepared system. We take a holistic view, expanding the work of designer: everything in the organization, the software, the data, the infrastructure, is a design candidate, and structures are riddled with binary oppositions, each featuring a privileged term, creating hierarchies, which create semantic glitches that we tend to gloss over, but which the software cannot. It is this that ultimately undermines the software in inadequacy or complication. We therefore deconstruct such structural binary oppositions, foreground the idea of the concept to be designed, and invite a collage of other lenses from other fields, to make better software.

The Four Ideals

We design software with these basic *ideals*:

- Our work is to *design concepts*, before designing software, rather than classify in taxonomies and falsely overlay simplicity in a single frozen layered picture. The concept is of the system.

- Our view is *comprehensive*: the organization, the project, the integrations, the documentation, the conversation, the data, the infrastructure, the metrics, as well as the software applications are systems as objects of design. We recognize the impossibility of this, as we work beyond monoliths, or any totalitarian idea of completeness and stability.

- Our mode is *de-centered, deconstructed*: it embraces imagination, diversity, context, complexity, contradiction, and change. Meaning in the system is not rigid, but deconstructed; it is generative. Requirements change and overlap in gaps of incompleteness and contradiction, so we embrace uncertainty and design for it. We employ lateral thinking, rhizomatic root systems over arborescent hierarchies, rather than thinking in traditional structures, in binary oppositions, and hierarchies of technology versus business; this ensures our concepts can continue to create themselves and to change in evolution: they are autonomous, learning, unfolding, multiplicative modes.

- Our focus is on *diverse customers*: we are highly focused on outcomes, the "difference that makes a difference" to customers, the result, over the process, over our own activity. We recognize the diversity of voices in the many "users" of the system, and make our systems accessible, foregrounding our algorithmic and design bias so we can subvert it.

The Key Practices

We follow these *practices* that are consistent with our ideals. Some are new, some are old, some gain power by their inclusion and juxtaposition here.

Concept design practices

- You focus on the concept: what is the world you are making that creates a context for the design that becomes the production factory?

- How do you invite, not reject constraints, to find grounding? How specific can you be while still saying only true things in all the names throughout the design?

- How can you invite nonbuilding metaphors to help you as a bricolage?

- You are engaging and alighting the curiosity and intellect and cross-pollinating vectors of thought in your *team*. You are encouraging and nurturing their thinking processes. That is the first element. Not to dictate and prescribe, but to inspire and alight according to the principles of X.

- Use Design Thinking when thinking about what to make.

- Use lateral thinking when thinking about how to implement it. This is about solving problems using an indirect and creative approach via reasoning that is not immediately obvious. It involves ideas that may not be obtainable using only traditional step-by-step logic. Lateral thinking is more concerned with the "movement value" of statements and ideas. Edward de Bono defines four types of thinking tools: 1) idea-generating tools intended to break current thinking patterns—routine patterns, the status quo; 2) focus tools intended to broaden where to search for new ideas; 3) harvest tools intended to ensure more value is received from idea generating output; and 4) treatment tools that promote consideration of real-world constraints, resources, and support.

- Use Strategic ideas, as in *Technology Strategy Patterns*, to ensure your concept aligns with the business vision: raise your visor and innovate at this level of the idea. We're not interested in arguing over frameworks. They don't matter.

- Use Oblique Strategies to challenge your own conventional or default view. Pick one in the standup each day, or send them to the team. You're activating critical and lateral thinking and imagination.

- Use deconstruction: look at the multiplicity of structures that start to arise in the system, find the binary oppositions that support those structures (Master/Slave, Center/Margin, Speech/Writing, Production/Development—development is production to the developers, Functional/nonfunctional Requirements), determine which of the terms is the privileged one, and show how the traces undermine that privileging. Then design something without marginalizing one of the terms.

- We do DevOps, as it is a deconstruction of that historical binary opposition.

- The system has many small pieces, with high cohesion following the Single Responsibility Principle.

- Keep a design scrapbook or lookbook as they are called in fashion houses. You will need a multiplicity of views and perspectives represented in different formats for varying time horizons, executives, customers, and developers.

- We do not freeze in time, which has perpetually frustrated software designers. Instead we admit that this never works, and instead foreground *Becoming*. What we design is not the system as is, but a process of change, flight, or movement within an assemblage. As Deleuze and Guattari explain:

  > The process of "becoming-" is not one of imitation or analogy, it is *generative* of a new way of being that is a function of influences rather than resemblances. The process is one of removing the element from its original functions and bringing about new ones. Hans is also taken up in an assemblage: his mother's bed, the paternal element, the house, the cafe across the street, the nearby warehouse, the street, the right to go out onto the street, the winning of this right, the pride of winning it, but also the dangers of winning it, the fall, shame…. These are not phantasies or subjective reveries: it is not a question of imitating a horse, "playing" horse, identifying with one, or even experiencing feelings of pity or sympathy. Neither does it have to do with an objective analogy between assemblages. The question is whether Little Hans can endow his own elements with the relations of movement and rest."

For architects, this means we resist the demands to freeze things in time. Things are not themselves: they are only ever *becoming-things*. So we design for *movement*, design for becoming, not now-ness, not false decideability and stasis. We know that we don't know the most important things, how it will be used, and we design an empty center to hold that not-knowing up front, on purpose, with care: this makes us foreground pluggability throughout the system.

Comprehensive view practices

- There is only one substance. Therefore everything which exists must be considered on the same plane, the same level, and analyzed by way of their relations, rather than by the "essence" of the "entity", as if it exists in a vacuum: that false assumption damages our designs. Despite its name, Relational Data Models privilege the essence, and relegate the relation to a second-class citizen. Deconstruction *loves* the relation, and see things not in an special essence, but in their relations of differences. We find ways in the design to foreground the relations and the differences.

- Graph databases are therefore an excellent tool, as are pub/sub, eventing streams that turn the database inside out, and modeling services as *contextual* agents, not essences. That is, we don't design the One True "Profile" service to rule them all. We instead abstract up and design the Persona service, wherein the single person with one tax ID has many different relevant modes of being in the world, and designing for that multiplicity aggregates nuances that improve the richness of the system.

- The elements of the architecture (business, application, data, infrastructure, as well as their representations) are not viewed as separate but in a unity, altogether, and their impact and forcefulness and intensities on each other are examined and considered and designed for.

- Make design decisions in empathetic thought of customer personas in different extremes, both valid.

- Design with the entire picture in mind: business, application, data, and infrastructure as systems. When designing, think of the monitoring as you implement an algorithm; consider the business implications of infrastructure choices; and consider the changing requirements when locking down a data modeling.

- We recognize our duty and responsibility and joy to design all the things, not just focus on the software: when subsystems are in harmony with each other and the broader concept, the product will be optimal across many concerns (-ilities, project concerns). Design the software together with the business design and the infrastructure and data design.

- The making of the software is one small piece of the puzzle; overindexing on software and thinking it will run separately when magical fairies whisk it away to the cloud is a recipe for failure.

- In considering infrastructure, we design pipelines.

- We radically automate the testing: we never manually test, but have test automation engineers. The tests are not ancillary to code: they are code, and are first-class citizens.

- Write automation tests against the infrastructure, too.

- Design in *extremes* such that if you are plotting out this event type, get two different points of view and put one stake in the ground and then a second one on a different extreme (how does ecommerce work for a sleep room, how does it work for a coffee mug).

- Code reviews are not about today's code and policing programming but about *encouraging the concept* and broadening its understanding and application. It is about mentoring, sharing, mapping to the principles and not scrutinizing junior developers but more like pair programming so others learn it and make less SPOKs and learn the principles and refactor the design.

- We do Pair Architecting: share a screen and review the design together, in a plain text file to get the words right. You're agreeing on metaphors that carve our semantic space and it should be MECE.

- Radical *immutability* in the architecture whereas the artifact that is built and deployed is totally immutable. Focusing on making things immutable every-where possible is the key to allowing movement and change and mutability, which is the hallmark of a manageable, monitorable, extensible, cost-effective system

- Write a Design Definition Document that compiles the views across business, application, software, and infrastructure stakes. This might be called a Petits Recits.

- Why wait for a week to demo code? When code is done, invite the team to demo it immediately, or in a very short amount of time, in an event-driven way, when your story is done—don't wait until the end of the sprint if you use those (though Kanban is more consistent). Make a party of it.

Decentered, deconstruction practices

- Defer the implementation: do not write precisely the requirements as given. First create a context in which those imagined requirements could come to life; then implement them as merely what happens to be the first known requirements (not even the "default"—that's always a false privileging). See what you're doing now, abstract up to the category, and make that first as the context, then implement whatever the stated requirement is, knowing it will change. Give names that recognize this.

- Design machine learning capabilities *throughout* the system. This is generative architecture, active design: embrace that. Yes, make your machine learning for customer product recommendations, but also for data clean up and rogue monitoring. Design learning into the system to make it truly organic. This suggests making feedback loops and machine learning pipelines. You don't decide the implementation up front even necessarily: let the system pick based on what it learns. You're recommending products to your customers without being asked: your system can, in an adversarial manner, learn, pick a champion, and deploy it in an ultra-dynamic manner. The radical pluggability supports this idea. You are designing the system that can do better, move, grow. We don't make frozen pictures of software or frozen software.

- Do not design with hierarchies or enums in the data model. These will almost always be proven to be false deconstructed in the world, so your software must reflect more *fluidity*.

- Assume your component will eventually be Decorated or have a Strategy injected. Instead of directly implementing any business logic, write it as the presumed first Strategy implementation.

- Prefer peer-to-peer protocols and systems without Master/Slave, such as Cassandra.

- Interfaces over inheritance.

- Do multivariate testing, canary deploys, multivariate deploys.

- Do not privilege production over staging: have a multiplicity of stagings, and automate learning which ones work best. Why have *one* production? Have many running at once. Use multi-armed bandits to explore and exploit. The world of X production is richly multidimensional.

- Do automation at the beginning of the project, not at the end.

- Define metrics at the beginning of the project, not at the end. Code toward success metrics.

- Break production on purpose: run Chaos Monkey to ensure you're breaking production. This makes your services more resilient.

- Design and use pipelines for Continuous Integration and Continuous Deployment. Design them up front, when your software is just Hello World, not at the end. This way you test them throughout the project. They are software, too. Make pipelines for your database (FlywayDB). Make a machine learning Pipeline for Continuous Learning.

- We know that we don't know, so we design for change, not fake frozen pictures, we design it to be *pluggable*.

- Design the *configuration* first, not last as we typically do, when things are most rigid: consider how this will be changed and design it for that change, not for fixing on arbitrary and changing requirements.

- Don't treat exceptions as exceptions (ancillaries, losers in the binary opposition) but rather as one of the valid paths requests will take through the system in its cyclomatic complexity. This will make your services more robust and resilient. You'll design Dead Letter Offices, consider retries and compensations and useful messages to quickly improve, and narrow your design appropriately. Accept exceptions, and invite them. If you don't give them power, they will take yours.

- Do not assume the single data tool: model your associations for change and becoming, with extensibility as the feature. This will mean there are many data models: the different database implementations, in which one may be suited for reads and one for writes under different services with different scalability needs and usage patterns. There are also different views of the same data: yes, use materialized views but also caches and denormalized patterns, which may differ.

- Use the Specification pattern (see "Specifications" on page 175) for decoupling external search criteria from the entity.

- Design for the team, the first user of the software, to maximize flow. You as a designer are making space for the rest of the team so they can do their work in parallel to maximize velocity and ownership. Design for the team too and then Conway's Law will work well, and the software will be well organized and developers can be accountable and have pride of ownership.

Diversity of customer practices

- Outcomes over activity.
- Value creation over process obedience.
- Employ use cases with an outside-in approach.
- Commit to the Value Chain and make it efficient towards outcomes. Do not focus on policing developers or preventative architecture review boards to ensure compliance with an arbitrary and academic committee that does not own an P&L.
- Your internal colleagues are your customers too: developers are the first users of the system; the Network Operations Center monitoring crew are users of the system; testers are users of the system. Everything you do in the design to support this diverse customer set will pay off.
- There are nearly 200 countries on earth, with thousands of languages. Externalize user strings and design for internationalization and localization from the beginning.
- If this is a web system, design it for a watch. If this is a phone app, design it for a game console, or for voice. Foreground varying UIs by creating a separate UI Package service. There is no "The UI."
- Use eventing liberally. We default to synchronous request/response models, as if we know the meaning, we know what should always happen. Instead, foreground asynchronous. This improves scalability and description of the system. But it also does something for you where you don't have to decide the meaning: you allow the "import" of the event to be deferred. This is powerful because the business changes their mind frequently, the system evolves, different customers need different things, things means something different to diverse audiences. Any reaction in your application should not be hardcoded. Use event handlers.
- Allow for a multiplicity of voices using polyglot persistence and polyglot programming: make them right for the job and there will be different kinds for different jobs in your application. This is the majesty of AND, not the tyranny of OR. This dramatically improves performance and prevents lock-in of contracts, licensing, and thinking.

Opening

Though perhaps counterintuitive when they were born, some of our most cherished and time-tested tools and ideas embody some form of these ideals, particularly in a field in which we didn't imagine why we needed to keep source code private, and we often just shipped for free with hardware products until the Copyright Act of 1976. This rich history includes even (again) our language, such as recursive definitions, as in, "GNU stands for GNU's Not Unix":

- BitTorrent, Cassandra database, and the World Wide Web itself, as peer networks
- Unix variants
- The Apache Foundation and open source projects
- Wikis
- Eclipse, Emacs
- Chaos engineering
- Servant leadership
- Quantum computing
- Blockchain

So in a sense, what we propose is a radical departure from the status quo, that few would recognize as the corporate enterprise architect job, and is *shocking* once fully understood. Yet in a sense we have intuited these things in our history, and in this way made some of the most important contributions to the field. Semantic Design, X Architecture, is scary-radical, such that the standard-issue business person paying even some attention might find it astonishing, preposterous. Yet it bears traces of some of the best work in our collective history, and looks backwards as it looks forward, and in this sense is nothing new, nothing to fear, tut tut. But practicing it as a framework, as a method, as a collection of job strategies as we put forth here will help us build the future better.

We have practiced this art, this craft, this design method, this strategy, this *way*, and it has proven to work well. Nothing is perfect. We will invite new problems in this, surely. But in making software this way, we find we can do more with less, we move quickly, our designs are better, our projects more successful, the software more sturdy, flexible, scalable, harmonious, even beautiful and delightful. Our customers do better. Our businesses do better. We do better.

The Semantic Design Toolbox

The Tools

Throughout this book, we have introduced new, and sometimes radical, ideas for how to approach software design. Many of these ideas are about thinking differently, using different language, and reconsidering the very job of software designers as what we used to call "architects."

Accompanying these ideas we have introduced many templates as well. These serve to bring this new approach of deconstructive software design into a pragmatic, practical realm so that you can apply it today in your own work. Deconstructive design is more a mindset and a "way of life" than a silver bullet; I don't advertise it as a silver bullet. It's hard work. You'll likely spend some time swimming upstream of your corporate culture to change how you approach software design in this new way.

These are the key components, templates, checklists, scorecards, and practical frameworks, that together form the semantic designer's toolbox. You can download the toolbox at *https://aletheastudio.com*.

Thinking Stage

For these tools, see Chapter 4.

- Persona Document
- Customer Journey Map

Concept Stage

For these, see Chapter 2.

- Lookbook
- Parti
- Concept Canvas

Design Stage

For these, see Chapter 5.

- Mural
- Vision box
- Mind map
- Use cases
- Principles
- Position paper
- Approach document
- RAID
- Design Definition Document

These tools help capture the ideas in Chapter 6:

- Business glossary
- Business capabilities model
- Process map
- System inventory

These are in Chapter 7:

- Guidelines list

Operations and Governance

These are the toolbox components in Chapters 10 and 11:

- Role of architect
- Lateral thinking guide
- Operational scorecard
- Service-oriented organization template
- Scalable business machine template
- Program management framework
- Change management framework
- Governance framework
- Service design checklist

In Chapter 12, the manifesto, the following is offered:

- Deconstruction design practice list

Together, these templates, frameworks, scorecards, and lists together form a complete and practical semantic designer's toolbox.

Further Reading

These books have shaped my work as a software developer, manager, architecture leader, chief architect, CIO, and CTO over many years. They have all, in various and sometimes tangential ways, informed the ideas in this book—sometimes as inspiration, sometimes as intellectual sparring partner. The ideas in this book are made possible by these wonderful works, particularly those in Philosophy. I encourage you to follow your curiosity with this list.

Architecture and Design Books

- Alexander, Christopher W. *The Phenomenon of Life: An Essay on the Art of Building and the Nature of the Universe*, Books I and II. The Center for Environmental Structure, 2002.

- Alexander, Christopher, et al. *A Pattern Language*. Oxford University Press, 1977.

- de Bono, Edward. *Lateral Thinking: Creativity Step by Step*. Harper, 2015.

- Box, Hal. *Think Like an Architect*. University of Texas Press, 2007.

- Brooks, Frederick P. *The Design of Design: Essays from a Computer Scientist*. Addison-Wesley, 2010.

- Dal Monte, Luca, et al. *Maserati: A Century of History*. Giorgio Nada Editore, 2014.

- Frederick, Matthew. *101 Things I Learned in Architecture School*. The MIT Press, 2007.

- Glancey, Jonathan. *Architecture: A Visual History*. DK, 2017.

- Goldberger, Paul. *Why Architecture Matters*. Yale University Press, 2011.

- Karjaluoto, Eric. *The Design Method*. New Riders, 2013.

- Kossiakoff, Alexander, et al. *Systems Engineering: Principles and Practice*. Wiley, 2011.
- Lidwell, William, et al. *Universal Principles of Design*. Rockport Publishers, 2010.
- Lukic, Branko. *Nonobject*. The MIT Press, 2010.
- Norman, Don. *The Design of Everyday Things*. Basic Books, 2013.
- Patt, Doug. *How to Architect*. The MIT Press, 2012.
- Piano, Renzo. *Museums*. The Monacelli Press, 2007.
- Van Uffelen, Chris. *Bridge Architecture and Design*. Braun, 2009.

Philosophy Books

- Adams, Hazard, and Leroy Searle. *Critical Theory Since Plato*, 3rd Edition. Wadsworth Publishing, 2004.
- Appel, Andrew. *Alan Turing's Systems of Logic*. Princeton University Press, 2012.
- Aristotle. *Poetics*. Penguin Classics, 1997.
- Auden, W. H. *Lectures of Shakespeare*. Princeton University Press, 2000.
- Bachelard, Gaston. *The Poetics of Space*. Penguin Classics, 2014.
- Bataille, Georges. *The Accursed Share*. Zone Books, 1991.
- Berkeley, George. *Three Dialogues between Hylas and Philonous*. Hackett Classics, 1979.
- Blanchot, Maurice. *The Space of Literature*. University of Nebraska Press, 1989.
- Boole, George. *An Investigation of the Laws of Thought*. Dover, 1862.
- Borges, Jorge Luis. *Labyrinths*. New Directions, 2007.
- Brecht, Bertolt, and John Willett. *Brecht on Theater*. Hill and Wang, 1977.
- Brown, Alison Leigh. *Fear, Truth, Writing: From Paper Village to Electronic Community*. SUNY Press, 1995.
- Brown, Alison Leigh. *Subjects of Deceit: A Phenomenology of Lying*. SUNY Press, 1998.
- Butler, Judith. *Gender Trouble: Feminism and the Subversion of Identity*. Routledge, 2006.
- Campbell, Joseph. *The Hero with a Thousand Faces*. Princeton University Press, 1973.
- Cixous, Hélène. *Coming to Writing and Other Essays*. Harvard University Press, 1992.

- Cixous, Hélène. *Rootprints*. Routledge, 1997.
- Crary, Jonathan, and Sanford Kwinter. *Zone: Incorporations*. Zone Books, 1992.
- Culler, Jonathan. *On Deconstruction*. Cornell University Press, 2008.
- Descartes, Rene. *Discourse on Method and Related Writings*. Penguin Classics, 2000.
- Deleuze, Gilles. *Cinema II: The Time-Image*. University of Minnesota Press, 1989.
- Deleuze, Gilles. *Difference and Repetition*. Columbia University Press, 1995.
- Deleuze, Gilles. *Negotiations*. Columbia University Press, 1997.
- Deleuze, Gilles, and Felix Guattari. *Anti-Oedipus: Capitalism and Schizophrenia*. Penguin Classics, 2009.
- Deleuze, Gilles, and Felix Guattari. *A Thousand Plateaus*. University of Minnesota Press, 1987.
- Deleuze, Gilles, and Felix Guattari. *What is Philosophy?* Columbia University Press, 1996.
- Derrida, Jacques. *Aporias*. Stanford University Press, 1993.
- Derrida, Jacques. *Cinders*. University of Minnesota Press, 2014.
- Derrida, Jacques. *Dissemination*. University of Chicago Press, 2017.
- Derrida, Jacques. *Glas*. University of Nebraska Press, 1990.
- Derrida, Jacques. *Margins of Philosophy*. University of Chicago Press, 1985.
- Derrida, Jacques. *Of Grammatology*. Johns Hopkins University Press, 2016.
- Derrida, Jacques. *Speech and Phenomena*. Northwestern University Press, 1973.
- Derrida, Jacques. *The Truth in Painting*. University of Chicago Press, 1987.
- Derrida, Jacques. *Writing and Difference*. University of Chicago Press, 1978.
- Eagleton, Terry. *The Ideology of the Aesthetic*. Blackwell Publishers, 1991.
- Eagleton, Terry. *Literary Theory: An Introduction*. University of Minnesota Press, 2008.
- Eagleton, Terry. *Marxist Literary Theory: A Reader*. Wiley-Blackwell, 1996.
- Elderfield, John. *Modern Painting and Sculpture*. The Museum of Modern Art, 2010.
- Foucault, Michel. *Discipline and Punish: The Birth of the Prison*. Vintage, 1995.
- Foucault, Michel. *Madness and Civilization: A History of Insanity in the Age of Reason*. Vintage, 1988.
- Foucault, Michel. *The Order of Things: An Archaeology of the Human Sciences*. Vintage, 2012.

- Frankl, Viktor E. *Man's Search for Meaning*. Touchstone, 1984.

- Freud, Sigmund. *The Future of an Illusion*. W.W. Norton & Company, 1975.

- Frye, Northrop. *The Educated Imagination*. Indiana University Press, 1964.

- Haack, Susan. *Deviant Logic, Fuzzy Logic: Beyond the Formalism*. University of Chicago Press, 1996.

- Hacking, Ian. *An Introduction to Probability and Inductive Logic*. Cambridge University Press, 2001.

- Halmos, Paul R. *Naive Set Theory*. Martino Fine Books, 2011.

- Hegel, Georg. *The Phenomenology of Spirit*. Oxford University Press, 1977.

- Heidegger, Martin. *On the Way to Language*. HarperOne, 1982.

- Heidegger, Martin. *Poetry, Language, Thought*. Harper Perennial Modern Classics, 2013.

- Irigaray, Luce. *This Sex Which Is Not One*. Cornell University Press, 1985.

- Kant, Immmanuel. *The Critique of Pure Reason*. Penguin Classics, 2008.

- Keller, Thomas. *The French Laundry Cookbook*. Artisan, 1999.

- Kierkegaard, Søren. *Concluding Unscientific Postscript*. Princeton University Press, 1992.

- Lacan, Jacques. *Ecrits*. W.W. Norton & Company, 2007.

- Locke, John. *An Essay Concerning Human Understanding*. Prometheus Books, 1995.

- Lyotard, Jean-Francois. *The Postmodern Condition*. University of Minnesota Press, 1984.

- Makaryk, Irena. *Encyclopedia of Contemporary Literary Theory*. University of Toronto Press, 1993.

- Meadows, Donella H. *Thinking in Systems*. Chelsea Green Publishing, 2008.

- Minsky, Marvin. *The Society of Mind*. Simon & Schuster, 1987.

- Nelson, Ted. *Computer Lib: Dream Machines*. Tempus Books, 1987.

- Rousseau, Jacques. *Emile, or On Education*. Penguin Classics, 2007.

- Sallis, John. *Deconstruction and Philosophy: The Texts of Jacques Derrida*. University of Chicago Press, 1989.

- Shakespeare, William. *The Complete Works of William Shakespeare*.

- Shyer, Laurence. *Robert Wilson and His Collaborators*. Theatre Communications Group, 1993.

- Smith, Adam. *The Theory of Moral Sentiments*. Liberty Fund Inc., 1985.

- de Spinoza, Benedict. *The Ethics*. Penguin Classics, 2005.
- Sterne, Laurence. *The Life and Opinions of Tristram Shandy, Gentleman*. Penguin Classics, 2003.
- Stoppard, Tom. *Rosencrantz and Guildenstern are Dead*. Grove Press, 2017.
- Weinberg, Gerald M. *An Introduction to General Systems Thinking*. Dorset House, 2001.
- Wilde, Oscar. *The Artist as Critic*. University of Chicago Press, 1982.
- Winterson, Jeanette. *Art Objects: Essays on Ecstasy and Effrontery*. Vintage, 1997.
- Wittgenstein, Ludwig. *Tractatus Logico-Philosophicus*. Dover Publications, 1998.
- Wolfram, Stephen. *A New Kind of Science*. Wolfram Media, 2002.
- Zizek, Slavoj. *The Plague of Fantasies*. Verso, 2009.
- Zizek, Slavoj. *Tarrying with the Negative*. Duke University Press, 1993.

Software Books

- Allamaraju, Subbu. *RESTful Web Services Cookbook*. O'Reilly Media, 2010.
- Bass, Len, et al. *Software Architecture in Practice*. Addison-Wesley, 2012.
- Beyer, Betsy, et al. *Site Reliability Engineering*. O'Reilly Media, 2016.
- Bloch, Joshua. *Effective Java*. Addison-Wesley, 2018.
- Brooks, Frederick P. *The Mythical Man Month*. Addison-Wesley, 1995.
- Campbell, Laine, and Charity Majors. *Database Reliability Engineering*. O'Reilly Media, 2017.
- Daigneau, Robert. *Service Design Patterns*. Addison-Wesley, 2011.
- Erl, Thomas. *SOA Design Patterns*. Prentice Hall, 2008.
- Fowler, Martin. *Domain-Specific Languages*. Addison-Wesley, 2010.
- Fowler, Martin. *Patterns of Enterprise Application Architecture*. Addison-Wesley, 2002.
- Fowler, Martin. *Refactoring*. Addison-Wesley, 2018.
- Glass, Robert L. *Facts and Fallacies of Software Engineering*. Addison-Wesley, 2002.
- Hanmer, Robert. *Patterns of Fault Tolerant Software*. Wiley, 2007.
- Harvard Business Review. *Aligning Technology with Strategy*. Harvard Business Review Press, 2011.

- Hewitt, Eben. *Technology Strategy Patterns: Architecture as Strategy*. O'Reilly Media, 2018.
- Hohpe, Gregor, and Bobby Woolf. *Enterprise Integration Patterns*. Addison-Wesley, 2003.
- Jacobson, Daniel, et al. *APIs: A Strategy Guide*. O'Reilly Media, 2011.
- Kejariwal, Arun, and John Allspaw. *The Art of Capacity Planning*, 2nd Edition. O'Reilly Media, 2017.
- Kroll, Per, and Phillippe Kruchten. *The Rational Unified Process Made Easy*. Addison-Wesley, 2003.
- Lamport, Leslie. *Specifying Systems*. Addison-Wesley, 2002.
- Larman, Craig. *Agile and Iterative Development*. Addison-Wesley, 2003.
- Leffingwell, Dean, and Don Widrig. *Managing Software Requirements*. Addison-Wesley, 2003.
- McConnell, Steve. *Software Project Survival Guide*. Microsoft Press, 1997.
- McGovern, James, et al. *A Practical Guide to Enterprise Architecture*. Prentice Hall, 2003.
- Monson-Haefel, Richard (editor). *97 Things Every Software Architect Should Know*. O'Reilly Media, 2009.
- Morris, Kief. *Infrastructure as Code*. O'Reilly Media, 2016.
- Narayan, Sriram. *Agile IT Organization and Design*. Addison-Wesley, 2015.
- The Open Group. *TOGAF Version 9*. Van Haren Publishing, 2015.
- Pilone, Dan, and Neil Pitman. *UML 2.0 in a Nutshell*. O'Reilly Media, 2005.
- Schlossnagle, Theo. *Scalable Internet Architectures*. Sams Publishing, 2006.
- Sessions, Roger. *Simple Architectures for Complex Enterprises*. Microsoft Press, 2008.
- Stephens, Rod. *Beginning Software Engineering*. Wrox, 2015.
- Taylor, Hugh, et al. *Event-Driven Architecture*. Addison-Wesley, 2009.
- Taylor, R.N., et al. *Software Architecture: Foundations, Theory, and Practice*. Wiley, 2009. (You can get the PowerPoint slides here (*https://www.softwarearchitecture book.com/svn/main/slides/ppt/*).)
- Tulach, Jaroslav. *Practical API Design*. Apress, 2008.

Index

A

acceptance criteria, 179
access control lists (ACLs), 223
accessibility requirements, 207
accidental complexity, 54
accomplishing something, 26
activities, observing for users or personas, 78
advertising, creative directors in, 238
aesthetics, semantic designer's skills and background in, 232
affordance, 57
Agile, 46, 282
alignment
    business strategic objectives and tactical demands, 122-123
    concept's alignment with strategy, 29
Amazon Alexa, premise of, 81
Amazon Web Services (AWS), 143
    APIs, naming of, 145
    AWS CloudFormation templating system, 214
    using Amazon S3 with interactive documentation, 157
Americans with Disabilities Act (ADA), 135
    compliance with, 207
Ansible, 214
Apache Cassandra (see Cassandra distributed database)
Apache TinkerPop Gremlin, 200
Apache tools for stream processing, 192
APIs
    considering for use in different contexts, 65
    guidelines for, 147
    reviewing popular service APIs, 145

separating from implementation, 171
service API, 98
Application Design section, Design Definition Document, 103-105
applications, 139-181
    anatomy of a service, 158-165
        engines, 161-165
        orchestrations, 158
        serverless, 164
        UI packages, 158
    API guidelines, 147
    application-specific services, 153
    business architecture in, 133-136
    cacheability and idempotence, 149
    comments in code, 179-180
    communication through services, 154
    compliance maps, 217
    contextual services and service mixins, 168-170
    data as point of, 188
    decoupling user interfaces, 141
    design that harmonizes business and application systems, 119
    designing for resilience, 155-157
    embracing constraints, 140-141
    eventing, 165-168
    expecting externalization of services, 154
    independently buildable services, 151
    interactive documentation, 157
    languages, 172
    metrics for, 216
    performance improvement checklist, 170
    platform design, 142-144
    radical immutability in, 173-175

separating API from implementation, 171
service resources and representations, 144
specifications, 175-178
strategies and configurable services, 151-153
test automation, 178
tools for, 294
versioning, deconstructed, 148-149
approaches, 99
situations requiring creation of, 100
arborescent, 253, 285
Archer, L. Bruce, 72
de Architectura (Vitruvius), 23
architecture
books on, 297
building and design, 17
architecture (software)
architect, use of term, 5
architects, role of, 235
architecture as non-necessary metaphor in
technology, 8
design thinking as context for applied architecting, 74
elements of, 288
forgetting the conceptual legacy of architecture, 242
infrastructure considerations for architects,
209-211
origins of, 3-15
semantics and, 20
arts, semantic designer's background in, 232
assumptions, 112
expecting externalization of services, 154
for solution success, 102
asynchronous operations, 164
basic anatomy of asynchronous service
components, 166
publisher/subscriber or pub/sub, 165
wise use of asynchronous calls, 167
Athena, travel industry software based on
(example), 35
attributes, 184
auditing, 207
automatic retries, 156
automation, 226
defining automated pipelines first, 217
service design checklist, 273
autoscaling, 224
availability
metrics for applications, 216

service design checklist for, 277
avoiding something, 26
axiom of pairing, 44

B

becoming, 287
behavior, driven by metrics, 132
Bernini sculpture The Ecstasy of Saint Teresa,
90
Bezos, Jeff, 143, 154
binary oppositions, 51, 224, 286
Brooks, Fred, 54
budgeting and financial planning (for infrastructure in cloud environments), 210
bulkheading, 156
business
business context, elements of, 120
design that harmonizes business, application, and data, 61
designing software to operate within, 118
platform as business framework, 66
scalable business machine, designing,
263-266
semantic designer's understanding of, 232
treating as a system and applying design
principles to it, 117-120
writing business glossary, 125, 183
questions and guidelines for, 185
business architecture
defined, 120
definition by Object Management Group,
120
in applications, 133-136
tools, 294
Business Design section, Design Definition
Document, 102
business idea, 26
Business Process Modeling Notation (BPMN),
130
business processes, 275
business strategy, 26
capturing, 120-123
aligning strategic objectives and tactical
demands, 122-123
providing a common understanding,
120-122
business system design
creating business capabilities model,
126-129

creating organizational map, 125
creating process map, 129
creating the business glossary, 125
defining metrics for successful processes, 131
framework, introducing for, 123-124
instituting appropriate process governance, 132
reengineering processes, 129-131
taking inventory of systems, 131

C

cacheability, 149
cacheable URIs, 148
caching
  data model for the cache, 190
  response, 156
capabilities, 102
  business processes versus, 127
  creating business capabilities model, 126-129
  support by systems, 131
capacity planning, 210
Cassandra distributed database, 60, 188, 196
  checklist for determining suitability of, 196
  services for which it's the wrong choice, 197
  wrapping services as managed components, 227
category mistakes, 10
challenge idea tool, 249
change management, 267-269
chaos engineering, 64, 225
Chef, 214
chief semanticist, 241
circuit breaking, 156
Claim Check pattern, 167
clarification (in design thinking), 73
Clarks, Jonathan, 66
classpath deployment and network proxies (data accessors), 195
clients
  major version changes breaking clients, 149
  rebuilding, 151
  service-client subproject, 99
cloud, 59
  deployment tools for cloud environments, 214
  infrastructure considerations for architects, 210

  infrastructure design checklist, 222
  money spent on cloud providers, 257
clustering, 170
code coverage, 203
code reviews, 254-255
collaboration (in design thinking), 74
collections (on web APIs), 170
comments, 179-180
commodities, 5
communication, semantic designer's skills in, 232
compensation, 156
competition and innovation, 10
complement, 44
complexity
  caused by oversimplifying, 55
  essential and accidental, 54
  inherent in the world, representing in design, 42
  simplicity versus, 41
compliance map, 217
comprehensive view, semantic design, 285, 287
computers, prices of, 4
computing, future of, 242
Concept Canvas template, 26-30
concept statement, 29
concepts, 15
  concept stage tools, 294
  conceptual tests, 252-253
  design practices, 286
  designer of, 194
  designing, 285
  extra-synthetic conceptual work in murals, 90
  formal methods and innovative models for viewing, 233
  lateral thinking and, 248-251
  organizing in mind maps, 94
  production of, 17-47
    advantages of semantic design, 45-47
    architecture and design, 18
    context, 41-42
    creative director in fashion, 236
    defining a concept, 25-30
    designers as producers of concepts, 23-24
    expressing the concept in a parti, 33-37
    fit to purpose, 32
    ideas captured in a lookbook, 30-32

and competition in technology, 10
and concept of architecture, 18
inputs (scalable business machine), 264
insights
    forming in design thinking, 79
    generating in design thinking, 83
integrated development environments (IDEs)
    Eclipse, 60
    refactorings and recommendations in, 254
integration tests, 218
intention and use value, giving to negative
    space, 58-61
interaction features, 194
interactive documentation, 157
internal consistency, testing concepts for, 253
internationalization and localization
    currency exchange rate, 145
    languages in applications and services, 172
Internet of Things (IoT), 141
    streaming data, 192
Interpreter pattern, 175
intersection, 44
issues, 112

J

Java, 168
    API and implementation in same package,
        171
    comment examples in APIs, 180
    managed components, 227
    multi-armed bandit library for, 222
Java Database Connectivity (JDBC), 172, 200
JavaScript and CSS files, combining and mini-
    fying, 170
JavaScript frameworks (UI), 141
Jenkins, 214

K

Kahn, Louis, 58, 64
Kanban, 255
Keller, Pyzdek, 131
key management, 223
Knapsack problem, 176
Kubernetes, 214

L

language
    in software development, 20

languages in applications and services, 172
    role in shaping thinking and practice, 8
    study of, in semantics, 20
    using properly in design, 64-65
latency, 104, 107
    in Apache tools for stream processing, 192
    in cloud environments, 223
    measured in service response testing, 276
    per service, 216
lateral thinking, 248-251, 253, 286
    vertical thinking versus, 248
leadership skills of semantic designers, 233
Lean Six Sigma, 9
legal and regulatory requirements, 102, 135
    Americans with Disabilities Act (ADA)
        compliance, 207
Levi Strauss, IT project (2008), 14
licensing, 111, 218
    for graph databases, 199
Liu, Jason, 222
load balancers, 223
logging, 155
    data model for logs-as-data, 190
    design of log messages, 227
lookbook, 287
    capturing ideas in, 30-32
        possible contents, 31
    extra-synthetic conceptual work in, 90
lookup registry to support service discovery, 61
Lucidchart, 94
lunar landing system, concept sketch of (parti
    example), 34

M

machine learning, 289
    data model per use case, per service, 190
    data pipelines, 203-206
    determining customer clusters, 169
    feature engineering for, 193-195
    multi-armed bandits and infinite feature
        toggles with, 221
major version change, 149
Malkovich, John, 30
managed components, 227
management, governance, and operations
MapReduce algorithm, 63
marketing, 232, 234
Marx, Karl, 17
master/slave databases, 196

Python, 111, 168, 179
    separating API from implementation, 172

Q
quality assurance, 277
quarantine or embassy, creating, 63

R
radical immutability (see immutability, radical)
RAID document, 112
Raiders of the Lost Ark (movie), 237
random inputs, 250
range, 44
rate limiting, 156
reading further, resources for, 297-302
recovery
    disaster recovery, 210
    mean time to recovery, 216
reflexive, 44
regulatory requirements, 102, 135
    Americans with Disabilities Act (ADA)
        compliance, 207
relational databases, 187
relations, 44, 184
representations and resources (services),
    144-147
requests
    chaos engineering with, 225
    toggle router component setting Toggle
        Context, 220
requirements, 45
    functional and nonfunctional, 96
    myth of, 19
resilience, 104
    designing for, 155-157
    externalized services and, 154
resilience4j, 156
resources
    chaos engineering with, 225
    resource tagging, 223
    service resources and representations, 144
response caching, 156
REST
    APIs observance of HATEOAS principle,
        150
    Open API documentation for services, 157
    orientation around resources and represen-
        tations, 145
retries (automatic), 156

reveals, parti based on, 37
reversal method, 249
rhizomatic, 218, 253, 285
risks
    business risks in software project, 103
    defined, 112
    RAID (Risks, Assumptions, Issues, Depen-
        dencies) document, 112
roles
    approach to production in business, 9
    in software production, 9
    role clarity, challenges of, 231

S
scalability
    ensuring proper design of software for, 155
    high-scalability case studies, 164
    of engines, 162
    representing, 163
scalable business machine (SBM), designing,
    263-266
scaling infrastructure, 223
    IaC and, 210
Schmidt, Peter, 247
science, software design and, 10
search
    disappearing web search engines, 66
    for candidate objects based on criteria,
        175-178
security
    auditing mechanisms, 207
    for externalized services, 154
    OSWAP secure coding reports, 215
    security data model per service, 190
    service design checklist for, 276
security groups, 223
semantic design manifesto, 281-292
    four ideals, 285
    key practices, 286
        comprehensive view practices, 287
        concept design, 286
        decentered, deconstruction practices,
            289
        diversity of customer practices, 291
    opening, 292
semantic design toolbox, 293-295
    concept stage, 294
    design stage, 294
    thinking stage, 293

U

UIs (user interfaces)
  creating UI packages, 142
  decoupling from applications, 141
  rebuilding UI package application, 151
  UI packages, 158
Unified Modeling Language (UML) diagrams, 95
union, 44
unit tests, 218
URIs
  cacheable, 148
  testing with cUrl program, 149
use cases, 95
  for streaming data, 191
use value and intention, giving to negative space, 58-61
use value, questioning, 77
user acceptance testing, 179
user interfaces (see UIs)
users, 65
  determining in design thinking, 75
  extreme users, 77
  observing users' actions in design thinking, 75
utilities, 98

V

Vagrant, 213
value
  creating in your organization, 234
  creating, capturing, and delivering, 120
  creation for customers by technology creative director, 239

value stream, considering in process reengineering, 130
Value Proposition Design (Osterwalder et al.), 79
variants, 42
versioning, 148-149
vertical scaling, 162
vertical thinking versus lateral thinking, 248
video games, creative directors, 238
viewpoints, multiple, 114
virtualization, 224
vision box, 93
Vitruvius, 23

W

waterfall, 46
Web Content Accessibility Guidelines 2.0 (WCAG), 207
web ecommerce clickstreams, 191
WebSockets, 157
words, testing, interrogating, and challenging, 186
workflow, drawing out, 160

X

XMind, 94

Y

YAML, 179
  use by AWS CloudFormation, 214

About the Author

Eben Hewitt is the chief architect and CTO at Sabre Hospitality where he is responsible for the technology strategy, designing large-scale, mission-critical systems, and leading teams to build them. He works at the intersection of innovation, architecture and design, leadership, and global enterprise business development. He has served as CTO at one of the world's largest hotel companies and as CIO of O'Reilly Media. Eben has originated architecture departments at three companies. He is also the author of *Technology Strategy Patterns* (2018) and *Cassandra: The Definitive Guide* (two editions, translated into Chinese), and several other books on architecture, services, Java, and web development. He has won awards for innovation and been an invited presenter to Amazon AWS, Oracle headquarters, and conferences around the world. He is a full member of the Dramatists Guild, with his first full-length play produced in New York City.

Colophon

The animal on the cover of *Semantic Software Design* is an African forest buffalo (*Syncerus caffer nanus*), a subspecies of the Cape buffalo found in Africa. This type of buffalo lives in rainforests throughout the western and central parts of the continent, in contrast to the other three subspecies who roam the savanna.

African forest buffalo are the smallest subspecies at 550–700 pounds (compared to 880–1760 pounds for the Cape buffalo). They have red-brown hides with dark faces. The shape and size of their horns is also distinct from their larger cousins, as the horns are smaller, grow in a different direction, and do not fuse in the center. The buffalo feed on grass and various plants in clearings around the forest. As deforestation occurs, the buffalo have also adapted to graze near human roads or recently logged areas where grass is now able to grow.

Herds of forest buffalo are relatively small at no more than 30 individuals, and are typically made up of 1–2 bulls and several females, juveniles, and calves. The bulls stay with this group the entire year rather than cycling through a bachelor herd. The herd size is usually a deterrent to predators, as most cannot kill an adult buffalo. One notable exception is the Nile crocodile.

Many of the animals on O'Reilly covers are endangered; all of them are important to the world.

The cover illustration is by Jose Marzan, based on a black and white engraving from Lydekker's *Royal Natural History*. The cover fonts are Gilroy Semibold and Guardian Sans. The text font is Adobe Minion Pro; the heading font is Adobe Myriad Condensed; and the code font is Dalton Maag's Ubuntu Mono.

O'REILLY®

There's much more where this came from.

Experience books, videos, live online training courses, and more from O'Reilly and our 200+ partners—all in one place.

Learn more at oreilly.com/online-learning

©2019 O'Reilly Media, Inc. O'Reilly is a registered trademark of O'Reilly Media, Inc. | 175